Exploring the
Four Corners Region

Exploring the Four Corners Region

A Guide to the Southwestern United States Region of Arizona, Southern Utah, Southwestern Colorado & Northern/Southwestern New Mexico

5th Edition

James A. Schwarz

ORDERING INFORMATION

Telephone   928.853.3641
Email   jims@tqs-sim.com

Cover design and map by Leanna Johnson
Photo of author by AM Geyer (Andrea Geyer)
Blazin' M photo courtesy Blazin' M Ranch
All other photos by James Schwarz
Thanks to Michelle Lerman for input on New Mexico

ISBN 978-0-9794538-2-3

PRINTED IN THE UNITED STATES OF AMERICA

Dedicated to my mother
Gloria Kinney Schwarz,
who lived to travel.
Her love of travel and exploring
new places rubbed off on me –
I am thankful for that wonderful gift.

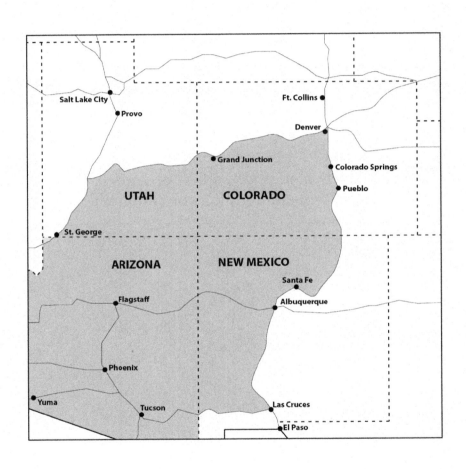

TABLE OF CONTENTS

TABLE OF CONTENTS _____ 1

INTRODUCTION _____ 7

ARIZONA _____ 11

Phoenix Area - Valley of the Sun _____ 11

Northern Arizona _____ 31
Payson _____ 31
Prescott _____ 33
Cottonwood/Jerome _____ 36
Sedona _____ 40

Route 66 (I-40) _____ 46
Seligman _____ 46
Williams – Grand Canyon Gateway _____ 47
Flagstaff _____ 48
Winslow – Standin' on the Corner _____ 65
Holbrook – Petrified Forest Gateway _____ 66

Grand Canyon _____ 67
South Rim _____ 67
North Rim _____ 70

Northeastern Arizona _____ 73
Page – Gateway to Lake Powell _____ 73
Fredonia _____ 76
Navajo & Hopi Reservations _____ 77

Southern & Eastern Arizona _____ 83
Globe/Superior _____ 83
White Mountains _____ 85
Florence _____ 86

Tucson _____ 90

South of Tucson _____ 101
Patagonia _____ 102
Elgin – Wine Country _____ 103
Sierra Vista _____ 104

Tombstone _____ 106
Bisbee _____ 106
Chiricahua National Monument _____ 111

Scenic Drives in Southern Arizona _____ 112

Yuma _____ 113

SOUTHERN UTAH _____ 117

St. George _____ 117
Hurricane/La Verkin _____ 120

Cedar City – Shakespeare Festival _____ 121

Springdale – Gateway to Zion _____ 123

Kanab _____ 127

Scenic Route – State Highway 12 _____ 130
Panguitch _____ 130
Red Canyon Area _____ 130
Bryce Canyon Area _____ 131
Cannonville _____ 132
Escalante _____ 132
Boulder _____ 133
Torrey _____ 134
Hanksville _____ 137

Highway 191 Corridor _____ 140
Bluff _____ 140
Mexican Hat _____ 141
Blanding _____ 142
Monticello _____ 143
Moab _____ 143

I-70 Corridor _____ 149

Ancient Rock Art and Ruins _____ 153

Southern Utah National Parks & Recreation Areas _____ 155
Cedar Breaks National Monument _____ 155
Zion National Park _____ 156
Bryce Canyon National Park _____ 157
Capitol Reef National Park _____ 158
Lake Powell _____ 160
Arches National Park _____ 160

Canyonlands National Park _____ 162
Hovenweep National Monument _____ 163

Scenic Drives _____ 164

Salt Lake City _____ 166

SOUTHWESTERN COLORADO _____ 169

Front Range _____ 169
Denver _____ 170
I-76 Corridor (Denver to Nebraska) _____ 174
Boulder _____ 175
Golden _____ 176
Colorado Springs _____ 177
Pueblo _____ 181
Cañon City _____ 181

Central Mountains _____ 183
I-70 Corridor – Denver to Tunnel _____ 183
Silverthorne/Dillon/Breckenridge _____ 185
Vail _____ 186
Glenwood Springs _____ 188
Aspen _____ 190
Leadville _____ 201
Salida _____ 202
Gunnison _____ 203
Crested Butte _____ 204

San Luis Valley _____ 206
Alamosa _____ 206
Crestone _____ 207
Saguache _____ 207

Southwest Mountains _____ 208
Telluride _____ 208
Cortez Area – Mesa Verde Gateway _____ 215
Pagosa Springs – Hot Springs _____ 218

Highway 550 – Million Dollar Highway _____ 220
Montrose _____ 220
Ridgway _____ 227
Ouray _____ 231
Durango _____ 236

Grand Mesa Country _____ 240
  I-70 Corridor Grand Junction to Glenwood Springs _____ 240
  Grand Junction _____ 241
  Fruita _____ 248
  Palisade – Peach & Wine Capital _____ 249
  Cedaredge & Grand Mesa _____ 252
  Paonia/Hotchkiss _____ 255
  Delta _____ 260

Scenic drives _____ 265

NORTHERN & SOUTHWESTERN NEW MEXICO _____ 267

Route 66 (I-40) _____ 269
  Gallup _____ 269
  Grants _____ 270
  Albuquerque _____ 271

Turquoise Trail – New Mexico 14 _____ 275
  Madrid _____ 275

Santa Fe – Art & Culture Mecca _____ 276

North of Santa Fe _____ 282
  Ojo Caliente – Hot Springs _____ 282
  Taos _____ 283
  Las Vegas _____ 284

Highway 550 _____ 285
  Aztec _____ 285
  Farmington _____ 285
  Cuba _____ 286
  Jemez Pueblo _____ 286

Southwestern New Mexico _____ 287
  Silver City _____ 287

I-25 Albuquerque to Las Cruces _____ 288
  Truth or Consequences _____ 288
  Mesilla _____ 290

SOME THINGS TO DO BY CATEGORY _____ 291

Museums/Tours _____ 291

Shopping _____ 293

Interesting Towns _____ 294

Outdoors/Scenery _____ 296

Spas/Hot Springs _____ 299

Archeology _____ 301

Spiritual Spots_____ 302

RESOURCES _____ 303

Getting Additional Information _____ 303
   Hiking & Tour Books _____ 303
   Federal Visitor Centers _____ 303
   Municipal & State Visitor Centers _____ 304

Grocery Stores _____ 306

Ski Areas_____ 308

Gear _____ 309
   Traveling by Car _____ 310

Kids _____ 312

INTRODUCTION

I have spent over 35 years exploring the Southwestern part of the United States, having lived in Colorado Springs, Vail, Phoenix, Flagstaff, and currently Montrose/Telluride. Plus my parents lived in Tucson for 15 years. Through my experiences, I have found many unique and interesting spots. This book shares some of those places. My interests range from hiking, backpacking, cycling (road and mountain), and skiing (alpine and x-c) to fine dining, music and the theatre. I hope you will glean out some interesting spots to explore on your own.

This started out as a travel *"pick list"* of places to give to friends visiting me. The idea to start it came from a colleague of mine in Toronto, Don Witchell, giving me a similar list two-page list for the Toronto area. It was great fun using his list to explore one of my favorite cities. I decided to do the same for my area since I never could remember all the fun spots to see when a visiting friend was asking about them. The list has grown over the years, to the point I have turned it into a book. Many people have supported me doing this, including significant input into this book – thanks!

One specific incident triggered me to consider publishing this work. We were spending Thanksgiving at a picnic site in Oak Creek Canyon (near Sedona, Arizona) with friends. When heading out I found I had left my lights on my vintage 1967 Ford Galaxie XL and the battery had run down. Luckily a couple from Texas pulled right in front of my car. They thought my distress was their parking below me. After explaining my dilemma, the offered to jump start my car. During the process, I gave them a copy of my notes on sites to see as a thank you. They loved it and said it was what they had been looking for in a tour book (they had a stack in the back seat).

If you have any ideas on places to add to the list or have found a place that has closed or doesn't provide the same experience, contact me at jschw@mindspring.com. I don't have the chance to travel to many of these spots annually so feedback on current conditions would be appreciated.

The book focuses on Arizona and includes the Four Corners region (Southwestern Colorado, Southern Utah and Northern/Southwestern New Mexico). In the fifth edition I still haven't included the entire states of Colorado, Utah or New Mexico. A map in the front of the table of contents shows the areas covered by this book.

FYI - there is an actual **Four Corners Monument** *(off of US Highway 160) where Arizona, Utah, Colorado and New Mexico meet. It is a popular photo spot with smiling families spanning four states in one shot. I personally prefer the parking area, on US 160 just inside Colorado, above the north side of the San Juan River, where you can frequently see landmarks in all four states (Shiprock, NM; Sleeping Ute Mountain, CO; Blue Mountains, UT; and the Chuskas/Lukachukais, AZ).*

I have attempted to include lodging and restaurant information for most areas, however it is not meant to be a complete list, rather it includes places I have found interesting or unique. Lodging is especially personal and many people prefer certain types of accommodations or are hooked into loyalty to a certain chain due to their frequent travel program. Most of these areas have a good variety of possibilities, established chains (though in peak seasons, reservations are recommended).

In the future the book will be expanded to include other areas in the Four Corners states as well as new "finds" on my travels. If you find an interesting place, again please, please, share it with me! Also updates on existing entries are appreciated.

If venturing out for a hike, bike ride, ski or other outdoor activity make sure to be adequately prepared and know your personal limitations. Consulting experts or books dedicated to the activity is recommended. Also be aware distances between gas stations and other services can be over 100 miles in certain areas so also make sure your vehicle is ready for the trip. Cellular telephone service can also be problematic in rural areas. Be prepared for deer and other animals on the roads.

Jim Schwarz – June 2017

©2015 AM Geyer (Andrea Geyer) www.amgeyer.com

Thanks to Andrea Geyer for this shot of me in a ski lesson with her family up at Telluride.

ARIZONA

Arizona has such a wide variety of terrain to explore. In just 2-3 hours you can completely change the seasons. Flagstaff, where I lived for 13 years has real winters, similar to the Front Range in Colorado. If I was frustrated with winter, I could be in spring weather in Sedona or the Phoenix Metro Area (Valley of the Sun).

Phoenix is growing up and becoming a real city. In the past, it lacked a wide range of cultural activities. Its smaller sisters, Tucson and Flagstaff, on the other hand have had a stronger history of cultural events.

PHOENIX AREA - VALLEY OF THE SUN

I lived in the Phoenix area for almost seven years. At first I found the area intimidating, since it is so spread out and many of the gems of the city are hidden in nondescript strip malls which dominate the roadsides. And notes for the Phoenix area include the metro area communities of: Scottsdale, Mesa, Tempe and Glendale

Things to do

Downtown Phoenix – remember the light rail runs right through downtown and is a fun way to access these sites.

Heard Museum – An excellent museum for Native American artifacts and current art work by Native American artists – not to be missed. Right on Central Avenue in downtown – you can now take light rail there too (the stop is almost directly in front of the museum). It has had free nights to Arizona residents (call to confirm). *I went there recently after almost 20 years – still an amazing museum. I* *would venture to say this is one of the few world class museums in Arizona.* The museum store/gallery is a treat in itself (I bought a raven print the last visit).

Science Museum - Downtown Phoenix, nearby the convention center. It is a beautiful building with tons of 'neato' things for adults and kids to play with.

Herberger Theatre and Orchestra Hall - They are the cultural heart of Phoenix and are across the street. The Herberger is a good performing arts theatre, worth a visit if a good show is playing. Also the **Hyatt Regency – Compass Arizona Grill** across the street from Orchestra Hall has nice views from the rooftop revolving restaurant/bar (you can get coffee or a drink for fairly low $$ and still enjoy the view without paying big $$ for dinner). You can't miss the round restaurant section on the top of the building. The Civic Center plaza connects these two buildings to the convention center.

Phoenix Art Museum – Phoenix's art museum has happily been improving as years go on, with examples of many masters (though it is still not close to the caliber of Chicago, New York, Philadelphia or Minneapolis where I grew up). They took over the Phoenix central library space (the library moved south a few blocks) and increased exhibit space. Special shows have been improving too – one was a collection of masterpieces from the D.C. based Phillips collection. It is at McDowell and Central Avenue.

> **Phoenix Theatre** – It is in the same complex as the Phoenix Art Museum and does higher-level productions along with the Little Theatre that does children's type productions.

> **Palette at Phoenix Art Museum** –A good place for a bite while at the museum. 602.257.2191

Burton Barr Central Library – This is a really well designed library with an art gallery on the first floor and a special teen section as well. Their rare book room has a collection of artist designed art books – must call for an appointment 602.262.6110. A walkway connects it to the Phoenix Art Museum with statues and quotes of cancer survivors.

First Fridays – The city of Phoenix almost killed this wonderful event. It is unlike many other art walk events in that it is part open galleries with wine but part street fair with tables set up all over the place and live music in many places. Thousands show up. FYI – it gets less tame as the night wears on. Main area is on Roosevelt either side of Central Avenue. Roosevelt is just north of I-10 in downtown – and note they closed some of the access from 7th St and 7th Ave when leaving the area. *Haven't been since moving to Colorado but still looks like it is going strong – here is a website with shuttle info: http://artlinkphoenix.com/first-fridays/* .

Japanese Friendship Garden – Haven't been here yet but the information sounds intriguing. Do formal tea ceremonies once a month (2nd Saturday) and 3 acres of gardens. Open Saturday 10-4 and Sunday 12-5 ($3) and first Friday of every month free 4-7PM. Also other times by appointment. 1125 N. 3rd Ave. – 602.256.3204. Also you can visit the **Chinese Cultural Center** on 668. N. 44th St. (just South of the 202 freeway) – 602.275.8578 – they have several restaurants, shops and sporadic events (e.g., Chinese New Year) plus a huge Asian supermarket. Other good Asian markets are on 17th Ave. and Camelback (NW corner) and **Lee Lee's** on Dobson and Warner (NE corner).

Professional Sports - Downtown Phoenix is home to the **Talking Stick Resort Arena** where the Suns play as well as Chase Field where the Arizona Diamondbacks play. **Chase Field** is a covered baseball field with a retractable roof and there is even a swimming pool that can be rented that you can watch games from. *I took my dad to a baseball game here many years ago now. He loved it (we had killer seats right behind home plate courtesy of a friend).*

Pueblo Grande Museum - Just northeast of the Phoenix airport at 4619 E. Washington (at the 143 freeway Washington exit) is the ruins of a Hohokom pueblo, Southern neighbors to the Anasazi people of Mesa Verde. This cultural group built extensive canals in the Valley of the Sun and the structure at Casa Grande National Monument. Surprising find in the middle of a large city, though you will find better ruin sites elsewhere, this one is very convenient.

Musical Instrument Museum (MIM) – I finally was able to go winter of 2017 after hearing nothing but positive comments about this museum. It is wonderful. I wouldn't try to do it all in one day as there are exhibits for many different country's traditional music forms. Your headset switches to the music of the current exhibit. 4725 E. Mayo Boulevard in Phoenix 480.478.6000

Taliesen West - Was created by Frank Lloyd Wright - on my list of places to see. He had a large influence in the valley, creating the beautiful **ASU Gammage Auditorium** in Tempe (at the intersections of Mill and Apache and the Biltmore Hotel off of 24th Street (North of Camelback). It is worth trying to go to an event at Gammage as well.

Mesa Arts Center (MAC) – It is a wonderful 2005 addition to downtown Mesa at Main and Center (east of Country Club). Incredible building with a gallery, art studios and several theaters. It is a wonderful example of modern design. Hopefully it will help change the environment of downtown Mesa. *I recently went to a play there and was impressed that there were three separate events going on in the different stages MAC has.* www.mesaartscenter.com

Scottsdale Art Walk - It is on most Thursday nights in the galleries North of Indian School and West of Scottsdale Blvd. Some really interesting art pieces are in some of the galleries. Make sure to walk around the Center for the Arts and the library (the library is a beautiful building) - they have wonderful fountains and park areas!

Christmas

Tumbleweed Christmas Tree – Downtown Chandler Christmastime has a tree made out of tumbleweeds. The time I saw it they even offered a picture with the tree.

Tempe – Town Lake – Mid-December (Saturday December 9th in 2017) there is a Fantasy of Lights boat parade. www.downtowntempe.com

Christmas Lights - In the valley many neighborhoods really dress up for Christmas:

> **Mesa** - Some of the "snow bird" trailer parks have some wonderful displays.

> **Tempe – Downtown** - Between Apache and the Salt River Bridge on Mill Street.

Botanical Gardens – Has a traditional luminaria display. *Las Noches de las Luminarias* runs through December. 480.941.1225 - www.dbg.org

Zoolights – The Phoenix Zoo has a large lighting display, including animal sculptures.

Coral Gables Avenue - Just North of Thunderbird Avenue (East of 19th Avenue), drive up Coral Gables - wonderful decorations.

Outdoor Activities

For being a large metropolitan area, there are a lot of outdoor things to do. South Mountain Park is probably the largest city park in the country that actually has large wilderness areas!

Bicycling - The Phoenix valley at one time was rated very poorly by Bicycling magazine. I really feel it has come a long way. The trick is to be creative in route choices. Do not pick major roads for travel! Rather pick the in-between roads (often called "half mile" roads).

Half Mile Roads – Generally Good Bicycle Routes - For instance Maryland Avenue (South of Glendale), Oak or Sweetwater (North of Cactus) are excellent half mile roads to travel on. None of these roads have crossings over I-17 - only the canal path does this at Metro Center (see Corps of Engineers path). Maryland has a tunnel that goes underneath the Highway 51 - Piestewa Freeway (just to the left of where Maryland terminates). Oak traverses the entire city from downtown Phoenix to Scottsdale, with a bridge crossing the Piestewa Freeway. When traveling Oak, you will pass through some marginal areas and I would not recommend night travel.

Scottsdale Greenbelt - located East of downtown Scottsdale, near Miller and on the north end terminating with Hayden, is a wonderful bike path system that terminates at the Phoenix Zoo/Botanical Gardens but then can link south via the water treatment facility to Tempe Town lake.

Corps of Engineers/County Bike Path - Running from near the Arrowhead Mall (83rd Ave and Bell) to the Arizona Biltmore Hotel (near 24th St and Camelback) is a canal system that includes a wonderful bike trail. Most major road crossings have a tunnel to avoid crossing the road (including a tunnel at Metrocenter, for I-17, by the amusement park). A word of caution, I would not travel the route after dark, as is the case with most routes in the valley - be aware when riding of suspicious people and of course unaware motorists. There also is a newer spur connection trail going NE on Skunk Wash that connects to the main trail in the NW section.

Consolidated Canal Shared-Use Pathway — Runs through Mesa. Connects to the **Western Canal Path** in Gilbert.

Hiking - A wide range of hiking exists in the valley area, though most will want to hike between October and April. If hiking in the hot months, make sure to bring a lot of water.

Camelback Mountain - Just East of the intersection of Tatum, McDonald and 44th Street (after it bends to the East) is the entrance (on the south side of the road) to the hiking trail to the top of Camelback Mountain. I prefer this to hiking to the top of Squaw Peak, but it is strenuous. Fewer people use this trail then Squaw Peak, but still can be very busy and parking can be difficult. You can also take another trail — parking on Invergordon and hiking the east side of the mountain.

Piestewa Peak Park - This is a hiking and picnic area in the heart of the Phoenix (it used to be called Squaw Peak). Between the Highway 51 and 24th St. on Glendale Ave. (called Lincoln in Scottsdale), go north on Squaw Peak

Drive to the park entrance. This is the first light west of 24th St. or the 2nd light east of Highway 51. Follow the road up past the residential area.

Main Summit Trail - You will see the main trail to the left, once inside the park. This is a strenuous hike with a lot of people on the trail. Often it is hard to find parking near this trailhead on busy mornings.

Nature Loop & Other Trails - Otherwise continue to the end of the road and park. There are a lot of trails in this area, consult the map. I prefer this area due to its more quiet nature and in certain areas on the trails you don't even know you're in the city. This area a good picnic spot with built in BBQs and covered tables, called "ramadas" (nice at sunset with the BBQ going) - the ramadas can be reserved through the Phoenix Parks and Recreation Department.

South Mountain Park – Pima Canyon Trailhead - *Wonderful spot in the middle of the city* - To get there, take 48th Street South from I-10 and go past Baseline into the

Arizona Grand Resort & Spa complex (formerly Pointe South Mountain Resort). Baseline also intersects I-10 just to the East of 48th street. You will go past Rustler's Roost restaurant and a town house area on 48th Street. Before reaching Guadeloupe there is a booth or kiosk (for the park entrance) and a golf course on the right. Take that road (East Pima Canyon Road), west to the parking lot. Hike up the dirt road until it dead ends. Then find the trail sign and take the main trail (National) to Hidden Valley Trail. Fat Man's Pass is a spot on Hidden Valley Trail. Fat Man's pass is about 5 miles round-trip from your car. There are many other trails from the trail-head that you can also explore.

Superstition Mountains - Canyon Lake - A nice drive that takes about an hour. Even if you are not a hiker, the scenery is wonderful. You can also rent boats to see the lake. From Apache Junction (West of Phoenix), take Apache Trail (number 88) going northeast.

> **Hiking** - Nice hiking trail after the 2nd one lane bridge to boulder canyon (about 1 mile in affords wonderful views). If hiking remember to follow the trail up the hill and don't take the fisherman trail at the trail head.

> **Boating** – You can rent boats (Precision Marine on Canyon 986-0969, Sahuaro Lake or Roosevelt Lake 467-2245) or do an organized boat tour at the lake.

> **Restaurants** - There is a restaurant at Canyon Lake as well. If you continue driving on 88 past the lake, you will come to Tortilla Flat, a "small" town - trailer park, restaurant, and post office. I never had a meal there, though it would be a fun stop for a drink or burger. I knew one of the people that "owned" the town in the 40's when they were building the dams for the reservoirs (Canyon Lake...).

Superstition Mountains - First Water - Before canyon lake, on Apache trail, just past Lost Dutchman State Park (about 3-4miles outside Apache Junction is the First Water trail head, turn right and drive 2-3 miles on a dirt road (passenger passable - though don't drive too fast). The trail head is at the end of the road. Normally I take a right at the first "T" intersection (about 1/3 mile in) and back track after I have had enough. Sometimes I do a large loop, though this is too confusing to explain, call me if you want details on this. Many neat trails in this area, though watch which way you go and return by the same route, since many of the trails are large loops where you could get lost if you are not paying attention. Lots of people hike this on the weekends.

> *NOTE: In the Superstitions or any desert hiking, take water!!!! Bring at least 2 quarts in late spring. Be careful and watch for snakes once it gets warm (i.e. April), especially during the week when there are very few people on the trails. The weekends seem to be less of a problem. They normally are not out in the winter, since it usually is too cold for them. Also dogs and cactus don't mix well – be prepared to deal with a dog that finds them plus take plenty of water for them too. Please stay on existing trails, as the desert plant life is very fragile and doesn't recover like "wetter" climes.*

Shopping and Night Life

Arizona Mills – This is a factory outlet type shopping center with much more and the newest major mall in the heart of the valley. Tons of shops and it has been busy since the day it opened. There is a huge Harkins movie theater complex, IMAX theater and the Rainforest Café is a great place to eat (kids will love it). It is on I-10 at Baseline Road (South of the airport by about 3 miles). On the other side of I-10 on Baseline Road is

Biltmore Fashion Park - is located on 24th St. and Camelback (NE corner). Some great restaurants too. Great Sax 5th Avenue store.

Fashion Square - is located on Scottsdale Road and Camelback (NW corner). Niemann Marcus, Nordstoms and other high end department stores.

> **Harkins Camelview Theater** – This used to be the spot for art and foreign flicks. With the recent renovation they appear to still have some of those films along with mainstream showing. They also owned the original Cine Capri near Biltmore Fashion Park (was my favorite theater in town before being torn down) which reo-opened in a new location off of the 101 that I have not been to.

El Pedregal - At the Boulders, at Scottsdale Road and Carefree Highway, North of town. Trendy shops and sometimes they have live entertainment in the center court.

Arizona Center - Located on 3rd St. and Van Buren, in downtown Phoenix. It has interesting shops as well as great night life with several bars. Handy location if downtown, but for major shopping I'd try some of the other spotes.

Downtown Tempe - At the intersection of Mill and University, the downtown area ends at the Salt River. It has a nice movie theatre complex (Harkins) plus a wide range of eateries; it is a hopping place on weekends. My Big Fat Greek restaurant and Rúla Búla pub are fun – right on Mill. Now that the project at the Salt River is completed below Tempe, there is a waterfront area – **Town Lake**. The bike path system from Scottsdale down links into the north end of the lake. *Sadly downtown over the years has become more corporate than I'd like with icons leaving – most recently Coffee Plantation.*

Downtown Glendale – Known for its antique shops, it also has an awesome chocolate company and I hear they have an annual chocolate festival – Cerreta (5345 W Glendale Ave - www.cerreta.com - 623.930.9000)

Downtown Gilbert – Fun trendy place for a meal or hanging out – Gilbert Rd. south of Guadalupe Rd. **Western Canal Path** at north end of downtown connects to Tempe, Chandler and Mesa. The **Art Intersection Gallery** at 207 N. Gilbert Road is worth a visit (480.361.1118). Downtown art walk 1st/3rd Saturdays – October-March.

Old Town Scottsdale and 5th Avenue - The area around Indian School and Scottsdale road. Many galleries in old town as well as specialty shops on 5th avenue.

Fry's Electronics (no not the grocery store). This has to be the biggest retail electronics store in the state. If it is anything electronic or an appliance – they sell it. It is worth a visit if you are a gizmo fanatic. It is a pretty manic environment inside and not all the sale staff seem to be happy campers but for selection, no one can beat them. *I first shopped at them when they were only in California.*

My Sister's Closet & My Sister's Attic - Women's consignment store of designer clothing. Multiple Valley locations – one in Town and Country Mall.

Sun Devil Liquors – In Mesa on 235 North Country Club (just South of University) – heard they have a great wine selection downstairs with a lot of wine tasting events.

Hyatt Gainey Ranch Resort – In Scottsdale on the weekends, in the past a Jazz group Nuance played that was pretty talented. I heard them at a concert in Sierra Vista. 602.861.4961 or www.nuancejazztrio.com are contacts for the group Nuance.

Pointe Hilton Tapatio Cliffs - This hotel/development is North of Dunlap Ave., on 7th. Street, on the east side of the road. The bar at the Pointe (Terrace Room at the **Different Pointe of View restaurant**) is at the top of the rock, above the hotel, with nice views from the outdoor patio. I didn't go there often, but it was a treat to sit out on a nice evening. It is open evenings unless there is a special event. 602.866.6350

Greater Phoenix Swing Dance Club - lessons on West Coast Swing 6 P.M. Sundays at VFW – 4853 E. Thomas. Lessons are $10 (less for members) and open dancing after. http://www.greaterphoenixswingdanceclub.com

Water Parks – **Golfland Sunsplash** (Mesa) and **Big Surf Waterpark** (Tempe). Open in the summer (if you're crazy enough to be in Phoenix area in the summer). The **Kiwanis Recreation Center** also has an indoor wave pool. It is in Kiwanis Park (a city of Tempe park) on the south side of Baseline Road (between Rural and Kyrene).

Coffee Houses

The coffee houses in Phoenix are good but until recently did not approach Macy's in Flagstaff for the best coffee, in my opinion. Happily that has changed in recent years!

Bergies Coffee Roast House – In downtown Gilbert is a <u>wonderful</u> coffee house with nice patio area. Great espresso. 309 N Gilbert Rd

Cartel Coffee Lab – This is one I haven't tried but was recommended. In downtown Tempe. 225 W University Dr. (corner of Ash and University). There also is a downtown Phoenix one on 1 N. 1st St.

Cave Creek Coffee Co. & Wine Purveyors – 6033 E. Cave Creek Road – 480.488.0603 – www.cavecreekcoffee.com. A friend really loved this place and they recently got a super write up for smaller music venues in the Valley. It is on the very north end of the Valley and you can also take Carefree Highway from I-17 East to Cave Creek road.

Crepe Bar – On the NW corner of Rural and Elliot in Tempe. They are known for their crepes (so a good breakfast place). But I had an 'A-list' espresso drink there – something I rarely find. Next door is also a shop specializing in croissants (**P. Croissant**) so possible to keep everybody happy!

Luci's Healthy Market Place – On the NW corner of 16th St and Bethany Home is a great hang out spot that serves up breakfast/lunch and a pretty good coffee bar. The location is what makes it with garage style doors that open up on a hospitable day.

Restaurants

Since I don't live in the valley anymore, some of the restaurants may have changed completely or service shifted. Let me know of your experiences. For instance a neighborhood favorite, Richardson's caught fire and never re-opened.

Chinese/Oriental/Indian

Deli Palace – ate there after a many year hiatus. In a much newer building with very good food. 5104 E. McDowell – 602.244.8181

Gourmet House of Hong Kong - Phoenix on 1438 E. McDowell just west of 16th St. 602.253.4859. I had dinner there recently – this has to be one of the best Chinese restaurants in the valley – and authentic. The décor is very plain but the food is spectacular and they offer many unusual dishes that you can't get other places.

Malee's Thai Bistro - Scottsdale on 7131 E. Main St. - just South of Indian School and West of Scottsdale Road - wonderful Thai food (my favorite). Reservation needed for the winter. 480.947.6042.

Loving Hut – Vegan cuisine. Same location used to be **Supreme Master Ching Hai** also vegetarian. Loving Hut is a chain of vegan restaurants. 3239 E Indian School Rd – 602.264.3480 - www.lovinghut.us

Italian/Mediterranean

Bella Luna – In Goodyear (west end of the Valley) on 14175 W. Indian School Road - 623.535.4642.

Café Boa – 398 S. Mill in Tempe comes recommended from a friend. Haven't tried it yet myself but Judy has and she liked it. 480.968.9112.

Crazy Jim's Restaurant – 305 W. Washington (downtown Phoenix) 254-6550 or 4041 N. 15th Avenue 264-4777 or 1401 E. Bell Road 467-1111. Great place for Gyros or salads – good food and not pricey. One of my customers, Joel turned me onto the place and still good when I drop by with work downtown.

Golden Greek – 7126 N. 35th Ave just North of Glendale (on Westside of road) - nice Italian and Greek food in family atmosphere - great homemade pita bread. *Still one of my favorite spots as they keep turning out good food and keep it small and cozy.* 841-7849

Haji Baba - 1513 East Apache in Tempe (West of McClintock), great Middle Eastern food! 894-1905. Haji Baba also has a wonderful deli and you can purchase olives and feta cheeses from several countries. Also try **King Tut Café** on 1044. S Terrace Road (921-1670 - it is Southeast of the Rural and University intersection in an apartment and residential area) that has wonderful Middle Eastern food as well and attracts a large group of people from the Arabic community (they have a big screen TV with Arabic stations on it). Also **Princess Market** on 2620 W. Broadway (just east of Highway 101) that has a nice market section and serves food too.

Middle Eastern Bakery and Deli - On the west side of 16th Street between Thomas and Indian School (3052 N. 16th St.). They bake their own pita bread and have a good selection of prepared foods and Middle Eastern grocery items (not as extensive as Haji Baba but still very good). Open Tuesday-Saturday - 277-4927

Pita Jungle – On East Apache, West of McClintock on the north side of the road also one on Southern just east of Dobson. Good array of Middle Eastern and other eclectic options. If you have a vegetarian friend, they will find many things to choose from.   Though their service can be up/down. A plus is their happy hour and reverse happy hour with affordable apps and wine specials.

Pizzeria Bianco – Downtown near the science museum – in an old machine shop building (623 E. Adams St.). My friend Denise raved about the place. 602.258.8300. They have a sister sandwich shop **Pane Bianco** on 4404 N. Central (602.234.2100).

Ray's Pizza - Great NY style pizza on 59th Ave and Greenway (NE corner) 602.938.4065 (they also now have several other valley locations). Also try **Nello's** on 4710 E Warner Rd (the Tempe on McClintock and Southern store closed summer 2016).

Riazzi's Italian Gardens - 2700 Mill Ave. - South of Broadway - nice family run Italian restaurant that has been in the Valley for years. 731-9464. *This is one of my spots to hit when I come down from Flag – good value, good food and good service.*

Romanelli's Deli - 3437 W. Dunlap (249-9030) has an extensive Italian deli that includes imported cheeses, baked goods and prepared sandwiches. Based on the intersection of 35th and Dunlap you would not think of shopping for food there, but it probably has the most complete selection of Italian foods in the valley.

Romeo's Euro Café – Wonderful Mediterranean eatery with a to die for pastry case. Select wines $6/glass till 6PM. 207 N Gilbert Rd - 480.962.4224

Yusef's Middle Eastern Deli – 15238 North Cave Creek – in 2010 I found out about this great deli. They also serve up food too – probably their appetizers are a better deal. They have great feta cheese and olives at affordable prices. 602.867.2957

Mexican/Central American/Southwestern

Blue Adobe Grille – 144 N. Country Club (north of Main in Mesa). 480.962.1000.

Carlsbad Tavern – Recommended by a local as the best they had found for Mexican in the valley (3313 North Hayden Road - 480.970.8164) though it is more New Mexican oriented. Haven't tried it. Also the chain of **Rubio's** is very good – many in the valley (one is just West of the Rose Garden exit off of I-17 – left at first road and near where Target strip mall is). They started in San Diego area and have very fresh food. **Manuel's** - in my opinion, was the best Mexican restaurant chain in the valley (http://www.manuelsstore.com) but haven't tried Rubio's yet. Their meals are closer to authentic, with a very nice atmosphere. Try the green corn tamales.

Dick's Hideaway – Next to Luci's Healthy Marketplace on the NW corner or 16th Street and Bethany Home is a Southwest eatery that is open all day. No outside sign to mark the location, just a posted menu. The bar is dark and the wait can be long – so you might need something to drink while you wait. Happy hour is 3-6 and 9-close. (6008 N. 16th Street – 602.241.1881). http://richardsonsnm.com/

Eliana's - El Salvadorian cuisine, family run, on 24thStreet on the east side of the street, just north of McDowell Road (next to Pep Boys at 1627 N. 24th. St.). Try their "papusas" and "platano con frijoles y crema". 225-2925. *I had a chance to recently eat there again – still friendly service and wonderful food.*

Paletas Betty – Downtown Chandler on 96 W. Boston Street (just west of the plaza on a side street). They also have a Tempe location (425 S. Mill).

Parilla Suiza – Mexican food from the country's capital – restaurants in Phoenix (13001 N. Tatum and 3508 W. Peoria - 602.978.8334) as well as Tucson (5602 E Speedway, 2720 N. Oracle and 4250 W. Ina). Have enjoyed the meals there and they have a wider variety of menu options.

Raul and Teresa's - On the south side of Buckeye Road - 519 W. Main (Hwy. 85), just East of Litchfield Road (West valley) - 932-1120.

Restaurant Sinaloa – we happened on this small restaurant at 2601 E. Bell – 953-0430 (also one on 45 W. Broadway Rd. in Mesa – 464-0024). It had good food that was pretty authentic and had reasonable prices.

Fine Dining

Vincent on Camelback – Recommended by a friend in Flagstaff as a nice place for a meal. I haven't tried it yet. 3930 E. Camelback – 602.224.0225

Tarbells - 3213 E. Camelback – supposedly super good food – haven't tried it yet.

Razz's – Recommended restaurant that I haven't tried. Get a reservation. 10315 N. Scottsdale Rd. - 480.905.1308.

Other Places to Eat

U.S. Egg – Great place for breakfast - 131 E. Baseline – 480.831.0070 - 6:30 AM-2:30 PM. **First Watch** is another popular breakfast place.

Flancer's – <u>Amazing sandwiches</u>. 610 N Gilbert Rd **Lulu's Taco Shop** across the parking lot is also yummy.

Frasher's Smokehouse – Owner moved his Scottsdale steakhouse here and is hands on making great BBQ., 602.314.5599 – 3222 E. Indian School.

Karsen's Grill – 7246 East 1st Street in Old Town Scottsdale. It is a small intimate bar/eatery that has later food than some in downtown Scottsdale. Friendly staff too.

Old Station Sub Shop – At 1301 W. Jefferson on the south side of the street (near the state capitol). Not the best neighborhood but great sandwiches for lunch. 253-7665

Joe's Real BBQ – Downtown Gilbert on the east side (301 N. Gilbert Road) – closed on Sundays. Also has great homemade root beer.

Pomegranate Café – A wonderful vegetarian oriented café in Ahwatukee. They strive to provide local ingredients, including wine. Even raw food offerings. Expect a little slower service since many items prepared from scratch. It is on the SW corner of Chandler Blvd and South 40th Street (west of I-10). *This is a favorite of my friend Mary Ann. Cassie, one of the owners, is a wonderful spirit with passion for making yummy and healthy food.* 480.706.7472 - www.pomegranatecafe.com   Another nice vegetarian oriented restaurant is **24 Carrots – Café & Juice Bar** on 1701 East Guadalupe Road in Tempe. 480.753.4411

Rúla Búla Pub – Downtown Tempe – friends had dessert there and like it. Friendly spot for a beer. 480.929.9500.

Lodging

Biltmore Hotel – It is off of 24th Street (about 1/3 of a mile North of Camelback). This is a landmark Frank Lloyd Wright structure. The hotel is not cheap to stay at so you may opt to dine there instead, just to have the experience.

The Buttes - Not inexpensive, but it has, in my opinion, the nicest pool in the city and is centrally located near the airport. Good lunch buffet in the café.

Royal Palm Inn - On 5200 E. Camelback, about 2 mi. west of downtown Scottsdale. It is an older in that still has the flavor of the resorts that were popular here in the 40's/50's. *Note: This hotel has been completely renovated since I have been there last, so the experience may be very different.*

The Wigwam Resort – Upscale resort on the west end of town. Has had a good reputation for years – go north on Litchfield to Wigwam Blvd and turn right (east). 623.935.3811. They have had lower summer rates.

NOTE: There are many nice places to stay in Phoenix metro area. I recommend being near downtown Scottsdale or in downtown Tempe. Be careful with low and even medium $$ hotels as they may be in undesirable areas of town (i.e. Van Buren Ave.).

NORTHERN ARIZONA

Northern Arizona is completely different from the southern part of the state. It comprises the largest contiguous Ponderosa pine forest in the world and yes it does receive snow. When Phoenix is hitting 105 degrees, Flagstaff normally has 80-85 degree days. Yet driving 30-40 minutes from Flagstaff to Sedona, the temperatures can rise to the 95-100 degree range on the same day! The **Colorado Plateau** has some high desert areas that are sparsely vegetated (less than even the Tucson area). There are also a lot fewer people with Flagstaff at almost 70,000 inhabitants being the largest "city" for 140 miles. Prescott to the southwest of Flagstaff is the next biggest community. - lower in elevation so it has milder winters and more typically in the 90's in the summer.

PAYSON

Payson itself is mostly recent strip-mall like construction and their downtown historic area is nothing close to Bisbee, Yuma, Flagstaff or Prescott. It is located in a pretty area in the woods and there are some interesting restaurants and things to do if you dig around. Probably the closest spot to hit from Phoenix if you want to get to the woods (one of my customers commuted to Mesa every day from Payson). And a good shopping spot if camping on the Mogollon Rim.

Barnhardt Trail - The Mazatzal range (pronounced 'matazal' by locals – I'm not clear how that pronunciation developed), South of Payson is a pretty area, though rugged. The Barnhardt trailhead is a several mile drive in on a rough road (passenger vehicles worked last time I was in – though I went slow) from the main Beeline Highway (south of Payson). The trail itself is very pretty about a mile in.

Mogollon Rim - Driving up the Beeline Highway (87) to Payson then Highway 260 (towards Christopher Creek and then onto the rim itself is very nice). Sadly the quaint two-lane road is now becoming a 4-lane monster. You can also get to rim country from Flagstaff via Mormon Lake or the Verde Valley via Highway 260.

Some very good hiking in that area too, though be careful on where you park your car if in Christopher Creek itself (though it was years ago I have heard the locals can be pretty picky on where you leave it). A nice trail more-or-less follows the rim. Once you get on top of the rim on Highway 260, take the first road to the left onto Rim Road (Forest Road 300). At one of the overlooks, park and walk along the rim. Really great views!

PRESCOTT

Prescott is a wonderful town, originally slated to be the state capital (Phoenix won that political battle). With its famous Whiskey Row it draws weekend partiers. Yet the wide variety of shops and eateries provides a wide range of activities.

Downtown Prescott

Courthouse Square – The central town square downtown. It has a beautiful courthouse and bandstand. This really is a cornerstone to the community with many places to sit and catch up. Often with events - neat to visit during Christmas. **Hassayampa Inn** just off the plaza on Gurley Street is another historic landmark.

Whiskey Row – Is the grouping of old historic bars on Montezuma Street directly across from the Courthouse Square. Tons of antique consignment stores.

Prescott Center for the Arts - Performing arts center doing community theater. Art gallery in the basement. My dear friend Noelene paints sets for their shows. 208 N Marina St - 928.445.3286

Tis Art Center and Gallery – Nice gallery on 105 S. Cortez Street (928.775.0223).

Perigrine Book Company – 219 N. Cortez Street.

Hiking Shack - On 104 N Montezuma has quality outdoor gear and information on the Prescott area. Plus shoe experts to help fit sometimes pesky hiking shoes. 928.443.8565

Events

Prescott Folk Music Festival – The first weekend in October is the annual folk music festival in Prescott at Sharlott Hall (couple of blocks from the main downtown plaza). Formal events plus lots of people playing everywhere make this a fun afternoon (both Saturday and Sunday during the day). The historic buildings at Sharlott Hall alone are worth seeing.

Contra Dancing – Normally the third Saturday of every month during September-May is a Contra dance (folk dancing done in lines) and is usually at the town meeting hall (right at the corner as you turn right to enter old town Cottonwood. Starts around 7:30 PM but they sometimes have a pot-luck or meet for dinner beforehand. In Prescott it is normally the first Friday of the month at the Armory (on Gurley Street about ½ mile from downtown). It is a fun mixed crowd in a non-smoking and non-alcohol environment.

Getting Outdoors

Prescott has pretty good access to the outdoors. Other sites not mentioned below are: Granite Dells or hike Thumb Butte. The Prescott website has a lot of information on local trails: http://cityofprescott.net/services/parks/trails/

Circle Trail – You can get a **City of Prescott Trails and Outdoor Recreation map** for $1 from the Hiking Shack or other spots in town. The map includes the Circle Trail and other trails.

Prescott Peavine National Recreation Trail – A nice six mile graded dirt path that is right in town (fine for cross or mountain bikes). Take Hwy 89 to Prescott Lakes Parkway, then to Sundog Ranch Road. FYI - $2 fee to park (but a nice parking lot with a restroom). There are other places to park for free. Photo to the right.

Mingus Mountain – A really pretty hike is when you summit Mingus mountain (between Prescott Valley and Jerome) is to go north. Do not go into the campground (stay left) and you will get to a cattle gate. Go through and go about ½ mile more and on your right is a trail-head that will give you great views of Sedona and the San Francisco peaks. Think it is called Wood Chute trail related to and old flume that used to carry timber into Jerome. The campground is also nice.

Restaurants

El Gato Azul – Fun tapas style restaurant a couple of blocks off of the Prescott plaza. Had live music outside the night we dined there. FYI – I liked it though the kitchen is a little chaotic and might not be liked by some.

Gurley St. Grill – In downtown Prescott. They have their own brewery and great food/service. On 230 W. Gurley Street, 1 block west of the main courthouse plaza. 928.445.3388.

Maya Mexican Restaurant – Great local eatery in Prescott on 512 South Montezuma Street. When I was there I remember they didn't have a liquor license but let people bring in their own beverages (I'd check before going if you want to do that). 928.776.8346

Murphy's – Longstanding eatery in Prescott. Fun to have a drink at the bar. 201 N. Cortez – 928.445.4044

Raven Cafe – Wonderful spot serving up great food with organic/local focus including beer & wine. Have live music too! Nice upstairs patio. 142 N Cortez S – 928.717.0009 - www.ravencafe.com

Wild Iris – A great coffee shop in downtown Prescott on 124 South Granite Street (one street west of the courthouse plaza). Also great desserts.

COTTONWOOD/JEROME

Jerome is the mining town that sits above Cottonwood on the slope of Mingus Mountain. You can also drive over to Prescott from Jerome on State Route 89A. If you take that drive, see the note under Prescott for a pretty hike on Mingus Mountain. **Clarkdale** is another cute town near Cottonwood.

Verde Canyon Railroad - On my list to do, more scenic than the Grand Canyon railroad and supposedly can see eagles at certain times of the year. 800.293.7245.

Arizona Botanical Gardens - North of Cottonwood off of Highway 89. Nursery with nice cacti greenhouses and example plantings. Closed December to mid-Feburary. 928.634.2166

Dead Horse Ranch State Park – Below **Tuzigoot National Monument** – though you take an earlier turn off to get there. Good picnic areas and trails.

Tavasci Marsh – At Tuzigoot National Monument, is one of the best spots to see birds in the state - especially during migration.

Blazin' M Ranch – Outside of Cottonwood is a fun, Western-themed frontier town that is great for couples, families or groups. With meals, ranch adventures, entertainment, and special events. 928.634.0334 - https://www.blazinm.com/

Native American Ruin Sites

Montezuma's Castle National Monument – On I-17 before the exit for Sedona. It is a Sinagua culture cliff dwelling from around 1100 AD. It's just a few minutes from the freeway and worth seeing. *When my grandfather saw it in the 1940's, you could still tour the actual cliff dwelling – now you can only view it from below.*

Tuzigoot National Monument – Just outside Cottonwood is another ruin site that is worth seeing from the Sinagua culture. The Sinaguans were part of a trade network that included cultures to the south and the better known Anasazi of Mesa Verde National Park.

Shopping

Old Town Cottonwood – Wow! Cottonwood has really evolved. The old town area has had a huge influx of shops in the past couple of years. Worth walking around.

Jim & Ellen's Rock Shop – Funky rock shop that has been in Old Town for years.

Wineries – Several vineyards have tasting rooms in Old Town. Plus you can visit others touring around the area. One I liked is **Alcantara Vineyards and Winery** – out of town a bit on the Verde River with a nice patio. 3445 South Grapevine Way (off of Thousand Trails Rd.) - 928.649.8463

Clay Art Studio (Cornville) – Cute gallery plus studio where clay classes are tought. 9435 Cornville Road – 928.852.4481

Jerome – Up 89A south past Cottonwood is a neat mining town called Jerome with all kinds of cute stores. I enjoy wandering the streets with the historic buildings – like Bisbee there are many sets of stairs to navigate the hillside town. Jerome is getting gentrified – when I went there in the 1990's there were a few shops with many buildings in poor shape. Now many buildings have been restored and there is a variety of shopping, including several wineries. You can continue on 89A over Mingus Mountain to Prescott and down to Wickenburg. This is a very nice drive with lots of scenery.

    Spirit Room – This bar has been supporting live music for years. Fun to hang out if there is a band you like.

Restaurants

Annie's – Good spot for a diner breakfast. 660 E. Mingus Ave.

Crema Café – in Old-town Cottonwood (917 N. Main Street). A nice place that makes a good cup of coffee and upscale breakfasts. Though it is a bit pricey in my opinion. I'll go back since it is local and good however. 928.649.5785

Colt Grill – New BBQ joint in Old Town Cottonwood.

Haunted Hamburger House - In Jerome above the police station (take the stairs at the station end of the small park in town center). Great views of the San Francisco Peaks and great burgers, steaks and ribs. Just don't ask for vegetables!

Manzanita Inn (Cornville) – 11425 E. Cornville Road – wonderful restaurant in the community of Cornville – 928.634.8851. *The service was stellar – and in Cornville of all places!* You can get there from 89A between Cottonwood/Sedona (stoplight a few miles out of Cottonwood go east) or exit 293 off of I-17. I'd recommend reservations.

Nic's Italian Steak and Crab House – Mainstay in Old Town Cottonwood. Nice Italian eatery with upscale feel. Large portions. 928.634.9626

Su Casa Mexican Restaurant (Clarkdale) – In downtown Clarkdale is a good, family run Mexican restaurant on the same side of the street as the old gas station. *I saw some poor reviews on the web – this is not an upscale restaurant and serves family style Mexican and is as much about the atmosphere as the food, being a long-time local place. It may not be what you want but I like going there.* 928.634.2771

Thai Palace (Cottonwood) - A new Thai restaurant is in old town Cottonwood – 704 N. Balboa St. – 928.639.0444 (just up from the spot where the road takes a hard right as it enters the old town shopping area). Friends feel it is the best Thai in the state – they may be right. Great service too. They have a sister restaurant in Uptown Sedona – 260 Van Doren Road – 928.282.THAI.

SEDONA

Sedona is located about 40 miles South of Flagstaff (1 hour) or about 100 miles North of Phoenix (about 1 ½ to 2 hours by car). The beautiful red rocks draw millions of tourists a year. It has wonderful hiking, scenery, shopping and restaurants. However, there is not much night life, if you are looking for a "hopping" resort. *At busy times, traffic in/out of town can be crazy, especially if coming down from Flagstaff or up from Village of Oak Creek – afternoons seem the worst.*

NOTE: Sedona has many places to explore via foot, bicycle, horse or jeep. Please remember to stay on established trails or roadways. The high desert environment is very fragile. There is a type of plant that covers the soil (Cryptobiotic soil) and resembles a lichen, walking on it can kill it, allowing the soil it protects to blow or erode away.

Things to do

Chapel of the Holy Cross - Church built into the red rock. Take Chapel Road off of 179 (right if coming in from Phoenix).

Sedona Heritage Museum – For those not wanting a jeep tour, hike, or shopping experience; this might be of interest to you. A preserved family farmstead and a center for regional history. 735 Jordan Rd - www.sedonamuseum.org - 928.282.7038

Events

Sedona Film Festival – This has grown into a major event (and sadly not as inexpensive as in its infancy). It is in early March and in the past was at the Harkins Theatres in West Sedona. I have heard that if you don't get VIP passes, all the good seats get taken by VIP pass holders. www.sedonafilmfestival.com

Christmas Lights - Tlaquepaque Mall - During Christmas time (December 1 – January 1) they have a special light display and events. *They took it over from the* **Los Abrigados Resort** *next door, which had an amazing display where owners would compete for the best display – sadly they no longer do that.*

Getting Out & Seeing Red Rock Country

Sunset at Sedona Airport – There is a parking lot at the top of the mesa the airport is on (to your left). You can walk over to some incredible views of Sedona – worth doing if there is a good sunset (or sunrise too).

Red Rock Crossing - Off of upper Red Rock Loop - follow signs. See water (creek) side of famous Cathedral Rock -trails, wading, picnic areas.

Schnebly Hill Vista - Take Schnebly hill road (across Oak Creek bridge from Tlaquepaque) - about 1 mile of rough road. You can continue on this road to Flagstaff - though it is very rough.

Sedona Photo Tours - Photo tips, history, flora and fauna through the red rocks in yellow jeeps.

Oak Creek Canyon - Drive from Sedona to Flagstaff through Oak Creek Canyon on 89A is really neat. The U.S. Forest Service loans a tape describing the canyon during the drive, the local office may have one (I got mine in the Flagstaff Supervisor station on 4th Street 527-3600 - they also have as small bookstore and trail information for Sedona and Flagstaff areas). Beautiful fall colors (usually peaks end of October/early November). *Please note that to park in the canyon, most places require a* **Red Rocks Pass** *– some locals are very upset about it and protest the pass. Passes are sold in many places, including the observation overlook at the top of the canyon.*

West Fork of the Oak Creek - is a _really_ incredible hike, about 10 miles North of Sedona (look for big parking lot on left - sign will say 'PARKING 500 FEET' and the road makes a sharp turn to the right at the entrance to the parking lot). Bring wet water shoes if you plan on hiking more than 3 miles in, up to that point you can normally keep your feet dry at the stream crossings. Parking lot now has a fee to park - get there early as it is a popular spot to explore. For backpacking enthusiasts camp beyond 7 miles out (climb up hillside on right of camping area to a cave - interesting supplies are usually left by kind campers). Also if you want the place to yourself and get a parking place, you want to get there as early as possible (you will still have lots of people on the way out). If you get there early, remember to bring cash to pay for parking as you will need to put it in an envelope and have the exact amount (around $5 but that can change).

Sterling Pass – Almost directly across from the Mazanita Campground is the Sterling Pass trail. There is very limited parking on the road. This is the back way into **Vultee Arch** on the other side of the pass. Until the spur to the arch trailhead on the other side of the pass, you won't see many people. It has a fair bit of climbing but worth it for views and varied vegetation. _This may be closed due to the recent fire in the canyon._

Slide Rock State Park - is also popular, though very crowded in the summer. They normally sell apples in the fall since the park was an old apple orchard. Bring your swimsuits to slide on natural water slide - though a summertime event since water can be cold. If water quality poor they close creek to bathers.

Grasshopper Point - Has wall jumping - into Oak Creek. Be very careful of underwater boulders dragged in from early 1990'sfloods!

Midgley Bridge - located about 2-3 miles North of Sedona on 89A. It is the first bridge north of town and has choices of canyon and mountain hiking. Many stop just for a photo. Can hike up to Mount Wilson (also from Encinoso picnic area).

Shopping

Garland's Indian Jewelry – A wonderful store that sells high quality Native American jewelry, pottery, baskets and paintings. It is in Oak Creek Canyon next to **Garland's Indian Gardens Café and Market.** 928.282.6632

Garland's Navajo Rugs – The sister store to the jewelry store in the canyon. It is on the roundabout across from Tlaquepaque mall. Their rug collection is superb! 411 State Route 179 - 928.282.4070

Tlaquepaque mall - It has all kinds of neat expensive stuff (it is on 179 just south of the "T" intersection of 179 and 89A in Sedona). It is next to the Los Abrigados resort. Don't miss the **Rowe Gallery** - In the tower section at the front of the mall has a nice mix of sculpture and paintings (http://rowegallery.com/).

Uptown Sedona - There are scores of art galleries and gift shops -the "Uptown" area (just north of the "T" intersection on89A) is a popular area to browse. Two stores I like are the **Worm Book Store** (928.282.3471) and the **Blue-Eyed Bear** which sells jewelry and decorative items (928.282.1158). *FYI – the Worm has relocated to the Village of Oak Creek Outlet Center but still worth a visit.*

Hoel's Indian Shop – in Oak Creek Canyon. 928.282.3925 – it is just South a bit from the West Fork trailhead in a house. This is a very upscale shop with very high quality items.

Restaurants

Elote – on 179 South of Tlaquepaque mall about ½ mile at the King's Ransom Hotel property. Great chef grade Mexican food. Jeff the chef/owner is very attentive and wrote a great cookbook (2010 Xmas present for my sister). *Friend Denise loves this place.* 928.203.0105

Garland's Indian Gardens Café & Market – Popular stopping spot four miles north of Sedona on Hwy 89A. The most recent incarnation is trendier with coffee, breakfast, & lunch items. 928.282.7702 http://indiangardens.com/ *Next door is* **Garland's Indian Jewelry**.

Orchard Canyon on Oak Creek (formerly Garland's Oak Creek Lodge) - In the canyon above Slide Rock (Banjo Bill picnic area is in front of it on the highway side of the creek). Fixed menu in the past. *Incredible food. Very well run and immaculate grounds. You must book ahead and weekends fill up around 6 weeks ahead of time and weekdays 2 weeks ahead of time (they are also not open year round). They* have a garden area and greenhouse for growing produce too. I have not tried them since the new owners took over. 928.890.4023

Mariposa Latin Inspired Grille – 700 AZ-89A (a bit west of the roundabout for the Sedona post office) - 928.862.4444 – www.mariposasedona.com

Oak Creek Brewing – The have the brewery near Basha's in West Sedona (2050 Yavapai Drive) and have a full restaurant in Tlaquepaque mall with very good food. The brewery is a local's hangout though it has expanded over the years and is known by tourists now.

Picazzo's Healthy Italian Kitchen Sedona - My friend Les's favorite lunch place. 1855 State Route 89A

Red Planet Diner – In West Sedona on the south side of the road. Fun diner experience – great meatloaf.

Rock Springs Inn – This is actually on I-17 at exit 242 (Black Canyon City area), south of the freeway exit on the frontage road on the west side of the freeway (if coming from Phoenix, you will exit and go left over the bridge and left on the frontage road for about ¼ mile). They have really <u>great</u> pie and pretty good BBQ sandwiches (the pie is what they are known for). A good stop off spot for a snack or lunch. *Recent feedback is the pie is not as wonderful as it used to be.*

Thai Spices – A great Thai restaurant at 2611 State Route 89A. They even have good vegetarian dishes. Closed on Sundays. 928.282.0599. *They have been in Sedona for over 2 decades – though haven't tried since their move. Would also consider the* **Thai Palace Uptown**.

Lodging

Orchard Canyon on Oak Creek (Formerly Garland's Oak Creek Lodge) - In the canyon above Slide Rock (Banjo Bill picnic area is in front of it on the highway side of the creek). 928.890.4023. FYI - *almost impossible to get a weekend there but weekdays are possible. Very well run and immaculate grounds.*

L'Auberge - Creek side and very romantic lodging, though very pricy. Ride the helitrope from creek side to Uptown area. Great honeymoon or weekend splurge spot. Gourmet French cuisine. Well worth the price and pampered by "tuxed" waiters. 800.905.5745

Sky Ranch Lodge and Motel - At the Sedona airport (it is not a major airport). Reasonable by Sedona standards with nice views from the mesa overlooking Sedona. Lately they have been up-scaling it a bit so it may not be the value it once was (though the stellar views are still there). 928.282.6400

ROUTE 66 (I-40)

Interstate Freeway I-40 has largely replaced nostalgic Route 66 in the Southwest. You can find bits of it in many of the towns that were along its way. Plus some sections still intact such as passing through Seligman and Oatman.

OATMAN

A small old mining town turned tourist town. Famous for its "wild" burros. I plan to stop there next year – it is a bit out of the way to visit.

SELIGMAN

This is a small community just North of I-40 on historic Route 66. It has worked to keep its Route 66 heritage intact.

Delgadillo's Sno Cap – *On the south side of Historic Route 66* **A must stop.** This place is known for its quirkily friendly service and classic drive-in fare (though it is a walk up window).

KINGMAN

Fast-growing town on I-40 – most strip malls and sprawling development. However the downtown area (south of the freeway) is quaint and has some nice little diners and potential for being even nicer.

Rosie's Den – On Highway 93 to Las Vegas is a small diner and curio shop with good affordable food and a friendly staff. It is on the west side of the highway.

ASHFORK

Lulu Belle's – Great BBQ. At exit 146 of I-40. 928.637.9818

WILLIAMS – GRAND CANYON GATEWAY

Williams has really evolved into a fun town. It is famous for the **Grand Canyon Railroad** that takes you from Williams to the Grand Canyon. A fun time to take the railroad is around Christmas when they do the Polar Express (800.843.8724).

Gallery in Williams – Artist cooperative. 145 W. Route 66.

Bearizona – Great family activity – www.bearizona.com

Planes of Fame Air Museum (in Valle) – www.planesoffame.org

Restaurants

Grand Canyon Coffee & Cafe – Great diner. Locals call it Anna's. 137 W Railroad Ave - 928.635.4907

Red Raven Restaurant – Spot for an upscale meal. Lunch/dinner. 135 Historic Route 66 - 928.635.4980

South Rims Wine & Beer Garage – Great spot for tap beer, wine or light meal. 514 E Route 66 - 928.635.5902

Hiking

Bill Williams Mountain – Go to the Forest Service station on the west end of Williams (west I-40 freeway exit for Williams). The trailhead is there. Best views are if the fire tower is manned and you are permitted to catch the view from there. This is a more strenuous hike, climbing 2,000+ vertical feet.

Sycamore Overlook and Sycamore Falls – From 4th street in downtown Williams go north about 8 miles to Forest Service 110. Now go about 6 miles (didn't clock it) to FS 109 & go left. Staying on this a few miles past the campground will take you to Sycamore Falls trailhead. A popular climbing area plus the trail along the ridge is super. At 'Y' for campground, you can go right to Sycamore Overlook – incredible view of Sycamore Canyon. You need a sturdy, high clearance vehicle.

FLAGSTAFF

Flagstaff is a fun mountain town with lots of things to do. It got its start as a timber and railroad town. From museums such as **Lowell Observatory** and the **Museum of Northern Arizona** to the **Arizona Snowbowl** ski area you can get your city or outdoors "fix". Because of the strong influence of the **Northern Arizona University (NAU)**, there is quite a mix of people here – their sports teams are called the Lumberjacks. The town is also surrounded by National Forest, allowing for camping, hiking, mountain biking, and skiing. There are several National Monuments in the area that are worth a visit.

Many people traveling to the **Grand Canyon** pass through Flagstaff, but never visit its quaint downtown with interesting shops and restaurants. Rather they hit a gas station at the entrance to the city along with a quick stop at a fast food joint along one of our less attractive stretches of road. Instead of doing a one-day marathon drive from Phoenix or another city to the Grand Canyon (over 10 hours in a car); why not spend a night in Flagstaff or Sedona, to the South? It allows you to see quite a bit more of this interesting part of the country.

Things to do

Downtown Flagstaff - It is fun just to walk around downtown and check out the shops. At night there are quite a few clubs worth checking out; several normally have live music on the weekends. The evening crowds have a wide range of ages in many of the clubs, not just early twenties.

Museum of Northern Arizona - On Highway 180 heading towards the Grand Canyon on the south side of the highway. A very good local museum that focuses on local items of interest, including some very good weekend "markets" in the summer that each focuses a different Native American tribe.

Riordan Mansion - Behind the Chase bank building on Milton road is a mansion of the timber barons Riordan Brothers. It was built at the turn of the century and unlike many historical buildings has much of its furnishings intact. It is decorated for Christmas and they do a special Halloween program (call on October 1 and it books quickly). To make reservations, call 928.779.4395. http://azstateparks.com/Parks/RIMA/

Lowell Observatory - Where the planet Pluto was found. On some nights, including Saturdays (weather permitting - have night viewing!!). I found the tour very interesting and viewing Saturn through the big telescope a real treat. Note: objects selected for night viewing vary by season. 774.2096 or http://www.lowell.edu.

The Arboretum at Flagstaff - 4001 S Woody Mountain Rd - 928.774.1442 (out of town a bit on a dirt road).

Sunset at Arizona Snowbowl - Note: *This is a great place any time of year to watch a sunset (if there is a good one brewing).* In fact I think it has one of the prettiest ones in the country. So if the ski area is closed, take a bottle of something, someday and enjoy one there. Further information on Snowbowl is below.

Lockett's Meadow - Take U.S. 89 towards Tuba City and go left at same intersection for Sunset Crater/Wupatki. About ¼ mile there is a road going to the right - this will take you to Lockett's Meadow. You can hike to the Inner Basin from a trailhead (heart of the volcano that made the San Francisco Peaks). The road is usually closed in the winter. Great place to see the aspen trees changing colors in the fall.

Grand Falls – Also called the Chocolate Niagara (though not as large). When running this may be one of the prettiest waterfalls in the 4 corners region. Typically this runs the middle of April till snowmelt runoff goes away – but check to be sure and we were out in January after some big snowfalls that were melting. You officially need a permit from Visitor Center to travel into the backcountry on the Navajo reservation – 928.679.2303 though I am not sure how strict they are with Grand Falls area as it is a popular area. Take Winona Road from Highway 89 (just North of Flagstaff). Go left on Leupp Road and then left at the Navajo Bible Church sign (about 15 miles from Winona road and right where the signs identify you are entering the reservation and you are about 15 miles from Leupp). Then go about 10 miles on rough dirt road. An alternate route is to go an additional 5 miles on Leupp road and turn left on 6910 (also a dirt road and the Arizona Gazetteer map has it mislabeled as 6920) – this will 'Y' with the other road and at that point go right. This road is in much better shape. At the falls, about ½ mile before the river crossing are several dirt tracks to the left.

One of the better ones takes you to a couple of overlook points – it has a small rock cairn as well. When coming back you can eat at **T-Bows 2 Bar 3 Historic Restaurant and Saloon** which is on 5877 Leupp Road to the east just before the intersection of Leupp and Winona roads (and after the auto salvage yard) – they have BBQ, sandwiches and pasta as well as a Sunday Brunch. 928.526.5388

National Monuments in the Flagstaff vicinity

Wupatki National Monument - Ruin sites north of Flagstaff on 89 (highway to Page). The Crack-in-rock ruin site is incredible. They only take 3-4 groups there on a two day backpack trip in the fall/spring (otherwise it is closed). People are selected via a lottery system (you must call ahead for the lottery). We did the trip and were impressed by the ruins we saw and the ranger that lead our group really made the trip special.

Sunset Crater National Monument – Next to Wupatki. Beautiful cinder cones and a cool lava flow. It is worth a detour if traveling from Flagstaff to Page. Do the loop through Wupatki. The hiking trails are very short. To hike **O'Leary Peak**, you head from the Highway 89 into the park but go left on a forest service road before entering the park (which can be closed in the winter so you park closer to the paved road).

Walnut Canyon National Monument – Off exit 204 on I-40. There are interesting ruins with a pretty hike (not a long hike but somewhat strenuous, since you must hike up and down several hundred feet on a paved path). They sometimes have special hikes on Saturday and Sunday, call for availability.

Events

Downtown Art Walk – First Friday of the month is art walk from 6-8PM. Well visited by locals. I'd start downtown on the galleries on San Francisco Street including **West of the Moon**. Sedona has a similar event but not sure of the dates.

Downtown New Year's - They drop a pinecone from the historic Weatherford hotel to bring in the New Year.

Fall Science Festival – Lectures and other events make this an interesting way to be exposed to interesting topics in science.

Flagstaff Mountain Film Festival – is definitely a local event that focuses on outdoor related films and slide presentations. I really enjoyed the event and it had an entertaining yet relaxed atmosphere. www.flagstaffmountainfilms.com

Heritage Square – Downtown plaza that has live music (typically Thursday evenings), outdoor movies (Saturday evenings) and other events during the summer. *They moved around movie night from Fridays to Saturdays so it doesn't interfere with Art Walk and other events.*

NAU Tuesday Night CAL (College of Arts & Letters) **Film Series** – During the school year a film series runs on Tuesday nights at the Cline Library auditorium (to the right as you enter the lobby of the library – past the coffee shop). It is free and they showcase great films. Believe start times are 7PM.

Riordan Mansion - It is decorated for Christmas and they do a special Halloween program (see more information on a prior page). Reservations are needed for special programs.

Evening Activities

Blendz Wine Bar – Barrels of single wine varietals are available to drink individually or make custom blends. You can create your own or use recipes from the staff. 21 East Aspen Avenue.

FLG Terroir (previously Wine Loft) – Wonderful wine selection. Some food options. On 17 N. San Francisco (2nd floor). Live music on some nights makes it livelier. The owner recently remodeled and changed the name to reflect the upgrade – still a great place for a glass of wine – 773.9463

Historic Brewing – Three locations – two downtown and in Williams. My favorite is the taproom in their brewing space on 4366 E. Huntington Dr. www.historicbrewingcompany.com

Nomad's Global Lounge – 19 W. Phoenix

Orpheum Theatre – On Aspen between Beaver and Leroux streets is a 1918 theater that runs various events – mostly traveling groups that do a show. Fun venue for a concert, though have to admit the sound system isn't as good as it used to be. Tickets at theatre are 928.556.1580.

Pay-N-Take – Right across from the Orpheum theatre is casual bar that serves wine, beer and espresso. It is a popular spot on Friday evenings and afternoons anytime in the summer.

Rendezvous – In the **Monte Vista Hotel** is a bar/coffee shop that works well for those of us over 35 that want a cool place to hang out. Right on the corner of San Francisco and Birch streets. *Plus last time I was in friends ordered some interesting cocktails – the bartenders play around with their own infusions.*

Root Public House – Restaurant and bar with nice upstairs patio seating. 101 S San Francisco St. - 928.774.1402

Wanderlust Brewing Company - Brew pub in a funky warehouse. Open Wed-Sat. It is in East Flag about a block north of Route 66 - 1519 N Main St - 928.351.7952

Uptown Pubhouse – A smoke free pool hall with a killer beer selection and plenty of tables. Music via jukebox isn't too loud. On Leroux street – 928.773.0551

Dancing

Contra Dancing – Normally the first Saturday of every month is a Contra dance (folk dancing done in lines) and usually at Mountain Charter School (located by Ponderosa Trails Park off Lake Mary Road) at 311 W. Cattle Drive Trail. Starts 7:00 PM (beginner lesson) and 7:30 dance. It is a fun mixed crowd in a non-smoking and non-alcohol environment. http://ffotm.org/contra-dances/

Galaxy Diner – When school is in session, Saturday nights from about 6PM on there is dancing in the lobby of the diner (on Route 66 just West of Milton road). They also meet at other locations in town. http://flagstaffswing.weebly.com/

Salsa Dancing – The NAU Latin Dance Club has had lessons on campus – in the past it was on Wednesdays and recently Tuesdays. When I went (years ago now) they then went down to South San Francisco street to dance later in the evening. They also promote things from the **Flagstaff Latin Dance Collective**.

Bicycling Around Flagstaff Area

Mountain bikes are king in Flagstaff. There are numerous trails and forest service logging roads to ride on, including Shultz Pass and many roads around the Lake Mary area. The Flagstaff Urban Trail System (**FUTS**) is mostly well-graded dirt trails that can take you from Ft. Tuthill (county fairgrounds), over Mars Hill (Lowell Observatory area that connects Thorpe Park into Railroad Springs off of Rte. 66) as well as out to Fisher Point. The system keeps getting better! A very good book describes mountain bike routes – **"Fat Tire Tales & Trails: Arizona Mountain Bike Trail"** by Cosmic Ray (he also has other books on hiking and mountain biking for the state).

Waterline road - One dirt ride worth mentioning for fall colors (typically late September to early October) is **Waterline road**

which is a dirt road that goes from Shultz Pass road (park about ¼ mile West of the Waterline road). You can ride up to the cabins (friends said about 9 miles) through some spectacular stands of Aspens then on up to the Inner Basin (heart of the San Francisco Peaks volcano) or out on other trails that link in. You can also hike up to the cabins from the Locketts Meadow trailhead. *Summer 2010 fire and later rains have closed the road – check on status.*

Road Bicycling

For road riding, the best routes are:

Lake Mary Road – Best is to drive to just before Lower Lake Mary and park if you want a shorter ride and hit the pretty section immediately (there is a wider paved area with mailboxes where cars doing this park). From the mailboxes, a loop out around Mormon Lake is about 48 miles. Mormon Lake Lodge has good breakfasts and heartier fare for lunch plus service was better the last time I was out (but be aware their serving schedule varies summer to winter and they may not serve some times of the day). *They recently widened the road from town so you can now safely ride from pretty much anywhere in Flag out to Mormon Lake. Also I'd recommend riding mid-week if you can – the traffic can get kinda busy on weekends and drivers aren't always considerate.*

Wupatki - The loop through Wupatki and Sunset Crater. I like going from Wupatki visitor center to Sunset Crater visitor center & back but you can do the whole loop going out on Highway 89. If not shuttling cars, make sure to park so you get your climbing out of the way first since it is about 2,000 vertical feet.

Arizona Snowbowl Road - (a killer climb)

Walnut Canyon National Monument – Take old Route 66 (recently repaved!) to I-40 crossing over into Walnut Canyon. Be aware of traffic on the stretch between the mall and I-40.

Designated Bike Routes - In town the city has may roads designated as bike routes, including Forest (which turns into Cedar and Lockett) and Butler.

Hiking

There are many super places to hike in the Flagstaff area. Remember to take water and rain gear. See hikes under nearby Williams too!

Mount Humphrey's – Tallest spot in Arizona. Drive up to the ski area – trailhead from ski are parking lot.

Kendrick Mountain (9+ miles) – Go out Hwy 180 past Snowbowl road, past the Nordic Center and take the first ungraded, forest service road to the left (1-2 miles further down). There are 1-2 before that but with gates and more of a track than a road. Go till the road 'T's and go right. Follow the signs to the trail head.

Veit Springs (1-2 miles) – Pretty aspen grove for fall colors and a short interesting hike to take newbie hikers on. Take Snowbowl road off of Hwy 180 (west of town about 6 miles) and go up about 5-6 miles. The road will have a straight section and turn to the left. At that spot is a pull off with a big metal gate behind it and park there. Go through the gate and follow the dirt road/track back up over Snowbowl road. You may notice a clearly defined trail that spurs off after the main trail/road curves away from Snowbowl road. That will take you to the powerlines and then into Veit springs area. There is a cabin, springs and pictographs as it was used by Native Americans as well as herders. The cabins are part of a hold sheep herding camp. *Note: you need a permit to park if the road is closed for roadside parking – normally this is in the winter when Snowbowl ski area is open but I'd check even in the summer. The Peaks Ranger district office can get you a permit (928.526.0866).*

Sledding & Snow Play

There are several designated places to sled in the forest – one is Wing Mountain off of Forest Road 222. My preferred spot has easier access is a cinder pit 1 mile North of the Arizona Nordic Village (go past another Forest Service on the west side and you'll see a sign that says Parking – just past that turn left to the West into the woods on a dirt road a short ways). The cinder pit hills work well if snow covered as there are less obstacles and you can park off of the highway. Both sites are accessed from Highway 180 from Flagstaff. I do not recommend parking on Highway 180 to snow play – it is a major accident waiting to happen. There are several other places to park off of Highway 180 – Forest Road 794 and the Wildlife Viewing Area just before Kendrick Park. Snowbowl Road is not open for parking any more – FYI.

Skiing

Please note that snow conditions can change quickly, especially for X-C centers, as they are lower than the downhill resorts. Snow permitting, there are many other ungroomed places to explore with X-C skis in the National Forest - best bet is on Highway 180 in the vicinity of the **Arizona Nordic Village**, since it is higher elevation than closer to Flagstaff. If you are new to Arizona, because of the varying snow conditions (unless you are skiing when it is snowing), wax-less skis perform much better overall than the waxable ones I loved in Minnesota.

There is also X-C skiing in the White Mountains, at **Hannigan's Meadow Lodge - Nordic Center** south of Alpine. The Lodge also has lodging and other activities (be aware that even if open they may not be prompt in calling back if you leave a message). Also many ungroomed sites near Sunrise Ski Area but it is National Forest trails (not a privately run center).

Arizona Nordic Village - Has great trails/skis. They are located 7 miles past Arizona Snowbowl ski area turnoff, on Highway 180. Hours (when open based on snow conditions) are 8AM-4PM Thursday-Sunday and major holidays and open till 5-7PM on Fridays. Now have yurts & cabins to rent year round. In good snow years they have had special events such as moonlight skis or an Eat, Drink, and Ski Merry (3 course meal with wine with short ski/snowshoe distances between courses). 928.220.0550 - www.arizonanordicvillage.com

X-C Skiing - Highway 180 – Forest Service Road 794 - Off of Highway 180 (road to the Grand Canyon from Flagstaff), besides the Nordic Center, many other good spots to ski for free are available. Before the Nordic Center on the right, look for Forest Service road 794. There is a good area to park right there (and off of Highway 180) and just ski up the road. It normally holds snow well and as long as people aren't driving on the road, it should be in good shape.

X-C Skiing - Highway 180 – Wildlife Viewing Area - Another spot is past the Nordic Center and just before the Chapel of the Holy Dove on the west side of Highway 180. There is a parking lot on the south side of Kendrick Park with a brown sign identifying wildlife viewing. Follow the wildlife-viewing trail on the west side of the parking lot (behind the outhouse, not the other trail to the South). It will link into many unused Forest Service roads. This seems to have the best snow I've found, even when you think there is no skiing left.

Jacob Lake - From Jacob Lake Lodge, drive south on Highway 67 till the road is closed for the winter and ski away – there are some forest service roads you can follow. Jacob Lake is on Alt 89A that connects Kanab to Marble Canyon via the Kaibab plateau instead of the main Highway 89 that goes through Page.

Arizona Snowbowl Ski Area - Great small ski area aimed at better than average skiers and snow boarders (1-2 days is enough for most people, unless you can handle the expert terrain, I personally enjoy skiing there). In the summer the ski lift takes hikers/sightseers to the top of the ski area with nice views (can see the rim of the Grand Canyon on a clear day) and can hike to the top of Humphrey's peak. I taught skiing there part time. In bad weather, the road will be restricted to chains/4WD. For sledding, they are now controlling most sledding off of Snowbowl road – there are other areas to sled a bit further out on Highway 180 past Baderville. 779-1951. *Note: This is a great place any time of year to watch a sunset (if there is a good one brewing).* In fact I think it has one of the prettiest ones in the country. So take a bottle of something someday and enjoy one there.

Shopping

Arne Ceramics – Fun, functional ceramic pieces – my parents love the coffee mugs he makes. It is on Route 66 West out of town (turn at Barnes and Noble and go West and is about ½ mile past the next stoplight on your right. He has variable hours - especially in the winter. He also has pieces for sale in the coop gallery downtown. 928.779.0429

Bookmans Entertainment Exchange – Great used book store that also sells CDs, DVDs, musical instruments and collectibles. It is behind Chase bank on Riordan Ranch Road (next to Michaels).

Downtown Flagstaff - North and also South of Route 66 between Beaver and San Francisco streets are a wide array of interesting shops.

>**Arizona Handmade Gallery -** On San Francisco street about ½ block North of Rte. 66. Friend Marcia has her clay animals in there and there is a good selection of a wide range of artists/styles. Two doors down is **The Artists**

Gallery that is a fine arts and crafts cooperative that also worth a visit.

Bright Side Bookshop – Nice local bookstore downtown. 18 N San Francisco St – 928.440.5041

Puchteca - 20 North San Francisco, 928.774.2414 - has a wonderful selection of high quality Native American artisan items at fair prices. If you want good value and not an inexpensive trinket – I'd stop by.

Sagebrush Trading – Quality casual outdoorsy clothes. 120 N. Leroux in the **Old Town Shops** (there are other neato shops there in what is the old J.C. Penney building).

Vino Loco – Great local wine shop on Birch Street, just west of the court house. They now have a wine bar too! – 928.226.1764.

West of the Moon Gallery – Nice gallery packed with neat stuff (a few doors down from Puchateca). Carolyn the owner may be working on beadwork – one of her specialties. 14 N San Francisco St - 928.774.0465

Winter Sun Herbs – The front of the shop sells wonderful Native American jewelry and Kachina dolls. The back of the shop is an herb shop with a variety of essential oils, tinctures and other herb products. They also sell the full line of Super Salve products. http://www.wintersun.com/

Coffee Houses

Coffee - Everyone knows about Starbucks. Here are some local places that serve up great coffee. **Fire Creek Coffee, Macy's** and **Late for the Train** locally roasts their own coffee and have their own bakeries.

Campus Coffee Bean - In the strip mall at University and Milton. I particularly like them for supporting local music and other events. They are also convenient if on Milton Road near I-40.

Fire Creek Coffee – Right downtown – another very fine place for a cup of coffee & friendly staff.

Late for the Train is another nice coffee house with a shop on Birch and San Francisco or on Highway 180 going out of town on the right. The Highway 180 stop is handy when going skiing or out of town hiking or to the canyon.

Macy's - On Beaver St. south of train station – for years the only place I could find a great espresso. Others have recently caught up. Has a wonderful bakery and inexpensive food (a lot is vegetarian). Great people watching. During the week they have happy hour on coffee drinks from 4-5PM. *It is a must stop for the "Flagstaff experience".* **I'd have to say Macy's is the standard I have placed all other coffee houses against, as it was the first really good cup of coffee I had in the USA, circa 1992.**

Restaurants

Sadly on my most recent visit to Flagstaff I noticed that the service in many places was a bit off. Staff in more than one spot seemed more focused on chatting with friends than taking care of other customers. I have also noticed this in ski towns. I still love Flagstaff and its eateries – just a warning to be patient.

Beaver Street Brewery - across from Macy's and Bellavia on Beaver Street (on west side of the street, 2 blocks south of the train station). New restaurant that brews own beer with good food (including stone fired pizzas). 779-0079

Black Bart's Steak House - Average to good steak house with a wonderful music review (the waiters are NAU music majors). My parents love going there and I only go if have guests in town that haven't been there.   779-3142 (they take reservations)

Criollo Latin Kitchen – took over the well-known old Cafe'Espress location and serves up tasty Latin food. 15 N. San Francisco. *It and its sister locations Brix and Proper strive to provide local and/or organic sourced foods when possible.*

Breakfast (or Lunch) Places

La Bellavia - two doors down from Macy's on Beaver Street - wonderful breakfasts (only open breakfast/lunch).

Brandy's - is located in the east end of town (on West and Cedar in the Safeway shopping center) and open some evenings for dinner. Menu is very similar to La Bellavia for breakfast/lunch as they used to have the same owners - with the addition of bakery and dinner items! 779-2187

MartAnne's - Has excellent Mexican breakfasts and lunch. Try the Chilaquiles or Huevos Rancheros. 112 Historic Route 66 - 773-4701 (now open Sundays). They are better known now so there could be a good wait, especially on the weekends.

Fine Dining

Brix – In my opinion the current best restaurant in town. It is on North San Francisco a few blocks north of downtown. 928.213.1021 *They change menus seasonally and service is top notch.*

The Cottage – Long standing upscale restaurant that recently got new owners. Dinner only and normally make reservations! *I have not tried new incarnation but friend raved about it.* One block west of Beaver Street & 2 blocks north of Butler. 126 W. Cottage Ave - 928.774.8431

Tinderbox Kitchen – on South San Francisco Street. I like eating in **The Annex** bar over the restaurant – still great food but more relaxed. Friend Denise loves this place.

Mexican

Los Alteños – On 1481 S. Milton Road (west side) in the same strip mall as Hickory's Smokehouse and BBQ. Great family run restaurant – my favorite for real Mexican food. *But it is not fancy and the TV is always on a Spanish channel and there may also be Mexican music going as they really cater to people from Mexico/Central America. Not the choice for a fancier date. Kinda stuck on the Birria – try it if you like lamb (but you can get it as a soup too).* Homemade chorizo. 226-7552.

Tacos Los Altos – On Rte. 66 between Fanning and the Country Club/I-40 overpass between Jack in the Box and Arby's. It is in my neighborhood and only recently tried it – the food is good and I can walk there! *Recently went back when visiting and the food is still good and affordable.*

Interesting and Eclectic Places

Morning Glory Cafe - 774-3705, open weekdays for lunch and I believe breakfast. Really great salads and soup. I normally get a tamale/soup combo. Menu seems to vary daily for salads and soups. On San Francisco, South of Route 66. *Maria the original owner passed away – a loved soul that served up great food. I recently went and the new owner is serving up the same great food and with an equally great smile.*

Dara Thai Restaurant - On 14 S. San Francisco Street, about 2 blocks south of the railroad tracks. The food is superb. It rivals anything in Phoenix. 928.774.0047. Another nice Thai restaurant is the **Little Thai Kitchen** on Milton Road next to the Crystal Creek sandwich shop (behind a gas station on the west side of Milton).

Hiro's – Great sushi on South Plaza Way across from Ross and Safeway. Only open lunch hours and dinner hours (gap in between and normally closed on Mondays). It lacks a little in ambiance (they need to get rid of the tacky fluorescent lighting). Another great place downtown is **Karma's** right on Rte. 66 – it is more upscale and date friendly than the other two but I prefer Hiro's for a mid-week relaxed dinner.

Pho MPM – got turned onto this place winter 2016 by friend's Patrice/Bruce. Affordable Vietnamese. 2112 N 4th St. - 928.714.9999

Red Curry Vegan Kitchen – 10 N San Francisco St.

Italian Restaurants (including Pizza)

Alpine Pizza - (downtown on Leroux, just North of Route 66). Good pizza in a fun, college atmosphere. Can order by the slice (with the toppings you want). 779-4109 For a slice of pizza my friend Karen prefers **NiMarco's Pizza** on 101 South Beaver Street – another long standing Flagstaff icon.

Mama Luisa's Italian Restaurant – At Route 66 and Steves Blvd. in East Flagstaff in a strip mall. It is about ¾ mile west from US 89. Excellent food and service in an unexpected spot. I've always had a good meal there though one friend sadly had the opposite. 2710 N. Steves Blvd. - 526-6809, reservations recommended.

Pasto - 19 E. Aspen 779-1937, long standing restaurant with great Italian food (between Leroux and San Francisco). Fun atmosphere. Reservations recommended.

Lodging

Starlight Pines Bed and Breakfast – Nice bed and breakfast on the east side on Lockett. It is about 2 blocks West of Fanning on Lockett. Michael and Richard put on a great breakfast and wonderful hospitality. 928.527.1912.

Little America – Very nice motor hotel with interesting (and spacious) rooms. A unique gem of a place – it also gets 4 stars from Mobil I believe. It also is a favorite of many who have stayed there, including myself when I lived in Phoenix and traveled here. It is off of the Butler Ave. freeway exit on I-40 just east of main I-17 and I-40 intersection. The property is situated in the forest and has nice walking trails too! Their gift shop was recently downsized – not as wonderful as it once was but still one of the best I've seen in a hotel. 928.779.7900

WINSLOW – STANDIN' ON THE CORNER

Besides being known in a song – 'standin on the corner in Winslow, Arizona' the town of Winslow is an old railroad town. **Standin' on the Corner Park** has a statue commemorating that song in the center of town (though the building behind it burned recently). The downtown has character but currently is not thriving – the railroad business isn't what it used to be.

La Posada Hotel - Just east of <u>the</u> stoplight in downtown is the restored La Posada that was an old Fred Harvey hotel. In its day it was a showplace. It is one of the nicest (or nicest) pieces of architecture in the Four Corners region. They even have a tour booklet about the history. *Since it was designed by Mary Colter as a railroad hotel, it is worth walking out to the railroad tracks and entering the hotel that way to give you a better idea of how the architect designed the property to be seen.* It is on Historic Route 66 (303 E. Second Street - 928.289.4366). They hotel also has a wonderful upscale restaurant called the **Turquoise Room** – I have eaten there several times and everyone I have been with has loved it (928.289.2888).

The Winslow Theater – Downtown they are currently showing main-run movies in the renovated theater. I think it is cooler than the Orpheum in Flagstaff. Sound system is good but not stellar. *I haven't been there in a few years but still showing first run movies.* http://www.winslowtheater.com/.

E&O Kitchen (at Winslow Airport) – Fun place for a meal (go south from the stoplight downtown to Airport road and take a right following it to the airport). I still miss Port Java (was a fun and unique little eatery) but happy to this equally good replacement at the airport. 928.289.5352 – closed Sundays. *The Winslow Municipal Airport in the early days of aviation was one of the key refueling stops for the airlines crossing the Southwest chosen by* **Charles Lindbergh**. *Lindbergh also stayed at the La Posada hotel. In fact from the air you can see the current and old runways – most are now derelict except the main one for current air traffic. Originally there were several runways pointing in different directions to help avoid planes landing in a cross wind by choosing a runway that pointed into the wind (not as critical with modern planes).*

HOLBROOK–PETRIFIED FOREST GATEWAY

Popular stopping spot on I-40 (East of Flagstaff) – crossroads to Mogollon Rim area to the south (State Routes 377 & 77). Gas prices in the past have varied significantly station to station – check around for better prices.

Petrified Forest National Park – Worth a visit, huge petrified logs are cool. Just east of town on I-40 or entrance off of Highway 180. Also Painted Desert viewpoints north of I-40.

Mesa Italiana Restaurant – Nice mom/pop Italian restaurant. You can also eat in the bar. 2318 Navajo Blvd - 928.524.6696

Old Bridge – There is a cool old one-lane bridge south of the town of Woodruff. Take Highway 77 south of Holbrook and go to Woodruff and follow dirt road south of town a few miles. It crosses the Little Colorado River.

GRAND CANYON

There is nothing quite like it in the world. It is really worth a visit. However, millions of other people also want to see the park each year and it can get very crowded. Going to the South Rim in the winter or visiting the North Rim (currently only open in the summer and the fall) is preferred.

If you do go, try to take time to really see it. I have heard that the average time viewing the canyon is in seconds or a few minutes. Staying for sunset really adds to the experience! If you decide to dine at the canyon, some places (e.g., El Tovar dining room) take reservations - make your reservation earlier in the day to insure a better chance of getting in.

SOUTH RIM

Get there via Flagstaff, going up Highway 180 to the main entrance or via Highway 89 and in via the Desert View side (turn off is 1 mile south of Cameron Trading Post). Several things to do there:

East Entrance

If you haven't been to the South Rim before, I recommend doing a loop that will take you in or out of the east entrance. This is going in from the East of 89 and 64 (via Cameron).

> **Cameron Trading Post** - If going in from the East, stop by and check out the store (1 mile south on 89 from the turnoff to the canyon on 64). Plenty of interesting stuff(new, antique and collectible). Make sure to see the gallery in the old two story rock building (some of the pieces are of museum quality!). The restaurant is fun too and not pricey with good food. Try a Navajo Fry Bread Taco.

> **Desert View** - Stop in and climb the tower (used to be $.25 – but was free the last time there) - it is touristy but a lot of fun and recommended. Tower based, in concept, on Anasazi (ala Mesa Verde)structures) and designed by the renowned architect Mary Colter. There are actual ruin sites in the canyon that can be visited as well, though better ones are up in the four corners region (Mesa Verde, Chaco Culture, Canyon de Chelley, Betatkin and Hovenweep).

El Tovar Hotel - One of the great old national park hotels. Beautiful log structure. Has a nice main dining room with wonderful food (though expensive) that does take reservations. Try breakfast or lunch if wanting to spend less $$. 928.638.2526 x6432 and central reservations are 928.638.2052. For less expensive dining, try the Bright Angel Lodge, a few minutes' walk to the West (though at popular eating times, the wait may be fairly long).

Shopping – Hopi House is a wonderful gift shop. It is directly next to the El Tovar hotel. **Verkamps** was my favorite gift shop (next to Hopi House). The Verkamps family was one of the original settlers at the canyon. *Sadly now the wonderful Verkamps shop is a visitor center and museum to the Verkamps* *family. This is due to issues with renewing their park contract in 2008 under 1998 law for park concessionaires.*

Grand Canyon Music Festival - Normally in August-September with wonderful performances (most are at Shrine of the Ages next to the South Rim visitor center and one typically in Flagstaff at the Orpheum). Not all concerts are classical. www.grandcanyonmusicfest.org.

Grand Canyon IMAX Theater- Just before the South Entrance on west side of the road. This is worth seeing (I was even impressed, originally thinking it was a tourist trap). Seasonal last show times (as early as 5-5:30 PM). 928.638.2203

Havasu Falls - It is located on the west end of the canyon is wonderful, though it is a 10 mile hike (can rent horses) to it. There is lodging and camping - but you must make reservations with the Havasupi Tribe - since it is on their reservation. Horses to carry packs can also be arranged. Once in the town, you must hike 2-2 miles further to get to the falls. April and September are usually the easiest months on your body. In hotter months it is important to hike out early in the morning to avoid hiking the last part in the heat (since the last section is a good climb up).

Colorado River Rafting - Advance reservations needed with professional companies (easiest to acquire is take in at Diamond Creek to Lake Mead). Most adventurous run is over rapids of Lava and Crystal. Commercial trips are usually 3-14 days. Sometimes you can run into non-commercial river runners in the old downtown Flagstaff bars for other trip choices (you need to be flexible as to when they go on a trip).

Hiking

I recommend hiking into the canyon (even 20 minutes) to really experience it. Remember the canyon can get very hot in the summer, especially the further down you go (into the100's at the bottom) - bring plenty of water!

South Kaibab trail - it follows the ridge line for better views and is a lot less crowded than Bright Angel, though steeper and no water. Some mule traffic. To get there, go right at the "Y" intersection inside the park (coming up 180). This road also goes to Desert View. Look for the sign for Kaibab trail (to the left) 1-2 miles from the intersection.

Bright Angel trailhead - (right out of the main village)has water at several stops, though expect a lot of people and several mule trains.

Hermits Trail - take the West rim shuttle (makes several stops at gorgeous overlooks) from the village to the last stop, Hermit's Rest (has gift shop and snacks). In the fall and spring you should be able to drive there. The trailhead is about 1/8 mile behind the Hermit's Rest off of a dirt road. This trail is not maintained, though still in fairly good condition as of 5/95. You will see even fewer people here than on Kaibab. Bring water!

NORTH RIM

It is up on the Kaibab plateau and about 1000 feet higher than the South Rim. Highway 67 only open in the summer (though can X-C ski in the winter - see skiing section for more information).

A good time to go up is in the fall after all the facilities close if you want solitude. There seems to be <u>much</u> less traffic then and the road to the North Rim (from Jacob Lake) one winter it was open until December 1 — talking with snowplow crews, they try to keep the road open till just after Thanksgiving so people can get Xmas trees. But going up the fall, if it snows, they may only plow it once a day and at some point they stop altogether. Remember there may be fewer overlooks to stop at and the lodge closes sometime in September or early October (their plumbing is not designed for really cold weather).

Lees Ferry – This is a major take-in to the Colorado River and a popular spot to launch fishing boat. It is managed by the US government and has camping as well as a small beach area along the river. The actual houses for the original ferry can be walked to and this will link into the Paria canyon area (permit needed).

Horseback Riding – This company also offers rides at the North Rim, Zion and Bryce Canyon parks. 435.679.8665 http://www.canyonrides.com/

Marble Canyon – This is the section of Highway Alt 89 between the turn off from US 89 (South of Page) and Jacob Lake. It is a beautiful drive. Below is a view looking back towards Marble Canyon from the view point heading up the Kaibab. A new modern bridge crosses the Colorado River. The old Navajo bridge across the canyon is now only open to pedestrian traffic and worth stopping to walk across.

Exploring the Four Corners Region

Jump Up Point - Another spot someone recommended that I haven't been to is Jump Up Point and directions as best I have them are to take the main forest service road west after Jacob Lake (should be 222) and turn onto FS 416 in the area where it goes by an old ranger cabin and where 416 'T's go right and then take your first left.

Lodging and Restaurants

Grand Canyon Lodge - Reservations for the main lodge, at the North Rim, are 928.638.2611 (within 48 hours) and 888.297.2757 if further out. The main restaurant also has really good food and an incredible view. Sit on the patio and have a beverage and watch the sunset!

Kaibab Lodge - Located 18 miles away from the rim and much more quiet. They also serve food though lately prefer the restaurant at the rim, Vermillion Cliffs or Jacob Lake. Beautiful meadows on the drive in from Jacob Lake. You may want to tie into a trip up to Zion National Park or Lake Powell. 928.638.2389. This is an odd little place that I would pick for location and not amenities. Closed in the winter.

Jacob Lake Inn - Is located where the highway to the canyon spurs from 89A. This is a fairly modest motel but has always been clean. They have great food as well. Their grilled cheese with onion and I believe bacon is killer. They are also the only gas station for many miles. 928.643.7232

Vermillion Cliffs Bar & Grille – This is a good restaurant and I stop there sometimes instead of up at Jacob Lake. 928.355.2231. Fun and friendly service as well plus a good beer selection. Charlie who works breakfast is a stitch. Proud of their BBQ ribs. Also the **Lees Ferry Lodge** is right there and has reasonable rates for quaint lodging sans TV (though it is popular with fisherman that fish in the Colorado below the dam so you might want to make a reservation). I also recommend it over restaurants right by the Navajo bridge.

NORTHEASTERN ARIZONA

PAGE – GATEWAY TO LAKE POWELL

The town itself is pretty plain but it is a jumping off point to many neato sections of Arizona and Utah.   You can stay in town or at the lodging right at Wahweap marina (though pricier there).   If you want to get directly to the core part of town, turn on North Lake Powell Blvd.   Where North Lake Powell Blvd crosses North Navajo Drive is where the visitor center is located and most of the better eateries in town.

Lake Powell

Also see notes under Utah (most of the lake is in Utah).   You can rent houseboats (plan ahead).   It is easy to get lost on the lake so I'd recommend taking an excursion tour to Rainbow Bridge instead if you have limited boating experience or might have trouble navigating a lake with many side canyons (that can all look the same).   I may not agree with the ecological issues of the dam (including that it will eventually fill with silt and become useless) but it is a beautiful place to recreate. Page, Arizona is a few miles from the main marina.

Wahweap Marina – This is the main marina on the lake and the easiest to get to from Arizona since it is right off of Highway 89. The marina has the monopoly on houseboat rentals out of Page and is run by ARAMARK which an authorized concessioner for the lake. Though you may be able to rent directly from owners – I even noticed them on AIRBNB. **888.896.3829** - http://www.lakepowell.com/

Skylite Rentals - 435.675.3795 will rent runabouts – it's like boating the Grand Canyon. Runabouts alone are expensive – years ago we spent over $300 to rent a boat for a day – including gas.

Rainbow Bridge National Monument - Is an incredible site to see part way up the lake. Take tour or rent a boat.

Wahweap Overlook – West on Highway 89 past the dam and turn off for Wahweap marina is a signed overlook. Drive down the dirt road to the parking area. Perfect to be there at sunset. Picture on prior page is from the overlook.

State Route 98 – This is a pretty drive that connects from Page back to Highway 160 (that highway goes through Tuba City, Kayenta and Cortez).

Navajo Route 20 – In 2013 this 28 mile section road was paved as an alternate route to Page when Highway 89 closed due to a significant landslide for several years. It is a nice alternate route to Page that crosses State Route 98 just before Page.

Antelope Canyon – South of town over by the power plant is one of the most beautiful slot canyons you can see. You can pay in town for a tour or drive out to the side and let the Navajo tribe shuttle you out. The latter is cheaper though they don't run shuttles out to the site too frequently so if time is important, take the more expensive tour. This site is a few miles in a dirt road from the highway. They drop you off right at the entrance. The actual slot canyon is about ½ mile long and easily walked.

4th of July Fireworks – They have them over the lake. We missed them but they must have been good based on the traffic jam we had to deal with. Ideal is to be out on a boat.

Short Walks

Trails Circling Town - There is a short walk you can do if you drive to Lake View Elementary school (at the end of N. Navajo (go left where Stombolli's Italian restaurant is to the end of the road). Hiking trails with views of the lake. Still on the edge of town but a good place to get quick exercise. Can do several walks – one out the end of potato hill (north) or looping east around town and the airport.

Horseshoe Bend – South of town on Highway 89 (south junction of State Route 98) is a clearly marked road to a short 1.5 mile round trip high that overlooks the horseshoe bend in the Colorado below the dam. Really pretty view. Best to do early in the morning during the summer months or close to sunset (no shade).

Mushroom Rocks – The Toadstool Trailhead is on the road between Page and Kanab. The trail is an easy hike (about 2 miles RT). For more information look under Kanab, Utah.

Page Restaurants

Page caters to the boating crowd so seems to be family oriented or beer oriented. There used to be an amazing Italian place there years ago Bella Napoli but it is gone! *I don't travel through Page as much in prior years, so happy to get new hints for good spots in Page.*

All of these eateries are on North Navajo Drive either side of North Lake Powell Blvd. Many are in the Dam Plaza on the SW corner of that intersection.

Bonkers – Nice sit down restaurant with variety of offerings including Italian. Open evenings March through October (closed Sundays and Mondays). 928.645.2706 - www.bonkerspageaz.com

Dam Bar and Grille – Sports bar feel with great tap beer selection and a really nice bar to sit at. Food and service when I was there was adequate but from on-line reviews it may not be a place to eat during busy summer months (I was there in February).

Ranch House Grille – For breakfast or lunch – a super diner experience for breakfast and popular with locals from what I can see. Even have French fry sauce – combination of ketchup and mayonnaise that I make on my own. 819 N. Navajo Drive (just off the main drag in town – about a block past Strombolli's) – 928.645.1420.

Strombolli's – This restaurant also has good food and more mid-scale. 711 N. Navajo Drive.

FREDONIA

This is a small community just south of Kanab – I frequently travel through there en route to the St. George/Cedar City area. They also have a Forest Service office with local area information (another office is up at Jacob Lake). The lodging here is more basic than that you'll find in Kanab or St. George – **Crazy Jug** seems to be a good choice (clean and fairly new but not fancy).

Nedra's Mexican Restaurant – This just reopened and had good food in the past. They also have Nedra's Too in Kanab but locals seem to think the original is better. Ate there years ago and the food was good but and recently went back and is still good and the staff is really friendly. http://www.nedrascafe.com/

Pipe Springs National Monument - If driving from the North Rim up to Zion, on Highway 389, is a preserved pioneer site just West of Fredonia. It was used by the Mormons to graze tithed sheep and is a good example of what life was like at the end of the 19th century.

Prairie Dog Pottery – In Fredonia at the intersection of the Highway 89 and Highway 389 is an old gas station (SW corner) that now houses a ceramics studio. The owners are very friendly and create some fun items. I don't know if they still do it now, but even after hours they leave out product and ask you to pay on an honor system. Neat to see that is still around.

NAVAJO & HOPI RESERVATIONS

This large area of land in the four corners region is distinct from most areas of the United States. Its culture is very different and rich while the level of Western development is lower, especially when getting off of the main roads (which often are the only paved roads). I feel it is worth exploring due to the beautiful landscape and interesting people. *And don't forget to watch for the wonderful skies that can be amazing with incredible cloud formations.*

NAVAJO RESERVATION

It is much larger than Hopi Land and it completely encircles their neighbors. The primary towns are Tuba City, Kayenta, Window Rock and Ship Rock. You can find jewelry shopping from roadside stands where prices and quality vary as well as neat scenery such as Monument Valley, Navajo National Monument, and Antelope Canyon. Classic rock formations in Monument Valley (North of Kayenta) have graced many a Western movie. The Northeastern side where the Chuska mountain range resides is a contrast to the high desert red rock country – the Chuskas have an extensive forest of pine, spruce and fir.

Native American Vendors - On 89 heading towards the reservation (or any other areas in the "Rez"), there are many Native Americans selling their wares. Normally this includes silver jewelry, pottery and rugs. There is quite a range in quality and prices so buyer beware, though it is a fun way of shopping and often you can really get great prices. My favorite style is Hopi jewelry - though on the Hopi reservation there are fewer roadside stands and more stores. With Hopi jewelry, make sure it is authentic, since it is expensive, if buying the real thing.

Cameron Trading Post - About 45 minutes North of Flagstaff is a historic trading post – celebrating 100 years! Be sure to explore the gallery in the 2 story stone building. Many pieces are of museum quality. The have lodging set around a nice courtyard. 800.338.7385 for lodging reservations.

Monument Valley – Between Kayenta and Mexican Hat on Highway 163 – famous rock formations. You see quite a bit driving on Highway 163 or take a tour of the area (I have not taken one of the tours). Leaving the valley to the north and looking south is the well-known shot in Forest Gump when he was running cross country (picture above – this was taken by a friend Jeannie from Page).

> **Goulding's** – Just west of Monument Valley. Long running operation – the owners during the Great Depression went to Hollywood and with luck met movie director John Ford, selling him on using Monument Valley, he made 10 movies there. Lodging and good food. 435.727.3231

Navajo National Monument – This is the home of Betatakin and Kiet Siel ruin sites (about 1100 A.D.). These are supposedly some of the best in condition in the Southwest. You can view the Betatakin ruin sites from the rim of a short hiking trail. Kiet Siel however requires a long hike/horseback ride and guide (normally can only book Memorial to Labor Day). Reservations are also needed for Kiet Siel.

CHINLE/GANADO AREA

This is the town at the mouth of Canyon de Chelly. Best food in town the locals like is the Junction in the Best Western motel complex.

Lodging – the **Holiday Inn** is the most upscale but I prefer the **Thunderbird Inn** right on the National Monument and a nice quiet spot (though the Best Western near the junction has a pool and internet access). The cafeteria at the Thunderbird Inn is fine for breakfast but would go elsewhere for dinner. Next to the Thunderbird Inn is the campground – when we were there it was free (not sure if that way year round).

Canyon De Chelly National Monument - Northeast corner of the state next to the town of Chinle. White House ruins are worth seeing - I'd recommend getting a guide for a better tour versus a group tour. 4WD is needed to drive in the canyon. Don't miss some of the overlooks too!

Chuska Mountains

The range goes from approximately Window rock and ends just south of Four Corners (if you include the Lukachukai Mountains directly North of the Chuska range). Normally you should look into a permit to really explore this area, though you can drive over Buffalo Pass that goes east of Lukachukai into Red Rock.

Beautiful drive – **N-13/BIA-13** – From Chinle drive to Tsalie where the Dine College is and then take the road to Lukachukai (N-12 or BIA-12). Now take the road over **Buffalo Pass** to Red Valley (Navajo 13 or BIA-13) and onto US 491 (about 10 miles south of the town Shiprock, NM) – this is a steep and windy but really beautiful road (**closed in the winter and not suitable for rigs with long trailers**). At the summit is a small picnic area with great views of Shiprock (large stand-alone rock butte). As you near US 491, you will pass the actual Shiprock (there also is an actual town called Shiprock north on Highway 491). Best time to do this drive is around sunrise or sunset. You can also drive down to Window Rock on the Eastern side of Canyon de Chelly on N-12 – this is also a pretty drive.

Chuska Challenge - An annual bicycle ride that supports a non-profit reservation youth group (Y.E.S.) is held in October. It is supported and gets into the heart of one of the prettiest places in the state. This ride is called the **Chuska Challenge** and the donation fee is $30 to do the ride (www.youth-empowerment-services.org is the web site of the Y.E.S. organization that will contain information about the Chuska ride along with a spring ride they sponsor). They also do a spring ride on the west side of the Rez. *I have done this ride five times now and always enjoy it, though be prepared for unpredictable weather.*

Hubbell Trading Post National Historic Site - Is near Ganado, on the way to Chinle and Canyon De Chelly, is a historic trading post that is worth the visit.

Restaurants on the Navajo Reservation

When driving through NE Arizona, there are not many opportunities to eat or get gas for that matter. It is a very rural area. FYI - there is fast food in Tuba City and Kayenta. There is a diner in downtown Tuba City called **Kate's** that is also good (North at stop light and then right at next major road and it is on the right) – *November 2011 note: sadly the place is closed and boarded up – possibly a fire or other problem.*

The Junction - In Chinle in the same parking lot as the Best Western. Good place for breakfast, about ½ mile from the US 91 intersection. The **Holiday Inn** is a bit better for dinner but pricier and has a good Navajo Taco. *Though I have to admit I prefer eating here and last trip the breakfast was still killer plus* they remodeled the restaurant – *might now be the best diner on the Rez.*

Anasazi Inn – Just west of Kayenta is a pretty good diner. *Sadly they burned down and still haven't rebuilt.*

Tuuvi Café – In Tuba City right at the main stoplight intersection is a small diner on the SW corner of intersection inside gas station. *Closed recently – may reopen.*

Cameron Trading Post - The main restaurant has good food – especially the Navajo tacos. It is about 45 minutes North of Flagstaff.

Goulding's – A few miles west of Highway 163 at Monument Valley (north of Kayenta) has good food and lodging.

HOPI RESERVATION

This is a really interesting place to explore. This reservation is totally surrounded by the Navajo Reservation (or 'REZ'). Unlike most Native Americans, they have kept much of their traditional ways intact. They are also amongst the poorest economically of the tribes, though I feel in life-style one of the richest. Try to leave you preconceptions behind and observe their culture. The 'pikki' bread is a local staple, try it if you get a chance (though you may not like it). If you can go during a dance/festival that is open to the public – take advantage of the opportunity. Though the schedules are often hard to determine.

Walapi is worth seeing, take time for the walking tour. Be sure to ask people you buy things from what clan they are from, their clan is important to them as our nationality is to us.

SOUTHERN & EASTERN ARIZONA

Southern Arizona, including Tucson area and I-10 corridor towards New Mexico includes beautiful stretches of the Sonoran desert as well as the "sky islands". The sky islands are mountains that rise above the desert floor, supporting pine forests. Mount Graham and the Chiricahuas are two of these oasis of green in the desert. See the Globe/Oracle/Florence for areas North of Tucson.

Also worth considering is the Mexican-border area South of Nogales. Nogales itself is a busy boarder town but going south the town of Magdalena with its wonderful plaza and church downtown is worth seeing. Also Hermosillo is prettier than most Mexican cities. I have heard that Alamos further south is also a wonderful jewel of colonial architecture (it is an old mining town). The area around San Carlos is touristy but nice – we used to go to the Club Med there (sadly closed). It was on Catch 22 beach (where parts of the movie was filmed). There are still nice places to stay and a really pretty beach (though hot in the summer and cool in the winter). To go South of Nogales, you will need to pass through an area where you will need to: get personal papers (birth certificate or passport is recommended), car insurance, photocopy all papers and then turn them back into a fourth spot where they will call your name to get a decal put on your car's window. Coming home, remember to drop of your decal.

GLOBE/SUPERIOR

This is the mining region SE of Metro Phoenix and North of Tucson. I have liked driving through these towns, either for a visit or as another way of getting between Tucson and Phoenix.

Things to do

Boyce Thompson Arboretum – Located on Highway 60 just outside Superior. It has a wonderful collection of desert plants.

Tonto National Monument - Neat cliff dwelling ruins site of the Salado culture. Call ahead to book a hike to the upper ruins (only in the fall/winter/spring). You get to the monument via State Highway 188 that spurs north off Highway 60 between Claypool and Globe. You can also take 188 to Roosevelt Lake and then head to Apache Junction on Highway 88 (Apache Trail – the first section down to Tortilla Flat is unpaved) or you can continue on Highway 188 to Highway 87, a 4-lane highway which heads up to Payson or down to Mesa.

Aravaipa Canyon - This must be hiked or backpacked to see, a really beautiful place. Permits from BLM 428.4040. If the canyon has recently flooded, a 4WD vehicle may be needed to access the trailhead, otherwise passenger vehicle is OK.

Downtown Globe - Like Florence, it isn't touristy, yet it has the feel of a real small town with turn of the century buildings. The courthouse is now a cooperative art gallery that you can walk around and explore.

Downtown Superior and Miami - Their downtown areas are not in the best condition, but still have the feel of the West in them. I sometimes cut through the downtown areas rather than take the main highway bypass.

Restaurants

I haven't tried the restaurants in this area for a while so not sure of current conditions – would appreciate feedback.

Blue Ribbon Cafe - Downtown Globe - great home-style food (pies...). *Not sure if they are still in business.*

Tortilla Factory - Downtown Miami - sells homemade tortillas. *I believe this sadly has closed.*

La Casita - In Globe, next to Blue Ribbon Cafe - great Chicken Chimichangas.

Little Sombrero – In Casa Grande on the main drag (419 E Florence Blvd.) – someone that grew up there is addicted to their food and goes there whenever in town. Casa Grande is on the west side of I-10 and South of Phoenix metro area.

WHITE MOUNTAINS

This includes the communities of Alpine, Pinetop, Showlow and Springerville.

Things to do

White Mountains – This area is especially beautiful South of Alpine on Highway 191 (i.e. Hannigan's Meadow - where cabins can be rented - not fancy though). Winter road maintenance is not 24/7 south of Hannigan's Meadow in the winter. Not heavily traveled like Pine Top is in the summer. *FYI – Highway 191 was renamed in 1992 from Highway 666 due to the nickname the Devils Highway.*

X-C Skiing - In the winter there is a lot of X-C skiing opportunities. **Hannigan's Meadow Lodge** has a Nordic Center with 26km of groomed trails. Plus other activities like snowmobiling and in the summer horseback riding. http://www.hannaganmeadow.com/

Sunrise Ski Area - A nice Arizona ski area - has some nice expert terrain (though short). Better intermediate skier mountain than Snowbowl in Flagstaff. Don't expect all the amenities of a Colorado/Utah resort but it has a fair amount of terrain and lifts. Stay in Springerville or Greer for better lodging rates (and less traffic into the ski area on a busy weekend). They also have some Nordic trails that I haven't tried.

Pine/Strawberry - Fossil Creek - clear water, swimming, wall diving. Ask for directions in town (9 miles on a dirt road).

Restaurants

Los Dos Molinos - Springerville - great Mexican food. *Recent web search shows they are closed. I recently noticed several restaurants in the Phoenix metro area with the same name – not sure if they expanded. Also recent online reviews aren't as good as I expected and haven't been back to verify.*

Lodging

Reed's Motor Lodge - nice, inexpensive motel in Springerville. 333-4323. *More recent mixed reviews – though it sounds like what it was 20 years ago. A basic fairly well run local motel. But not perfect or trying to be upscale. FYI - I haven't stayed there since I lived in Phoenix.*

Snowy Mountain Inn (previously Bear Pond Inn) – A nice place to stay in Greer (near Springerville). They rent cabins and rooms in the past fairly good restaurant. The cabins are not fancy but the setting is very nice (no other buildings visible with its own pond). *They are currently closed but should reopen in 2017.*

FLORENCE

Yes where the prison is but worth a visit. It was once the hot spot to live in Arizona early in the 20th century. I found it very quaint with territorial adobe buildings. I enjoyed walking around town had changed little over the years. I also love the style of their county courthouse. Because it is still rough on the edges and not polished up for major tourism, some may not enjoy its charm. *Though the feel reminds me much of Colonial Williamsburg in Virginia where they recreated a colonial town based on an area with many of the original buildings intact.*

They have been trying to fix up some of the historical buildings there. The old Silver King hotel was burnt down by arsons in 1995 and there was pressure to destroy it in favor of progress. Luckily it was lovingly restored. Plus another significant house that was close to ruins was also restored recently.

Casa Grande National Monument - Near Florence and Coolidge, is an interesting Hohokom ruin site (abandoned in about 1200 AD), worth visiting, if you are in the area. It is right off of the backway from Chandler to Coolidge and Florence (Highway 87 which turns in to South Arizona Avenue in Chandler).

McFarland Historical State Park - On the main street, on the east end of town. It was the old court house and later a hospital. It is worth a visit.

Silver King Hotel – Reopened in 2009, the hotel has several shops and a coffee place. The upstairs balcony is open and would be a nice place to drink a cup of coffee with good views of main street.

Bucks 4 Style – Is a fun clothing consignment shop.

Seconds Please on Main – Is a consignment boutique that has furniture, antiques and prison outlet items.

Historic Home Tour – Typically the 2nd Saturday in February they have an organized tour of historic houses that includes a booklet for the event. Contact the visitor center for more info.

Windmill Winery – This is an untried spot but added it in case you were looking for something else to do. Open seasonally Wed-Sat at 1PM. *Notes on-line said they had sporadic hours so I would call before popping out there.* 1140 W. Butte Ave - 520-858-6050

Biosphere - Not my cup of tea, but some people like it. Just outside of Oracle (east of Oracle Junction).

Restaurants

I haven't tried the restaurants in this area for a while so not sure of current conditions – would appreciate feedback.

LB Cantina - Just west of downtown on the main street. 520.868.9981

Mainstreet Vault – right downtown. Go there for the Rueben sandwich.

Mount Athos – Greek cuisine. 444 N. Pinal Parkway – 520.868.0735

A & M Pizza & Bakery - Just out of town on Highway 287 heading to Coolidge. 520.868.0170

Lodging

Baily Street Bed & Breakfast (Florence) – Funky B&B in downtown Florence in a historic building. There is a patio area behind the main building. 321 Baily Str. - 520.509.5827

Triangle L Guest Ranch (near Oracle) – It was a wonderful guest ranch just outside of Oracle (nice drive to Globe or Tucson).   The breakfast we had was superb.   623-6732 Tucson   number   or   896-2804   in   Oracle.   http://www.trianglelranch.com/   *Stayed there now 15 years ago so can't vouch for quality – though still looks very nice on the website. We stayed in the 'Guest House'.*

TUCSON

Things to do

Arizona Sonora Desert Museum - great zoo and gardens, a must! West of town near the Old Tucson studios (the studios had a large fire about several years ago). 520.883.1380.

Downtown Tucson – This is probably the most urban feeling downtown you'll find in the state. It in recent years has become very trendy. The Hotel Congress is sort of the hinge-pin to the area.

Old Tucson - fun movie set park for kids (shot many Westerns there and High Chaparral TV series). It may be too touristy for some palates though Western movie buffs will enjoy it. It has been rebuilt since a large fire several years ago.

Dia de los Muertos – All Souls Procession – This is a really big event in Tucson. One I want to visit soon. Website has info on the event and procession route. http://allsoulsprocession.org

Tucson Gem, Mineral & Fossil Showcase – End of January to mid-February is a colossal event for rock hounds, mineral/fossil collectors and jewelry and related items. My friend Mary Ann makes an annual pilgrimage to the event. It literally takes over much of the town and there are multiple locations to visit. http://www.tucsonshowguide.com/

Degrazia Gallery of the Sun – Celebrated artist Ettore "Ted" DeGrazia built this 10 acre gallery site in the 1950's. It is now a museum that celebrates his works. You can call ahead to schedule a tour. 6300 N. Swan Road - 520.299.9191 - http://degrazia.org/

Western National Parks Association - National Parks Store – This organization stocks many of the national parks shops in the visitor centers. This is their main store. They also have scheduled talks that my parents loved to go to. 12880 N Vistoso Village Dr. - 520.622.6014

Kitt Peak National Observatory – SW of Tucson off of State Route 86 is an amazing spot – having the largest array of optical and radio in the world. https://www.noao.edu/kpvc/

Farmers Market - On the SE corner of Campbell and River in the shopping complex there is a Sunday farmer's market. I believe the times vary a bit between summer and winter. A *warning now that I am used to farmers markets, I have found some selling shipped in produce rather than locally grown.*

Bicycling & Walking

Tucson is a pretty bike friendly town. I have ridden many times here – mainly on the Rillito River Park. That trail is also popular with walkers. But also road cyclists like to ride Oracle

Road on the north end of town when it turns into a highway with a good shoulder. https://www.tucsonaz.gov/bicycle/maps

Rillito River Park Shared Use Path – Starting up by I-10 (just south of Orange Grove connecting with Santa Cruz River Park) if follows the Rillito River all the way to Craycroft. This bike path and walking trail (sometimes separated on opposite sides of the river – normally dry) is a great way to cut through town. There are many trailheads to park your car (see Loop map on above website).

Santa Cruz River Park Shared Use Path – This follows the Santa Cruz River on the west side of I-10 and connects with the Rillito River Park Trail just south of Orange Grove.

Cañada del Oro River Park Trail – This trail is in Marana and Oro Valley starting at !-10 (connecting with Santa Cruz River Park near Ina Road), going by Steam Pump Ranch and terminating at Tangerine Road. My sister likes to stay at the Holiday Inn Express in Oro Valley (just north of Steam Pump Ranch) and the trail goes directly behind it.

The Loop – A system of linked paths and bicycle lanes that circles the city. It includes the Rillito River Park, Pantano River Park and Santa Cruz River Park trails.

El Tour de Tucson – In November (the 18th in 2017) is an annual road bicycle ride/race that has several distances you can ride. It is timed so if you ride a shorter distance you end up riding with people from the longer rides. This bicycle group also has other rides, including a spring ride in Phoenix but the Tucson ride is by far the biggest. http://www.pbaa.com is their web site.

Cinema/Theatre

The Loft – On Speedway (north side of the road) and East of Campus area. Runs art flicks.

Gaslight Theatre – Permanent theater on 7010 E. Broadway 520.886.9428. They do zaney melodrama type comedies. If you want corny, fun theatre – go! If you want serious theatre – it isn't your ticket. They can fill up so make reservations ahead of time. *It was a favorite of my parents.*

Nature Spots

Santa Catalina Mountain – The drive up to the top of the mountain from town is very pretty. Changes from desert to pines!

Sahuaro National Park - (both East and west sides) beautiful, from west side can see on way to Old Tucson and Arizona Sonora Desert Museum.

Sabino Canyon - nice hiking and pretty scenery on the Northeast edge of town (Ina which turns into Sunrise runs right into the park entrance about a mile East of Kolb road). There also is a tram that takes you into the park if you want to avoid a long walk.

Ventana Canyon - Another pretty hike in same general area as Sabino Canyon. Go north on Kolb from Sunrise. The trailhead is after you pass Ventana Canyon Resort (a funny note is Kolb turns into Craycroft Road at about this point arcing back to Sunrise). The parking area for the trailhead is at the end of an employee parking lot for the resort (clearly signed). Trail goes through private property so make sure to stay on the trail. The resort is also a wonderful place for a cocktail.

Catalina State Park – This is off of Oracle Road (about 10 miles south of Oracle Junction and about 1 mile south of Tangerine Road (Tangerine has an exit on I-10). There are great hiking trails that get you up into the mountains with some nice views. Lower key trails for giving someone a first-time desert walk. They also have a really nice group campground (must reserve) with hot showers.

Bach's Cactus Nursery – this is an amazing commercial nursery with numerous greenhouses with cacti being propagated. They have a wonderful selection and it is a neato place to wander. There is also a pond area you can sit by. It also isn't too fancied out. 8602 N. Thornydale Road (about 1.5 miles North of Ina Road – River Road becomes Thornydale at Orange Grove Road). 520.744.3333

Tohono Chul Park – Wonderful 49 acre park/preserve with great examples of desert plant life.

They also have a nice gallery, shop plus restaurant that I love sitting out on their patio for a meal. Off of Ina just west of Oracle. *If visiting Tucson, your membership in another botanical garden could have reciprocity here.* 520-742-6455 extension 0 - https://tohonochulpark.org/

Colossal Cave - one of the largest dry caves in the U.S. and the new **Karchner Caverns** have opened in southern Arizona as well – they are a wet cave that was discovered about 20 years ago but kept hidden until it could be formally protected.

Picacho Peak State Park - About 25 minutes North of Tucson on I-10, the big rock monolith on the west side of the freeway. Hiking trail to the top is about 1.5 miles long, though very steep (cables hooked in the rock are used to get up some sections). Beautiful view from the top. It will be hot to hike in the summer!

Nighttime

Outback - Dancing in downtown Tucson. Large renovated warehouse with laser lights, old movies on big screen TV's, large dance floor, stage dancing, pool tables, latest music.

Dancing - Arizona Ballroom – Craycroft & Grant – open dance Friday/Saturday at 8:00 PM. **Irene's Café Too** – Saturday Salsa/Sunday Tango – Downtown on Congress (south side of road). **El Parador** – Friday and Saturday Salsa on Broadway near Tucson Blvd. **Cactus Moon** – Craycroft and Broadway (South of Broadway on west side). Wednesday and Fridays.

Shopping

4th Avenue Business District - Eclectic shopping (near the university) in Tucson, funny yet treasures abound. It is west of campus a few blocks.

Sunlink Streetcar – Consider a day shopping via the streetcar. One idea is to start at **Mercado San Agustin** which has shops/restaurants (http://mercadosanagustin.com/). Then ride to downtown and optionally shop there. Then take the streetcar up to the **4th Avenue Business District**. You can get a one day SunGo ticket. http://www.sunlinkstreetcar.com/

Bookman's Used Bookstore – Is a wonderful used bookstore (also in Mesa and Flagstaff). There are three locations in Tucson. My favorite one is on East Speedway (SW corner of Speedway and Wilmot). A smaller one, **Bookmans Ina Entertainment Exchange** is on the SE corner or Thornydale and Ina.

Caravan Foods – great Middle Eastern store on 2817 N. Campbell. 520.323.6808. They have Greek items my friend likes. Also **Babylon Market** on Speedway had a nice selection of Middle Eastern items but Arabic focused.

Etherton Gallery – Downtown on 135 S. 6th Ave (upstairs) is a very chic gallery with high caliber art. It is above the Downtown Kitchen + Cocktails restaurant. 520.624.7370

Market Place - On I-19 between Tucson and Nogales. Great prices on Tarahumara Indian baskets - closes early.

Cata Vinos Wine Shoppe – recommended by locals as a great place for good affordable wine run by the owner Yvonne. 3063 North Alvernon Way – 520.323.3063

Restaurants

Arizona Inn – My father took me to this classic hotel many times for lunch (*it was his favorite lunch spot in town*). Great hotel to wander around in – including the gardens. Lunch menu is more reasonable priced too. Food is good but not stellar but ambiance is great – so recommend going for lunch. http://www.arizonainn.com/

Baggin's – This local sandwich chain has several shops (e.g., Oracle and Orange Grove – 575-8878) and wonderful sandwiches in the $4-5 range. They also offer limited free delivery.

Blue Willow – 2616 North Campbell – a great place for light meals at affordable prices. 520.327.7577. A few blocks up on the same side of the street (just before Glenn Street) is a good Korean soup place and an Indian grocery store in another small strip mall.

Café a la C'Art – Part of the Tucson Museum of Art complex. Great patio spot. Order at the counter – we had wonderful desserts there and a good lunch. FYI – there is free parking behind the museum on Washington (a small side street). *FYI the get busy for lunch so get one in the group to grab an open table while the other gets in line – I also noticed you may be able to reserve a table (but that could be for museum patrons).* 520.628.8533.

Café Poca Cosa – Upscale Mexican downtown – it was setting the trend when it opened and now there are others competing. It is at the first floor of a newer parking garage – 110 E. Pennington 520.622.6160. They have a very unique menu with unusual and creative Mexican fare. *FYI – have friends that don't like the way they have morphed Mexican cuisine so it isn't for everybody.* One sister owns Café Poca Cosa and another owns **The Little One** – which is a Mexican diner on 151 N Stone Ave that serves breakfast/lunch.

Cartel Coffee Lab – Downtown one is nice spot on 210 E. Broadway. Also location on Campbell and several in Metro Phoenix.

El Charro Café - The Original - Oldest continuously family owned restaurant in the US. Friend loves their machaca. I have been their newer locations but think the original one would be the best choice. 311 N. Court Ave

Claire's Café - In Catalina on Oracle Road, a few miles South of Oracle Junction. Good home-style cooking with reasonable prices. 520.825.2525. *When my parents lived in Oro Valley it was a place we liked for breakfast or lunch. Haven't eaten there in a while so not sure how it is though reviews are good.*

Contigo Latin Kitchen – Latin theme (their name kinda suggests it). Nice happy hour 4-6. They reopened on the the Westin La Paloma property (it is the building just past the main building and lobby if driving into the resort). 520.299.1540

Dao's Thai Palace – ON 446 N. Wilmot in front of St. Joseph's hospital (just South of Speedway on the east side of Wilmot). I ate there a bunch of times when my dad was in the hospital. Affordable, good service, good variety, and good food. Was a super place for a quick break between visits. 520.722.0055.

Downtown Kitchen + Cocktails – This is a place that looks fun that I haven't tried though upscale and pricey. 135 S 6th Ave. - 520.623.7700

Elvira's – Trendy Mexican fare. *Some dishes come with a specialty thick tortilla. It is yummy but not good for getting up the good stuff from the meal so you can ask for regular tortillas too.* 226 E. Congress – 520.499.2302

Feast – Nice relaxed bistro serving lunch/dinner on 3719 E. Speedway. *My sister normally stops here the day she arrives on vacation in Tucson for lunch.* 520.326.9693

Five Palms – upscale eatery that came recommended by friends.

Gavi Piazza – On 5445 N. Kolb (just South of Sunrise). Good Italian restaurant. They also put out a great breakfast and of course coffee (prefer breakfast over dinner). Large portions at dinner! *They normally serve a complimentary antipasto plate for dinner and at lunch when asked they brought us it.* 520.529.2156

Gentle Ben Brewing Company – 865 East University – 520.624.4177 – one I haven't tried but on my list. It is in a great location but heard their food isn't as great (right next to campus).

Guadalajara Original Grill – 1220 East Prince Road – a very kitschy place but with good food that is pretty authentic. Day I was there they also had a salsa cart and made salsa to order.

Horseshoe Cafe – Small town diner in downtown Benson on 4th. Street - Off of I-10 about 45 minutes East of Tucson. Great desserts and home-style cooking though the second time there wasn't as good as the first. 520.586.2872

India Dukka – Indian grocery store on 2754 N. Campbell – same strip mall as Pho 88.

John's Greek Kitchen – This isn't a real restaurant. I just get to talk a good friend from Greece (who now lives in Tucson) into making amazing home-made Greek food.

La Baguette Bakery – If you are looking for a traditional French bakery with bread and pastries, this is your spot.! FYI – its offerings differ from a typical American bakery. 1797 E. Prince Road (on NW corner of Campbell and Prince). 6:30 AM – 6:00 PM Tues-Sat. *The owner's daughter has a connected restaurant that has nice breakfasts and lunches and I believe she might be open Sunday mornings.*

Lerua's Fine Mexican Food – Per a good friend, they have wonderful tamales! 2005 East Broadway Boulevard 520.624.0322

Pho 88 – on 2246 N. Campbell – has good Vietnamese soups. Not a fancy place but well run and clean. 881.8883. I also equally like **Miss Saigon** at 1072 N. Campbell (the SE corner of Speedway and Campbell) – 520.320.9511 and there even though I love the Pho soups I get a bun catfish dish where you can roll food up with lettuce leaves.

Prep & Pastry - Great breakfast/brunch place. Serve cocktails so you can have the requisite Bloody Mary for brunch! 3073 N Campbell Ave - www.prepandpastry.com - 520.326.7737

Reilly Craft Pizza and Drink – Downtown trendy pizza place. 101 E Pennington St - 520.882.5550 - www.reillypizza.com

Café Lucé (previously Sparkroot) – 245 East Congress street (across street west side of Congress hotel). Great coffee place and has food. Ordering is a little slow so don't plan on being in a rush. Service though is very, very good. *FYI staff told me you can park in the parking garage off of 5th Avenue (behind them) for an hour for free. It may even be same overall building that Sparkroot is in (haven't tried this trick yet). Sparkroot owners recently sold to Café Lucé which has several other*

Tucson locations – so not haven't been able to check out the new owners..

Sushi Cho Restaurant – 1830 E. Broadway – 520.628.8800. Great sushi in a modest setting. *Took my dad there many times for lunch – great prices for their lunch boxes.*

Tohono Chul Garden Bistro – on 7366 N. Paseo Del Norte (just North of Ina road) 520.742.6455. They are only open till 5PM for lunch – but incredible desserts and wonderful food at very fair prices considering the quality. If warm enough eating out on the patio is a plus. *Walking a bit around the park after a meal is an added bonus as it houses a nice array of desert plants. Winter 2017 my sister Janet and I did a morning bird walk in the park that was a lot of fun – you have to pay admission to walk in the park (though reciprocal arrangements with other botanical gardens). You need to reserve ahead to do the bird walk (520-742-6455 extension 0).*

Wild Garlic Grill – American bistro. On 1st Ave north of Grants. Happy hour at bar 4-7 and closed Mondays. 520.206.0017 - http://www.wildgarlicgrill.com/

Lodging

Peppertrees B&B - Tucson - includes healthy gourmet breakfast. Victorian decor, English owner, near University (U of A). Brick home with guest house and courtyard. You have to share guest house. 520.622.7167

SOUTH OF TUCSON

The region south of Tucson is very scenic with interesting drives, cute towns, wineries, history and other adventures. One way to start exploring is from I-10 take Highway 83 south to Sonoita and then State Route 82 down to Nogales or over to Tombstone/Bisbee on State Route 80 (and back via Benson to make sort of a loop trip). A side trip through Elgin is worth it.

Green Valley Pecan Company Store — This was a favorite of my mom. Get off o I-19 at the Sahuarita exit and go west. 1625 E Sahuarita Rd - www.pecanstore.com - 520.791.2062

San Xavier del Bac Mission - Classic Spanish colonial period mission church. It is still on the reservation of the Native Americans it was built to serve. Between Tucson and Tubac of of I-19. Go on weekends to experience the museum too.

Tubac - South of Tucson - touristy artist community with lots of fun shops. My most recent trip fell during their February art festival. The town has grown significantly. A good day tour from Tucson would be **San Xavier del Bac mission**, Tubac and **Tumacácori National Historic Park**. Between Tuback and Tumacácori you can drive the old highway which is now the frontage road instead of getting on the freeway.

Nogales, Mexico – Souvenirs/. Pay to park on U.S. side (ask when lot closes and be careful with valuables in your car around the border area!!!). Be prepared for old, rundown buildings. *I haven't done this trek in a long time, even our favorite eatery has closed.*

PATAGONIA

The town of Patagonia is on State Route 82 between Sonoita and Nogales. It is worth a stop if sightseeing on this road. Most of the fun shops are on McKeown Avenue a block off of the main road.

Gathering Grounds – A nice local coffee shop with good (though not amazing) coffee. Considering it is the only place to get a decent cup of coffee for an hour in any direction, worth of stop if you need one.

Global Arts Gallery – Local artisan gallery next door to the coffee shop.

Paton's Hummingbird Haven - 477 Pennsylvania Ave. The Audubon Society took over this bird haven from the Paton Family. I haven't checked it out yet. This region is a birder's paradise. *I haven't been to this spot but intend to next trip.*

Ovens of Patagonia – One block off of the highway is a wonderful local bakery (277 W McKeown Ave). Their chocolate croissant was wonderful. 520.394.2330

Red Mountain Foods – An independent grocery store with a co-op type feel. Many organic things and local when possible.

ELGIN – WINE COUNTRY

This side trip is worth it and could be a day adventure on its own. Head towards Sonita (State Route 83 from I-10) and keep going past State Route 82 to Elgin Road and over to the town of Elgin. There are now many wineries in the area and fall/spring wine festivals. You can then backtrack to State Route 83 and continue your tour of Southern Arizona. There aren't any restaurants down in Elgin. One place to have lunch is **The Café** in Sonoita. It is on State Route 82 just east of the State Route 83 intersection.

Wineries – Wine tasting has significantly improved since my first trip here in the early 1990's. There are around a dozen vineyards now, enough that you could probably make two day trips out of it (depending on how much you want to partake). Arizona wineries charge to taste wine (state law) and last trip was $10 but they give you the glass you drink out of (or $7 if you reuse a glass from another winery you visited).

Callaghan Vineyards – An award winning vineyard with a nice selection of wines. Definitely one of the ones you should visit if visiting the area. It is also more popular so can be busier. http://callaghanvineyards.com/

Kief-Joshua Vineyards – Nearby to Callaghan Vineyards is another newer vineyard worth a visit. Their owner focuses on single varietal wines. I was impressed with his late season Zinfandel – sweeter due to the late harvest yet interesting and fun to drink. http://kj-vineyards.com/

Village of Elgin Winery – It is one of the original wineries in the area. We first visited it in the 1990's and we were surprised at the level and variety of wines the main winery in town. If buying their higher-level wines by the case they were offering a great price. The winery also has been offering monthly "Wine & Dine" events paired with their wine infrequently – call for availability. They normally close at 4PM. 520.455.9309 or www.elginwines.com

SIERRA VISTA

Connecting point to many places in the area and Fort Huachuca is an active Army base.

Brown Ranch – A historic ranch just outside Sierra Vista off of Ramsey Canyon Road. Brown Canyon Trailhead is also at the ranch. Website has directions: www.browncanyonranch.org

> **Ramsey Canyon Preserve** - Further up Ramsey Canyon Road past the turn off for Brown Ranch is the Nature Conservancy preserve which is a hummingbird mecca (fee for entrance - 520.378.2785).

Carr House – The restored house is a focal point for playing in the area plus has programs every other Sunday. From State Highway 92, go west on Carr Canyon Road (the turn off is between Ramsey Canyon Road and Hereford Road). Drive about 2 miles – it starts out as paved then turns to dirt as it enters the National Forest. The dirt section up to the house is generally in good condition. The house will be through the gates to the left. Open Sat/Sun April 1 through Thanksgiving. http://www.huachucamountains.org/carr-house/ *This area is a highly recommended spot I haven't been able to check out.*

Perimeter Trail – After Carr Canyon Road turns to dirt watch for a picnic area to your right. There will be the trailhead to the left.

Carr Canyon - The road continues for about six more miles up Carr Canyon. It becomes a very windy, narrow road with steep drop offs and no guard rails – check weather Recommend a high clearance vehicle. The road is closed in the winter just up past Carr House.

Sierra Vista Ranger District – Useful resource for the area. Just north of Carr Canyon Road, on Highway 92. 4070 S Avenida Saracino - 520.378.0311 – M-F 8-4:30

Landmark Café - has great diner food and on Friday/Saturday evenings they have free live music (sometimes it is a line to get in). On 400 W. Fry Blvd on the south side of the road in a small strip-mall.

Karchner Caverns – Wonderful cave tours. On State Route 90 between Benson and Sierra Vista. 520.586.2283

San Pedro River - a 110 mile undammed section of river in Southern Arizona. The town of Hereford (a friend has a ranch on the river) is at the south end of the 40 mile long BLM National Conservation Area 520.458.3559. The bird watching should be incredible due to the ideal habitat for birds and a mild climate. You can also take the **San Pedro and Southwestern Railroad** out of Benson (on Interstate 10) that includes a stop at a small ghost town - Fairbank. (800)269-6314 - trips Thursday-Sunday.

TOMBSTONE

Besides the well-known O.K. Corral, Tombstone has an interesting main street with turn of the century architecture. I'd make a day trip out of both Tombstone and Bisbee if staying in Tucson – or better yet stay over in Bisbee one night. You could also tie it to a tour on State Route 82 that includes Elgin wine country and driving down to Nogales.

Courthouse – Worth seeing county courthouse on one end of downtown.

Bird Cage Theatre – Great museum with the old theatre box seats (complete with peeling wallpaper), downstairs gaming area and brothel still intact.

Crystal Palace Bar – Neat old bar to have a drink in while the power shoppers continue their foray.

BISBEE

Bisbee Is a neat mining town with lots of turn of the century architecture. The town has a real hippie/artist feel to it since it drew in quite a few artists and people trying to escape from the world 20-30 years ago. Best bet is to stroll around town and check out the interesting selection of shops as well as brewery gulch. *One of my skiing friends grew up on a ranch near Bisbee and his grandmother ran a hotel in Bisbee – currently with the name Silver King Hotel. In the early 1900's I am told it was the largest city between St. Louis and San Francisco!*

The Copper Queen Hotel – Well known restored hotel in the center of town. 520.432.2216 or www.copperqueen.com. Also their restaurant has good food in the evenings.

In the picture above, the main part of Bisbee is above the mine in the valley (arrow points to it).

1000 Steps of Bisbee – There is an official route of 9 sections of stairs you can climb. It winds up then down back through town. You even can have a beer as you pass bars/eateries. This is a fun way to see the city as many houses are only accessible by foot via their stair system. Lots of neat photo opportunities too (see the photo to the right).

Library – The town library is a neat 100+ year old facility that (on 2nd floor). Went to a wonderful talk about a legendary local ranching family.

Shrine – Above town on the hill to the east of town is a family shrine that you can hike up to. It gives good views of the area. A local friend took me up there so I can't remember the exact route but think you cut past the small grocery store in town.

Old Bisbee Coffee Roasters - Seth Appell serves up FREE espresso in **Peddlers Alley** – guessing weekends and busy tourist times. Of course, he sells his coffee and I recommend it (he ships coffee often the same day he roasts). www.uniquecoffee.com There is a vegetarian Mexican restaurant in Peddlers' Alley that looks really good but I didn't get a chance to try.

Night Time in Bisbee

Club Kilimanjahro in the historic, wonderful, cavernous Odd Fellows Hall built in 1918 (432-7920 or 432-2732). Looks like it has become a special events space so check their FaceBook page for what is going on.

Stock Exchange – Not a bad place for a drink.

Hot Licks – Live music on the weekends it seems and a fun place to go out for the evening.

Restaurants

Café Roka – Great dining and not too pricey (we spent $100 w/o tip for 4 people though stayed mainly with an entree). Get a reservation if you want to eat there, as walk-ins are harder to manage and lately they are booked over a week out and currently open Thursday-Saturday nights! 35 Main Street - 520.432.5153 or www.caferoka.com.

Copper Queen Hotel – see above.

Neariah's Mexican Restaurant – just east of the traffic light for Naco Highway (Safeway on the SE corner) is a good little eatery my friends call the "No Name Restaurant" as the sign is hard to read. FYI – service can be a little slow. They have homemade horchata too.

San Jose Restaurant and Lounge (previously El Cobre Restaurant) – on 1002 Naco Highway, a little out of town. Great affordable Mexican restaurant. 520.432.7703. Now *(winder 2015) with an Indian owner so they still have good Mexican and good Indian (like their fish curry). Thursday tostada night is a deal!*

NACO, MEXICO

You can go into Naco, Mexico, just south of Bisbee. There is a wonderful bakery just past customs on the right side (if you have never tried Mexican sweet baked goods, you may be pleasantly surprised). *Not sure of current status of crossing the border. It may be better to park now on the US side & walk over.*

DOUGLAS

Nearby Douglas also has a lot of interesting architecture and is surprisingly better maintained than I'd thought. It was the smelter for Bisbee and mines in Mexico. They are trying to renovate the cool old Grand theatre (to the right).

WILCOX

Wilcox is right off of I-10 (on the way to Chiricahua Nat'l Monument).

Apple Annie's Country Store (Apple Annie's Orchard) - took over the old Stout's Cider Mill in Wilcox for great cider and apple pie. Hopefully just as good – haven't been to the new store but the old one was a must stop. Just north of the middle freeway exit by the tourist information bureau – the recently moved the freeway exit so a bit harder to find. 520.384.2084

Lodging

Mule Shoe Ranch - run by the Nature Conservancy, has a hot springs (in an old water tank) and hiking. Rent "casitas" (small cabins) - though you need to be a member of the Nature Conservancy. Off of I-10 near Wilcox. 520.212.4295

Portal Peak Lodge Store & Cafe - In Portal, AZ, North of Douglas. Clean, inexpensive (at least it was) B&B with shared bathrooms in an old ranch house. Lots of neat bird watching and scenery in this area! 520.558.2223 - http://portalpeaklodge.com/

SW Research Station - The Southwestern Research Station is a year-round field station under the direction of the American Museum of Natural History (NY, NY). Sometimes rents rooms that aren't used by scientists and college students in the summer months. This is also in the Portal area of the Chiricahuas. Check their website for specifics on lodging. 520.558.2396 - www.amnh.org/our-research/southwestern-research-station/

CHIRICAHUA NATIONAL MONUMENT

35 miles from Wilcox is wonderful. Take time for at least a 20 minute walk in the rocks from the top of the monument or go for it and hike to Heart of the Rocks or Inspiration Point. Very nice campground ($7.00/day) that fills quickly in high season (fall/spring seasons).

I was recently back to Chiricahua NM after over a decade. I had forgotten how truly magical it is there with different plant life (due to the different climate zones you can walk through) as well as the wonderful rock formations that make it a very unique spot to hike. Parts of the trail system must have been built by CCC crews in the 1930's since the stone work on them is superb.

The **Portal** side of the Chiricahuas is also worth visiting and there are fewer visitors to that side (you can drive over the Chiricahua range, though check road conditions as it is a low-maintenance dirt road!). You would drive New Mexico Route 80 south to Portal Road and go in that way. The **Chiricahua Desert Museum** is a museum that opened in 2009 at that intersection and may be worth a visit too (I haven't visited this spot yet). http://www.chiricahuadesertmuseum.com/

Scenic Drives in Southern AZ

Globe-Oracle - The drive between Globe and Oracle on State Route 77 or Superior and Oracle on State Route 177 are very nice. Though be prepared to see active mines. Both roads join in Kearny. To the East of Mammoth, AZ is a Mesquite Bosque (forest of mesquite trees) that is worth visiting if you are into seeing different types of desert plant live. A dirt road actually goes through the bosque and loops back to the main road. Though it is a bit circuitous (I believe it ends up near San Manuel) and not recommended if the river is high (due to river crossings). There are very few stands of mesquite left like this with trees in the 30-40 foot range since most were removed when the Southwest was settled.

Pinal Pioneer Parkway – State Route 79 - From Florence to Oracle Junction is another pretty drive in the high desert. If going between Tucson and Phoenix, I'd recommend taking this drive if you have a bit extra time (and if going to Oro Valley or East Valley of Phoenix it may be faster).

Globe-Showlow – US 60 - The drive through the Salt River Canyon on Highway 60 is a must. Spectacular views!

Patagonia-Sonita Scenic Road (State Route 82) – Per a friend that grew up in Bisbee, many of the ranches in this region have signed conservation easements so the area is not cut into small parcels of land. Makes for a very pretty scenic drive. Take State Route 83 (from I-10) to Sonoita then State Route 82 to Nogales then loop back on I-19 stopping at Tubac. The town of Patagonia is worth a stop on the way. You can go other direction from Sonoita on 82 towards Tombstone – which is also a scenic drive and take State Route 80 to Benson). http://www.arizonascenicroads.com/tucson/patagonia_sonoita _index.html

YUMA

Downtown Yuma has potential – it has some interesting historic buildings and now has several nice restaurants downtown. The collection of historic buildings is due to at one point Yuma being a territorial prison as well as river port for the Colorado River and thus a prospering town.

Yuma Territorial Prison State Historic Park – Museum of the territorial prison that spurred people to move to the area. Downtown on the Colorado River, accessed by Harold Gliss Parkway (East 8th Street).

Ocean to Ocean Bridge – The historic one-lane bridge crossing the Colorado River was re-opened over 10 years ago. You can access it from Penitentiary Road over by Gateway Park. *The bridge serves as easy access to the casino across the river – on-line comments mention to not exceed the speed limit in this area.*

Gateway Park – Below the railroad bridge and I-8 is a town park on the Colorado River. It also has the **Yuma Crossing Bike Path** that goes a few miles both directions on the river – changing names to the **East Wetlands** and **West Wetlands** paths. To the east it goes by the nice **Yuma East Wetlands** (close enough you can walk to it). The other direction takes the bike path past the visitor center. There also is the **East Main Canal Path** that connects to the West Wetlands path around Avenue A.

Yuma Jaycees Silver Spur Rodeo – February. They even have a fun parade through downtown. http://yumarodeo.com/

Yuma Symposium – Art gathering the end of February. The folks at Tompkins Pottery are heavily involved in the event. www.yumasymposium.org

Yuma Art Center – The town maintains the facility which includes the recently renovated historic Yuma Theatre. Plus it has a wonderful gallery for art shows.

http://www.yumaaz.gov/parks-and-recreation/venues/art-center.html

Tomkins Pottery – 78 West 2nd St. 928.782.1934 – Great local pottery by husband/wife ceramic artist team (she throws and he glazes). They make artistic as well as functional pieces. http://www.tomkinspottery.com/ Across the street is **Colorado River Pottery** making functional pottery.

Yuma Community Farmer's Market – Tuesdays on Main Street downtown. Late fall through early spring – check their Facebook page for current schedule.

Yuma Garden Company – Couple of market farmers decided to open up a store front to directly sell organic seasonal produce and healing herbs versus just selling them at the farmer's market. Noon-6PM (closed Sun-Mon). 1292 S. 5th Ave – 928.581.4614

> **Ranchero De Lux Organic Date Farm** – The folks at Yuma Garden Company were out of dates. So they helped us get out to the farm they get them from on our own. *Was a fun little journey.* They grow organic Medijool dates. 1452 W Parkman Rd, Winterhaven, CA. The Ross Corner Store is the closest landmark, you go north past the store up to Parkman Road where you turn right passing several intersections. With a bridge possibly being permanently out, you have to wiggle a bit to get to the farm. (Yuma is right on the California state line so this isn't too far away). 760.572.0168 – I would call before going out. Also check to see if the Yuma Garden Company has their dates in stock.

Historic Coronodo Motor Hotel – Clean and comfortable and walking distance to downtown. Think they have videos too. 233 South 4th Ave. http://www.coronadomotorhotel.com/ If you want something newer – we really liked the Radisson Hotel out on the I-8 freeway.

Restaurants

Da Boyz Italian Cuisine – In the old Kress building is a friendly, trendy Italian eatery known for its pizza and lasagna.

Lutes Casino Restaurant – A longstanding spot downtown. Originally a pool hall that was really man's hangout (no bathroom for women) and the men's bathroom had a window so you could watch your pool game to ensure no one messed with it. Now a funky fun bar/eatery for all with old memorabilia posted on the walls or hung from the ceiling. It is a popular spot so you might need to wait for a table.

North End Coffee House – A nice coffee house with friendly staff. 202 S 1st Ave - http://www.northendcoffeehouse.com/

Pint House Bar and Grill – 265 S. Main Street – 928.782.2499

Prison Hill Brewery – 278 S. Main Street.

SOUTHERN UTAH

Utah has such spectacular canyon country that I love to just drive through it. Along with California, it must have the edge, on the number of National Parks (Zion, Bryce, Capital Reef, Arches, and Canyonlands)

ST. GEORGE

Winter home of Brigham Young. His house and the LDS temple are both worth seeing. The temple is the oldest temple west of the Mississippi. Also if you are entering this region via St. George, it is the last town with major shopping till you get over to Grand Junction or down to Flagstaff.

Snow Canyon - Take St. George Blvd. to Bluff and go right. Follow the signs. This is a scenic area nearby St. George. There is a fee if you are going to stay in the park and use facilities – currently free to drive through. Also a nice bike path up Snow Canyon Parkway. An interesting side note – the canyon is not named for winter precipitation, rather for one of the prominent LDS families that settled there (same goes for Snowflake, Arizona – where Flake was also a prominent family).

Tuacahn - An outdoor amphitheater in beautiful red sandstone cliffs in St. George, now with several summer shows, usually musicals. Their quality is high – worth going to. I saw "Guys and Dolls" a few years ago and was fun and well done. Remember it is outdoors so weather can be an issue. https://www.tuacahn.org/

Inn on the Cliff – Next to Cliffside Restaurant is a wonderful converted 1970's hotel into trendy, tastefully decorated rooms with _amazing_ views. They have a swimming pool and hot tub too. 512 S. Airport Road - 435.216.5864

Downtown

Downtown St. George has really evolved. There are many more shops in the cute historic buildings that had been ignored or vacant for many years. Ancestor Square on the corner of St. George Blvd and Main Street has several nice eateries and shops. Main Street on the other side of St. George Blvd also has some nice shops and eateries as does Tabernacle Street in that area.

St. George Carousel & St. George Splash Pad – Both are in the Town Square park next to the Woodward School and the St. George Tabernacle. Nice area to take kids (supervised of course). Off of Main Street between Tabernacle Street and W 100 South Street.

The Electric Theater – Music & performing arts venue. 68 E Tabernacle St - 435.688.7469

Art & Soul Gallery – 55 North Main Street. One of a couple of galleries downtown.

Judd's Store – Cute shop with ice cream, vintage candy/sodas and light food items. 62 E Tabernacle – 435.628.2596

Bicycling

Crosby Family Confluence Park – This was previously called Confluence Trailhead. The redesigned and relocated trailhead anchors the Virgin River trail and several other trails at 2099 South Convention Center Drive. It is near the Dixie Convention Center.

Snow Canyon Loop – Paved trail with a short section on a road. The following site outlines all trails of the area. http://www.stgeorgechamber.com/visit-here/things-to-do/biking-trails/

Restaurants

China Palace – Del's daughter-in-law loves this place. Have to admit their sweet and sour pork is pretty good (first time he found it in the US like when he was in Singapore). Affordable and not too fancy but friendly service. Pot stickers look good too. 435.673.0068 – 195 S. Bluff Street. *Recent on-line reviews are mixed some love it and some don't.*

Cliffiside Restaurant – Great service, good food along with killer views overlooking St. George. Recommend a reservation. 511 S Airport Rd - 435.319.6005 – www.cliffsiderestaurant.com

George's Corner Restaurant – The owners of the Painted Pony created this family restaurant with killer breakfasts. Live music Wed, Fri and Sat. They are also open late many nights – nice to have a place to go to after a movie or other evening activity. In Ancestor Square. www.georgescornerrestaurant.com - 435.216.7311

Neilson's Frozen Custard – Good frozen custard but not as good as the one that closed in Tempe area. I also tried **Larsen's Frostop Drive-In** – they had new owners and did a good job of making a traditional drive-in friendly and fun.

Painted Pony – Upstairs in Ancestor Square (on St. George Blvd. about a mile from the freeway on the right). Open for lunch. 435.634.1700

Twentyfive Main Cafe & Cake - Quirky spot offering gourmet cupcakes plus pizza & sandwiches. 25 N Main St. - 435.628.7110 - www.25main.com

HURRICANE/LA VERKIN

Old agricultural community that has evolved into retirees and bedroom community for people working in St. George. Have the locals tell you the story about the town and the building of the canal. Wonderful apricots and other fruit when in season.

Three Falls - A local hike to three falls can be fun if the water is running.

Pah Tempe Hot Springs – This was a low key family oriented hot springs that appeals more to tourists. *Sadly they are permanently closed due to disputes over rights to the water. Per their website the Washington County Water Conservancy District now controls the waters.*

Conflence Park – In La Verkin just across the bridge (over the Virgin River) from Hurricane is a park that goes down to the river (I have not tried it yet but a local told me about it). It is on the same side of the road as **River Rock Roasting Company & Baked Goods**. Probably best to access it heading from La Verkin to Hurricane – there is a sign with a small parking area. You might be able to walk over from River Rock Roasting after your morning coffee.

Restaurants

Main Street Cafe (Hurricane) – Loved this place when it was the New Garden Café years ago. Still a great spot, though the quality has gone up and down in prior years but probably the best place to eat for a few miles. You can also sit out in the garden area next to the restaurant. The new owners seem to have passion for the place. 435.635.9080

River Rock Roasting Company & Baked Goods (La Verkin) – In La Verkin just across the bridge (over the Virgin River) from Hurricane is a fun spot for coffee, baked goods and beer. Soon to have pizza. They also have a drive through on the NE corner of the intersection Highway 9 and Highway 17. 394 S State St - 435.635.7625 – www.riverrockroasters.com

Stage Coach Grille (La Verkin) – On 99 State Street is a place I haven't tried but recommended by locals. In the past there wasn't a decent evening dining spot in the area. 435.635.7400

CEDAR CITY – SHAKESPEARE FESTIVAL

Cedar City is an upper elevation college town with very different weather to close by St. George.

Shakespeare Festival - Cedar has a _very_ well-run Shakespeare festival in the summer months and now has a fall series as well. This is very popular, so book tickets ahead of time. 800-PLAYTIX for reservations or www.bard.org. The shows are very well done, though my recommendation is to do two shows, one of the non-Shakespeare shows and one Shakespeare, since most people have a hard time digesting several Shakespeare productions, due to the olde English. Also make sure to hit the pre and post show discussions of the show - you really learn a lot. The **Greens Show** every night before the performances is free and are medieval types of performances that kids normally love. _Note: There are _not_ a lot of late night things to do though this has been getting better in recent years. In 2016 they finished a new theater complex – with a new Shakespeare theater (that has a retractable roof!)._

Southern Utah Museum of Art – Beautiful new art museum that opened on the new campus for the Shakespeare Festival. They have rotating shows including senior student shows in the spring. 435.586.5432

Utah State Summer Games – Every year in Cedar City in June is the Utah State Summer Games – a mini-Olympics. The fireworks were really, really good. There was a separate pow-wow event the same weekend.

Bike/Walking Path – Just east of down town on Center Street is a park (South Side) that has a very nice bike/walking path that goes up the canyon that goes to Cedar Breaks. Note: it is on the opposite side of the river from the highway and only has one crossing across the river about 2 miles out of town.

Cedar Breaks National Monument –Cedar Breaks is due east of down (take Center Street). You could tie it into a day drive up into the Dixie National Forest.

Kolob Canyons Section of Zion – Kolob Section right off of I-15 South of town (exit 40). See other information under the section on National Parks. I like to hike the **Taylor Creek Trail** which is an easy trail that follows the creek.

Groovacious – 195 West 650 South – a great 'real' record store. Prices are regular but get great advice on music. 435.867.9800. Open Tues-Sat at noon. *Though the last time I was in the owner didn't seem as friendly – sad to see since a knowledgeable, friendly staff is crucial for the few record stores that remain.*

Restaurants

It may be getting better but one thing Cedar seems to lack is a choice of good restaurants that aren't part of a major chain.

Brody's – near the south freeway exit for town (Cross Hollow Road then head North on Sage Road – it is behind the Hampton Inn). Good, affordable Mexican food with a great salsa bar and friendly service. 1166 S. Sage Dr Suite - 435.531.8773

Centro Woodfired Pizzeria - Was a great new find in 2015 for a meal. There can be long waits to eat as it is popular. They can be busy but do not take reservations however use the

NoWait app. 50 W Center St - 435.867.8123 - www.centropizzeria.com

The French Spot – It is a wonderful place for pastries or coffee in a cute kiosk with outside tables. Michael Attali, the owner is from Lyon, France - he trained as a chef and pastry chef there. He and his daughter Leah serve up wonderful treats. 5 North Main Street - http://www.thefrenchspotcafe.com/

Milts Stage Stop – Great classic Western steakhouse east of town on Highway 14 about five miles. 3560 East Highway 14

Pastry Pub – On Center Street just west of Main Street – wonderful desserts and they also make coffee/tea (have soy milk for people like me) plus sandwiches and salads.

The Grind Coffee House – Free Wi-Fi plus a few comfy chairs make this a great meeting spot. They also have live music – *though much of it seems Christian focused and may not be everyone's cup of tea.* On Main street just north of Center street. *Last time in the coffee wasn't as good – but one of the few places to get an espresso type drink.*

SPRINGDALE – GATEWAY TO ZION

Springdale is the gateway to Zion National Park, the town is right at the entrance to the park. Be aware that during busy times (that includes spring and fall) the town can get really busy. Reservations are recommended for restaurants and lunch places might be quieter than at dinner.

Pedestrian Access to Zion National Park – I prefer using this to access the park. If you get there early enough there is free parking nearby on the main road. Otherwise paid parking in the parking lot for the strip mall in front of the entrance (which is also where the Springdale Shuttle terminates). This strip mall has Cable Mountain Lodge and Zion Canyon Brew Pub in it – being just before the automobile park entrance.

Shuttle System — The shuttle system runs during busy times. It means a little more planning. It also allows you to use the pedestrian entrance to the park which I recommend over the main entrance you drive in on (you can use the pedestrian entrance if on a bike too than ride the Pa'rus Trail).

Springdale Shuttle — Springdale has a shuttle system that goes through town and ends at the pedestrian entrance to the park (this is a strip mall just below the west park entrance on Highway 9).

Zion Canyon Shuttle - Once you are in the park, either walking or driving through the west gate, at the visitor center is the starting point for the Zion Canyon Shuttle (you must walk between the two shuttle systems). The Zion Canyon Shuttle has nine stops. It goes completely up Zion Canyon — terminating at Temple of Sinawava. Note shuttles can fill up so if you get off at a stop, anticipate waiting to get back on the shuttle during busy times.

Bicycling/Walking — This is a good way to get around the area. Several shops rent bicycles.

Bike Trail Towards Rockville - There is now a bicycle trail that goes almost all the way to Rockville and Highway 9 for the last bit has a good shoulder.

Springdale Bike Lanes - In 2017, Springdale's main street (Highway 9) will be fully revamped with bicycle lanes, making it much more bike friendly. So consider bringing a bike.

Pa'rus Trail (Inside Zion National Park) - From the Visitor Center is a paved trail that follows the river past one of the campgrounds and terminates at Canyon Junction (stop #3 on the Zion Canyon Shuttle). It also is a pretty walk since it is away from the main road

Gooseberry Mesa – Wonderful mountain biking area set up by the BLM with some slick rock sections and nice views of Zion Park and surrounding mesa country. The middle route is the easiest and it as a beginner slick rock loop to the right after entering the trail system (friends call it 'Slick Rock 101'). Road to the parking lot is rough. Can come up either from Springdale or Hurricane. Should be able to rent bikes or go on a scheduled bike tour out of Springdale.

Grafton – Ghost town a few miles from town up a dirt road.

Zion Canyon Cinemax – Had the film, 'Treasure of the Gods' which covered Zion Park and other scenic areas in Utah. Plot of the film was a bit dicey but the scenery was worth seeing. *They are permanently closed.*

Joy Craft and Design – In the same house as **Deep Creek Coffee Company** is a cute gift shop. The location allows the shoppers to browse while those that don't can sit on the patio having a relaxing cup of coffee. 435.359.3845 – www.joycraftdesign.com

Sorella Gallery – Next to Zion Pizza and Noodle Company is a gallery that includes photographs by well-known photographer Michael Anderson plus many other interesting things. Teresa and Tonya have created a nice space. 435.772.0622

Lodging

Under the Eaves Bed and Breakfast – A local recommended this. It has beautiful gardens. 980 Zion – Mount Carmel Hwy - 435.772.3457

Holiday Inn Express Springdale – Nice place to stay – second floor rooms have nice vaulted ceilings. Try to get a room overlooking the river. 435.772.3200 – 1215 Zion Park Road. You can also stay in the park at the **Zion Lodge** 303.297.2757.

Food

Zion Pizza and Noodle Company - In the old brick schoolhouse (or church) on the north side of the street, in the middle of town, has very good food (though a bit pricey) in a very relaxed atmosphere (you order at the counter). Can be very busy in the summer. They are closed in the winter.

Oscar's Cafe – Up behind the Shell station on the north side of Highway 9. It has great lunch fare. 435.772.3232

Deep Creek Coffee Company – On Winderland Land and Highway 9 across the way from Oscars is a small coffee shop in a house shared with a couple of other businesses. 932 Zion Park Blvd - 435.767.0272 - http://deepcreekcoffee.com/

Bit N Spur - Great Tex Mex style restaurant. Food overall is super (though overcooked my tuna fish tacos) – go for their staples like the steak, fajitas and I loved their green chili (stew type dish). Service can be slow and sporadic. They also stay open later than other restaurants in town during busy summer times (10PM was the closing time I was there but they actually served till around 10:20PM). Lately closed in the winter.

Thai Sapa – Great fresh food. It is close to the park entrance and was open for lunch the day I was there (and not crushed with people). 435.772.0510

King's Landing (at Driftwood Motel) – For high end dining in Springdale, this is where you want to go. On the west end of town. 1515 Highway 9 – 435.772.7422

9 East - Italian restaurant several locals recommended. 709 Zion – Mount Carmel Hwy - 435.619.8200

Bumbleberry Gifts – In the back is a bakery that still sells the infamous **bumbleberry pie** that was served up at Grandma's Kitchen (now closed).

Kanab

A convenient stopping point if traveling the region of Lake Powell, Zion, Bryce and the North Rim of the Grand Canyon. Its claim to fame is that a lot of Westerns were filmed there. Not as much filming activity in recent years – though winter of 2017 they were filming a movie at Aikens Lodge (the lodge signs were changed to an owl based them for the fictitious motel). The historic area of town is quaint.

There are many places to stay – mostly tourist oriented. Have to admit due to squeaky floors the Holiday Inn Express can be noisy (stay on the top floor). Locals recommended the Shilo Motel and Viola's Garden B&B but I haven't tried either.

Best Friends – Animal's best friend! The have a huge sanctuary north of Kanab off of Highway 89, where they give rescued animals a home. They have tours plus a visitor center in Kanab next to the Holiday Inn Express. 235 S 100 E - 435.644.8584 - http://bestfriends.org/

Movie Theater – Shows PG-13 and below movies on the weekends and Monday/Tuesday shows classic Westerns (most I believe were ones filmed in the area).

Raven Heart Gallery – Nice gallery downtown Kanab. 57 West Center Street - 435.644.5644

Mushroom Rocks – This easy hike (about 2 miles RT) is on the road between Page and Kanab. If driving from Kanab to Page on Highway 89, about 1.5 miles past the BLM office/visitor center for the  Paria Canyon is a turnout on the north side of the road and is before there is a passing lane – there is also a sign identifying the trailhead - **Toadstools Trailhead**. The power lines are another good landmark for the turnout. It is a fairly good-sized parking area. Follow the trail through the opening in the fence (there is a sign-in box about 100 yards in). The trail initially follows the power lines then connects to a wash. You can either follow the wash itself or stay on the trail. It will take you to an area with mushroom like pillars (erosion resistant rocks sitting on softer sandstone). *Be aware if the ground is wet or it is raining – this trail gets really slippery due to clay soil. If there is water running in the wash, I'd skip it altogether.*

Maynard Dixon Home and Studio – This is run by the Thunderbird Foundation for the Arts and is located in Mt. Carmel north of Kanab on Highway 89. There is a gallery right off the highway that has artwork for sale (including two of Dixon's paintings when I was there). There is no fee to walk through the wonderful gallery. The home is up the hill from the gallery and is where Dixon spent the last years of his life after leaving San Francisco. May-October you can schedule a tour of the home (fee for the docent or self-guided tour). 435.648.2653.

Food

Escobar's Mexican Restaurant – Family run restaurant. It is a smaller place and can be busy. Comes recommended by a local. Closed Tuesdays. 373 E 300 S

Houston's Trails End Restaurant – Classic ranch fare. On my list to try – supposedly their chicken fried steak is awesome. On the same side of the street as the movie theater. 32 E Center Street – 435.644.2488

Jakey Leigh's Café and Bakery – A few years back Jakey took over a long time favorite spot for morning coffee and breakfast. Still great friendly service with a comfortable, homey feel to it. Plus nice outdoor seating in warmer weather. Most baked goods are homemade. They have vegan and vegetarian options. 435.644.8191

Kanab Creek Bakery – More upscale breakfast/lunch place on 238 W Center Street.

Willow Canyon Outdoor – A great little find. *I love stopping here when going through town or for a morning or late morning if I just need a cup of coffee (even if the hotel's is free).* It is part coffee shop, bookstore and outdoor gear store. Great place to stop to get advice on local outdoor places to explore. One of the owners also is involved with a hiking group that does infrequent outings. 263 S. 100 East (just north of the intersection of the Highway 89 to Page and State Route 89A to Fredonia) – 435.644.8884.

Sego Restaurant – This is one I want to try on my next trip though I hear their menu is a bit unique so may not be for everyone. More upscale. The **Canyons Boutique Hotel** is in the same building and looks like a nice place to stay plus they do a great breakfast. 190 N 300 W – 435.644.5480. Another upscale place is **Rocking V Café** on 97 W Center Street.

Scenic Route – State Highway 12

This is a very beautiful highway that spurs off of US Highway 89, just south of Panguitch and ends in the town of Torrey. https://www.scenicbyway12.com/

Panguitch

A town on Highway 89 about 7 miles north of where State Highway 12 starts.

Historic Houses – The town has some nice red brick Victorian houses so I recommend walking or driving through some of the neighborhoods near downtown.

Panguitch Valley Balloon Rally – Typically end of June. http://panguitch.com/panguitch-valley-balloon-rally/

Quilting Tour – Is in early June with a full schedule of events including classes that you can pre-register for. http://www.quiltwalk.org/

Cowboy Collectibles - 57 N Main St - 435.676.8060

Kenny Rays – Diner with adequate breakfast and sandwich fare. *I was not impressed with their homemade pies – I would wait if driving east and stop at Foster's for pie. Open in the winter.*

Red Canyon Area

This is the first dramatic section of red rocks you will encounter if driving east on Highway 12 from Highway 89. There are many turnouts to take photographs.

> **Thunder Mountain Trailhead** – Right where Red Canyon starts is a trailhead for several hiking trails. There is a big

Dixie National Forest sign at the parking area (more parking is behind the first set of parking). Photo below

Red Canyon Shared Path – At the Red Canyon **Thunder Mountain trail head,** there is a paved multiuse trail that goes to the Ruby Inn on State Highway 13. There is a connector route for a few blocks that connects this path with the **Bryce Canyon Shared Path** at the shuttle bus center. That path goes to Bryce Canyon National Park This trail is not plowed in the winter.

Red Canyon Campground – Is a first come, first served campground on the south side of the highway. Opens in May. Red Canyon Visitor Center - 435-676-2676

BRYCE CANYON AREA

Foster's Family Steakhouse – About 2 miles west of Highway 63 (road to Bryce Canyon) is a supermarket (closed winters), motel and steakhouse. This is a third generation business. The steakhouse has hand cut steaks and <u>wonderful</u> homemade pies. Angela, third generation working in the restaurant, said the pie recipe was her grandmothers. 435.834.5227

Bryce Canyon Shared Path – From the shuttle bus center there is a bike path to Bryce Canyon National Park. There is a connector route for a few blocks that connects this path with the **Red Canyon Shared Path.**

CANNONVILLE

Kodachrome Basin State Park – It is about 20 minutes south of Cannonville – 9 miles to the park entrance on a 30 mph road. Honestly Bryce Canyon and Zion are prettier parks but I fell in love with this one as it is a bit off the beaten path and its focus is hiking and camping. There is not a lot of paved road with turn-outs to take pictures. You really need to get out and explore!

> **Campground** - Campsites are available from March 1st to late November (you can book campsites up to 4 months ahead of time). 800.322.3770
>
> **Hiking** – This is a park meant to be hiked as there is only the main road that terminates at the campground. There are 12 miles of hiking trails.

ESCALANTE

Escalante Mercantile – Cute store in a brick historic house with coffee, fresh baked goods, grocery items, healthy pre-prepared salads and sandwiches. Mar 1 – Oct 31st. 210 W Main St - 435.826.4114

Escalante Outfitters – Lodging in cabins, campground, store and tours. The Esca-Latte Café is open summers and serves up good pizza. http://www.escalanteoutfitters.com/ - 435.826.4266

Utah Canyon Outdoors – Coffee, outdoor gear plus guide hikes and shuttle service. Closed winters – opens March 1st. 435-826-4967 - http://www.utahcanyonoutdoors.com/

Cliff Ruin at Road Side Turnout– Between mile markers 51 and 52 at the roadside turnout is a small ruin up high on the right side of the alcove overlooking the road – most likely a granary. This is west of the town of Escalante.

BOULDER

It is small town in the Southern Utah has wonderful canyon country heading towards Escalante and to heading to the north out of town it climbs over the shoulder of Boulder Mountain. The drive into Boulder from Escalante is one of the prettiest on the planet. Calf Creek Falls is a popular hiking trail.

Be very careful going over Boulder Mountain to Torrey for deer – the same driving Torrey through Capitol Reef National Park. In the winter, Boulder Mountain can get hit hard by snow storms so check weather before traveling.

Burr Trail Road – The Boulder section of this road is paved until it reaches Capitol Reef National Park. It heads through the park and then connects with **Nontom Road** and winds down to Lake Powell. Nontom Road goes up the east side of Capital Reef National Park and terminates at State Route 24 – most of the road is unpaved. If driving the dirt sections, I would recommend checking road conditions and avoid it if the roads are wet.

Upper Calf Creek Falls Trailhead – About 7 miles west of Boulder on State Highway 12 is the popular Calf Creek Falls trail. There are also campsites and picnic sites. Camping requires a fee to be paid. They do not recommend RV's over 25 feet long in the campground. It is a first come, first served spot and should be open year round.

Anasazi State Park Museum – Ruins of Anasazi village. On Highway 12 on north end of town. If you have extra time worth a visit but I wouldn't make it a destination.

Food

Hell's Backbone Grill – It is a wonderful place to eat – in fact one of my favorite places to eat. 435.335.7464 or http://www.hellsbackbonegrill.com. They are open seasonally (mid-April to mid-October) and the old room-mate of a good friend was the gardener there. They try to use locally sourced products and their own produce. Get a reservation!

Kiva Coffee House – Just above the highway a couple of miles west of Boulder just past the Calf Creek Falls Trailhead (a hike worth doing too!). They are open breakfast/lunch and have a great patio to sit on with a stellar view! Closed in the winter.

Sweetwater Kitchen – Another very nice restaurant in the region. Open May through October at **Boulder Mountain Guest Ranch**. 3621 Hells Backbone Rd, Boulder - 435.335.7482 - https://sweetwaterkitchen.com/

Lodging

Boulder Mountain Lodge (right next door to Hell's Backbone Grille) – It is a wonderful place to stay! A group of friends stayed there Spring 2012 and had a great time. It fills up quickly – book ahead. Binoculars can help to see it.

Calf Creek Campground – See Upper Calf Creek Falls Trailhead.

TORREY

A small town that serves the Capitol Reef National Park area. Most things are open mid-April to mid-October. You can get cell phone coverage in Torrey but loose it heading into Capitol

Reef Park at the overlook about 2 miles from the visitor center. Bicknell is just over 8 miles west of Torrey – another option for getting a meal, especially off-season.

Torrey Gallery – Gallery with nice mix of art and rugs. The owners may not be around so call them to see the gallery. 435.425.3909 - www.torreygallery.com

Bicknell Theater (previously Wayne Theater) – To the west of Torrey in Bicknell is a movie theater showing films generally on the weekends. In the past they have had the 'Best of the Worst' film festival in July each year. The new owners have lovingly updated the theater and also have a "dinner and a movie" option! 435.425.3493 (see their FaceBook page).

Bicknell State Package Agency – The only liquor store in the area (also one in Escalante). Open Tuesday-Saturday. This site shows where there are state liquor stores or contract stores: https://abc.utah.gov/stores/index.html

Restaurants

The Badger Den (Bicknell) – Pizza joint in Bicknell.125 N Highway 24 - 435.425.2500

Café El Diablo – On the west side of town. Wonderful higher end dining. Nice atmosphere. I had the elk steak and want to go back for the marinated lamb shank. Closed in winter months – opens in April. 599 W. Main Street - 435.425.3070 or www.cafediablo.net

Capitol Reef Inn and Café – Good basic fare but better prepared than most tourist based restaurants. Owners have built a kiva as a dream project. The motel has basic clean rooms with nice landscaped grounds. 435.425.3271 - https://www.capitolreefinn.com/

Castle Rock Coffee & Candy – At the intersection to go down to Bluff (Highway 24) – 435.425.2100. This quickly became my snack, coffee, and lunch favorite on the last trip — and wireless too. New owners are friendly and they have consistent hours (closed Nov 1-Mar 1). I tried to go to **Robber's Roost** twice in May (busy time for the area) and they were closed — I gave up and sadly will <u>never</u> give them my business since inconsistent hours aren't customer friendly (a local confirmed they have flakey hours).

Rim Rock Patio — On the east side of town is a small pizza and BBQ joint calling themselves a "spaghetti western café". The staff and locals are a hoot. They are closed in the winter but open a bit earlier than other places in town. They serve draft beer. 435.425.3389 It is on the same property as the **Rim Rock Inn & Restaurant.**

The Saddlery Cowboy Bar and Steakhouse — Like many locations in town closed in the winter so call to check if they are open. 422 UT-24 — 435.425.2424

SunGlow Motel and Family Restaurant — You go there for one reason, the pie! *On-line reviews were more sketchy about other items on the menu or the motel accommodations. Their pie is award winning — try the unusual pickle or pinto bean options (I'd stay away from fruit pies since like most diners in the region they used canned fruit).* 435.425.3821

CAINEVILLE

Mesa Farm Market — On the state Highway 24 between Torrey and Hanksville (mile marker 102) is a great bakery and farm market. They also serve up coffee. It is on the south side of the highway. Owners are quirky and interesting and serve up great coffee, baked goods and produce. Sweet rolls are to die for. Now they also have wonderful goat cheese (I loved the Tomme cheese). 435.487.9146. *Closed in the winter.*

Luna Mesa – Just west of Mesa Farm Market 1-2 miles is a small restaurant with camping. Sadly it was neglected as the owner approached retirement – her daughter has now taken it over and working with her husband to bring it back up to par. Serving hamburgers, fresh cut fries, her mother's salsa/chips and the European coffee they were well known for. Closed winters. Tues-Sat 11-9. *Friends stayed there on a cross-country bicycle ride years ago. Family legend is her father saw a UFO land behind the property years ago.*

Rodeway Inn Capitol Reef – New owners are doing a good job of making this a nice landing spot (right off of Highway 24) to pop into Capital Reef National Park the next morning. You are literally surrounded by cattle pasture across the road and public lands behind the motel (that you can walk on). This area is remote enough you won't have cell coverage. The hotel has WiFi. Nearest restaurants are Torrey or Hanksville so get dinner before heading to the hotel. They do provide grills if you want to BBQ. 435.456.9900

Camping – Lots of BLM spots between Caineville and Capitol Reef National Park. One is on 2130 East Road (sign also says River Ford – Cathedral Valley). This is a loop road that reconnects with the highway – part way in is a river ford you need a vehicle that can handle it. Also on Notom Road where it crosses a creek are a couple of spots (about 2 miles in from the highway).

HANKSVILLE

Utah State Route 95 (Bicentennial Highway) – This may be a fun optional route to consider. It starts in Hanksville and diagonals down to Highway 191 just south of Blanding. This route crosses the northeast end of Lake Powell at Hite Crossing Bridge. It also goes by **Natural Bridges National Monument** via State Route 275 and a little past that State Route 261 spurs to the south to Mexican Hat via the Moki-Dugway. FYI – be self-contained on this drive as there may be no food or gas available. Highway 95 was largely a dirt road until improved and paved for the 1976 Bicentennial – this project inspired Edward Abbey's novel *"The Monkey Wrench Gang."* Abbey was against opening up this remote wilderness to easy access via a paved road.

Carl's Critter Garden – Motel with funky lawn art – not recommending staying here, just fun to look at.

Hollow Mountain – Gas station and gift shop with very friendly and knowledgeable staff on the corner of Highway 24 and 95. Celeste, the manager, really knows the region, offering up good advice for those traveling the region. The store is literally carved into the red rock! If you want something unique, you will love it. If you want a new, modern convenience store you might prefer something else. It is a spot kids might get a kick out of seeing. They also have nice, clean bathrooms in back. 435.542.3253

Goblin Valley State Park – A really wonderful park! It is big playground of rocks. The main area is a parking lot with access to lots of short trails into the rock garden. They also have a campground with a few yurts for rent – the campground looks cute though may not be fun with high winds. Fee for entry. Access is off of Highway 24 between Hanksville and I-70 on Temple Mountain Road (the turn for Temple Mountain Road has good signage for Goblin Valley). No food services at the park (Hanksville is the closest).

Temple Wash Petroglyphs – About six miles in on Temple Mountain Road from the turn off on Highway 24 are a well signed set of barrier pictographs on the right side of the road. A mile before the pictographs is the intersection to head into Goblin Valley State Park (left turn). There is a big parking area just past the sign (the second turn into the parking lot is a little easier to manage).

NASA Mars Site – Near Hanksville is a site NASA uses for its Mars like atmosphere. Not sure about visitation options.

Burpee Dinosaur Quarry – Burpee Museum of Natural History has a quarry outside Hanksville on BLM land. Contact the BLM Utah Field Station in Hanksville about tours 435.542.3461

Duke's Slick Rock Grill – If you crave steaks or smoked chicken, turkey or brisket – this is your place. Also nice breakfasts. Just west on State Route 24 from the intersection of State Routes 24 and 95. 435.542.2052 - www.dukesslickrock.com Behind the grill is a nice campground that also has newly built cabins to rent. They also own **Stan's Burger Shak** which offers up burgers and great milkshakes.

Blondie's Eatery and Gift – Next door to Hollow Mountain is a nice low key diner. Open year round. 435.542.3255

HIGHWAY 191 CORRIDOR

BLUFF

A small community with a 100 year old feel. Most of the older houses are on large, horse oriented lots, just as they would have been when built.

Bluff Fort Historic Site – The fort is on the north side of Highway 191 and is free to visit. Worth wandering the ground to give a feel what it was like to settle here. It also serves as the visitor center.

San Juan River – The Sand Island BLM launch site for the San Juan River is just west of town just before Highway 191 heads south and crosses the river (see **Ancient Rock Art and Ruins** in the previous section). A nice two night river trip is from Bluff down to Mexican Hat – you will need permits and want time to explore. Below Mexican hat is the famous Gooseneck section of the San Juan (the photo on the next page is one I took when flying with my friend Arturo in his beloved Cessna 210 – what a view!).

Sand Island Campground (BLM)
- Is located at the Sand Island BLM launch site. It is open year round and has 27 campsites plus 2 group sites. Regular campsites are available on a "first come, first served" basis. Pit toilets and potable water. A group campsite may be reserved in advance for groups of 15 to 25 – 435.587.1504 to make a reservation.

Twin Rocks Café - Has good food and a friendly owner willing to share places to visit in the area.

Comb Ridge Bistro – This was one of my favorite coffee stops for years. Open Tues-Sun – closed winters. Lately have hit them on closed days. Best to call and check if open. 435.484.5555

Duke's Bistro – Wonderful upscale restaurant in Bluff. Probably the best food you will find between Flagstaff and Moab. FYI - it is closed in the winter. Located in the **Desert Rose Inn & Cabins** on the west side of town. The inn has newer upscale lodging behind the main building that is quite nice if you are looking for a nicer place to land for the night as well. 435.672.2303 for both the inn and restaurant.

MEXICAN HAT

Although not on Highway 191, it is an alternate route south from Bluff into Arizona. It is small town on the San Juan River and north of **Monument Valley**. There isn't much of interest there except for a wonderful motel and restaurant plus access point to Monument Valley and **Grand Gulch Primitive Area**.

San Juan Inn - The San Juan Inn's rooms are small but quaint and the property directly looks over the river and is right where the bridge crosses the river. Picnic tables and chairs allow for bringing your own food to snack on. Their hours change depending on the season. 800.447.2022

Moki-Dugway – See elsewhere – a great road that cuts right up the side of a large mesa. Just the section you climb is dirt; the rest of the route is paved. Dirt section is fine for passenger vehicles.

BLANDING

North of Bluff is another community on your drive to Moab.

Blanding Visitor's Center – Nice visitor center with a small historical museum. Great place for a pit stop too.

Edge of the Cedars State Park – Collection of Anasazi artifacts plus restored Puebloan village. West 400 North, Blanding, UT – 435.678.2238

Hunt's Trading Post – Just south of the visitor center is a wonderful trading post that includes Native American jewelry, rugs, baskets, old pawn and also serves coffee. They have an espresso machine and make nice drinks at affordable prices. *The owners have a strong family history in running trading posts – Wayne Day's grandfather was the famed Sam Day who learned to sing all of the Navajo medicine man ceremonies and Debbie Hunt's father mastered the Navajo language and worked in a trading post at an early age.* 435.678.2739

Hovenweep National Monument – See separate notes on this wonderful spot. You can get to it from Bluff or Cortez too.

Natural Bridges National Monument – This is a little off the beaten path - hopefully it continues to stay off of the radar of the masses which are overwhelming the bigger National Parks in the area. 40 miles west of Blanding on State Highway 95. Blanding is also the closest town with any services too – none at the park. Also your cell phone won't work here. There is a 13 site campground – first-come, first-served. *This is now part of the Bears Ears National Monument so not sure in the future how this spot will be designated.*

Patio Drive In - No frills spot with good burgers. 95 N Grayson Pkwy - 435.678.2177

Monticello

South of Moab is a small town at the base of the Blue Mountains (also called the Abajo Mountains). You can take a drive up to the mountains on a paved road that loops north and connects eventually with Highway 211 that goes into the Canyonlands Park and Newspaper rock. This road is not plowed in the winter. But you can drive from town to where it isn't plowed and go cross country skiing if there is snow. Monticello has much cooler temps than Blanding or Moab.

Moab

Moab is the launching point into two wonderful National Parks (**Arches** and **Canyonlands**) and is the mountain biking capital of the country (so they say). There are also incredible hikes as well as floating on the Colorado River nearby. It is also a mecca for off road enthusiasts!

Be aware that this area draws potentially incompatible large numbers of people – hikers, mountain bikers, 4WD enthusiasts and general tourists. There is a big 4WD jamboree in April that may or may not be your cup of tea. If you want peace and quiet – find out what trails are better for hiking (there are many quiet options). Wintertime is much quieter too.

The town itself has really changed a lot. It used to be a conservative mining town and has morphed itself into a trendy tourist town – almost too trendy. The outer areas of the town are sprawling and less attractive but the core of the town is cute and has a nice trail along the creek.

Things to do

Jeep Jamboree Moab – October off road event. The **Jeep Safari** is in April https://jeepjamboreeusa.com/trips/moab/

Moab Folk Festival – November. www.moabfolkfestival.com

Moab Music Festival – Early September. Mostly classical music. Some neat venues including the grotto concerts (seem to be mid-week) or ones at a resort on State Highway 128. Be prepared for higher hotel costs! www.moabmusicfest.org or 435.259.7003.

Moab's Sand Hill - A 100 ft. tall 100 ft. wide steep patch of sand that you can sled on! Cardboard can work too. The Moab Sand Hill is across the street from the entrance to Arches National Park. There is a large parking area. Careful pulling out of the sand dune parking area onto the highway, there are fast moving cars and trucks.

WabiSabi Thrift Stores – on 400 East across from Milt's is their upscale thrift store. An interesting selection of 'stuff'.

Ye Ol' Geezer Meat Shop - On the south side of town almost across from the ALCO store. They get locally raised beef and other meats so the quality is high. Also good beef jerky. 435.259.4378 – open Tues-Sat 10AM-6PM and will pre-package an order for you.

Exploring the Area

Arches & Canyonlands National Parks – See more information in the section on National Parks.

Kane Creek – Take Kane Creek Blvd going west out of town to see interesting petroglyphs. Kane Creek Blvd 'T's into Main Street south of downtown (McDonalds is on the corner). After turning onto Kane Creek Blvd, a several blocks later it will spur to the left when the main road becomes 500 West. Several trails also spur off of the road, which turns to dirt a few miles out of town. **Hunter Canyon** is one (several miles after the pavement ends with a parking area on the left before the road climbs out of a wash). Don't forget to see the petroglyphs and Anasazi ladder on the left (parking area) and birthing rock further out on the right (down below the rim of the road on a large boulder). FYI - the man made caves were part of an old chicken farm. Nice views of the river.

Highway 128 - Colorado River Drive – Driving north out of Moab, take State Highway 128 towards Cisco. The road follows the Colorado River most of the way and connects with I-70 near Cisco. Last time through I saw bald eagle fly right over the car. It is one of the prettiest drives you'll ever go on! It is a great side trip that doesn't take extra time, if going between Moab and Grand Junction. *Probably would skip it if*

going through after dark or snowy weather. Be aware of icy corners in the winter. Negro Bill canyon is on the left a few miles out of town and a popular hike (try to do during the week rather than the weekends).

Wild Horse Canyon - has world class petroglyphs - long drive on a dirt road and a 3 mile hike. Nice hiking area just out of Moab take the road going by the water tank (believe it's called Powerline) by the old movie theater and drive-in theater. Follow it up till it dead ends. Trail head is a bit rough since it is a party spot for teenagers, hiking in is worth it.

Wilson Arch – South of town on Highway 191 at about mile marker 100 is an arch on the east side of the highway. There are several places to park.

Road Bicycling – Moab is known as a mountain biking mecca. It also had great road bicycling. For mountain biking I'd recommend consulting with some of the local bike shops. A great, friendly bike shop is **Rim Cyclery** (the oldest shop in town) – 259-5333.

> **Moab Canyon Pathway** – This paved bike trail starts at the Colorado River and Highway 191 and Highway 128. It goes north past the entrance to Arches National Park and then to Highway 313 which is the road to Deadhorse Point.
>
> **Skinny Tire Events** – In the spring they have a skinny tire (road bike) festival in mid-March plus other bicycling events. http://www.skinnytireevents.com/

Restaurants

Desert Bistro – Is a nice upscale restaurant in Moab. Probably want reservations when busy in town. 435.259.0756

EclectiCafe – On the north side of town is a fun place for food or coffee and lunch. They have a mixed menu with items that cater to vegetarian needs. Speed of their friendly service can vary if they are busy so if you aren't in a patient mood go elsewhere – but it is worth the wait.

El Charro Loco – On 812 S. Main Street (south of the Kane Creek stoplight) is an affordable Mexican restaurant with friendly staff. Plus they have a panaderia (Mexican bakery) with cases of 'pan dulce' which is Mexican sweet breads that I like with coffee. Also another good Mexican restaurant, **Miguel's Baja Grill** on 51 N Main St is a favorite of my friend Marcia (435.259.6546 – can be busy so I'd call ahead)

Jailhouse Café - Popular spot for breakfast (might be closed in the winters). It is worth the visit as it is a local icon. They do serve up a pretty good breakfast too (though be prepared to wait for a table). Loved **Red Rock Bakery and Net Café** (they bake wonderful bread and other breakfast items – 259-5941 and are right downtown on the west side of the street).

Milt's – On 400 East is a great burger, fries and milkshake place. *A local favorite since 1954.* You order burgers at the window & sit at picnic tables. www.miltsstopandeat.com

Moab Coffee Roasters – It is in a t-shirt shop on the corner (post office next building on side street). I passed this place up for years thinking total tourist-zone. They make an amazing espresso (though I'd skip their decaf espresso – that isn't their focus). 90 North Main Street. Long lines in the summer – FYI.

Moab Diner - For comfort food and breakfast. It is on the main drag on the east side of the street.

Moonflower Market health food store – On 100 N across from the Post Office (just east of the main road). 435.259.5712 Really good selection of general items and some pre-made to-go food. For fresh juices and smoothies, however, I recommend **Peace Tree Juice** on 20 S. Main Street.

Lodging

Lodging in Moab includes a lot of mid-range motels that are pricy in the summer. In the winter prices are very competitive (and equally expensive for what you get at peak times).

Castlerock Inn – 435.259.8700 that was recently built and very clean as well.

Redstone Inn - 800.772.1972 that has good rates and pet friendly environment. At the Redstone Inn, if you go out the back way you can avoid walking to the center of town on the main road and cut through the walkway along the creek

Red Cliffs Lodge – on State Highway128 (about 20-25minutes out of town) is a lodge that also has a winery and restaurant. The restaurant serves up well made ranch style fare and the real treat are the views of the canyon from the restaurant. www.redcliffslodge.com or 866.812.2002. They also host 1-2 of the venues for the annual Moab Music Festival that runs in late August/early September (www.moabmusicfest.org).

Free Camping – Per a Moab local there is camping off of Willow Springs Road which is south of town, accessed by BLM 378 (turn to the east off of the highway). This is a non-paved road.

I-70 Corridor

Highway 128 - Colorado River Drive – If driving to Moab from Grand Junction, take this drive down to Moab on State Highway 128 (I-70 exit 204). Much of the drive follows the Colorado River on in intimate two-lane highway. See prior section for more info on this route.

Sego Pictographs & Petroglyphs – I finally went there - you get off on the I-70 Thompson Springs exit east of Crescent Junction (that exit goes down to Moab). Some of them are <u>really</u> old. Go North on the road from the freeway and follow the road as it curves around (you cross the railroad tracks). Drive till just past the road turns to dirt – 5-10 minutes. You will see some incredible rock art – there is a parking area (with an outhouse) on the left where some of the panels are. The panel in the picture above includes Barrier pictographs that are several thousand years' old and larger images 6 feet high!

Green River

John Wesley Powell River History Museum - In Green River a friend raved about a nice museum covering Powell's river expeditions. It includes examples of old school river boats.

Plus a nice gallery and gift shop. It is right on the Green River. 435.564.3427 - http://johnwesleypowell.com/

Ray's Tavern (Green River) - Established in 1943 great burger joint with hand-cut fries & local brews. 25 S Broadway – www.raystavern.com - 435.564.3511

Green River Coffee Co. – Cute little coffee spot on 25 East Main Street. Amy, the owner has a nice oasis in Green River. 435.564.3411

Melon Fruit Stands – Late summer there are a couple of stands selling local melons - Green River is famous for its melons. They also have **Green River Melon Days** (Fri-Sat) in mid-September. This includes a Melon Cruise for car lovers – this is a higher speed version of a traditional parade. http://melon-days.com/

I-70 WEST OF GREEN RIVER

The section of road west of Green River is quite dramatic and there are several rest areas worth stopping at to take in the views. Then when you get to Salina and Richfield you have dropped into an agricultural valley. It is over 100 miles between Green River and Salina and not one gas station – nice to have some open spaces like that on a freeway!

Black Dragon Canyon Petroglyphs – On I-70, two miles west of the turn off for Hanksville at mile marker 147 is the road that takes you to Black Dragon Canyon. Right at that mile marker is a big rock and directly past it the dirt road you turn off on (this is not a regular freeway exit). Unlock and go through the gate (and relock it). Now follow the main road as it serpentines left for one mile. Parts of the road are narrow so you will need to pay attention for oncoming traffic since you may be in a better position to pull over to let them through. FYI – about .6 mile in there is a short sandy section – I did fine on that in my passenger vehicle but it is a section I would carefully drive straight through. Then at 1 mile you will see a sign for the Black Dragon Canyon Petroglyphs, go up about .2 mile and park your car. At this point the canyon narrows and you will need a jeep to go further. Walk up the road about 15 minutes until you see a wooden rail fence on the right. The petroglyphs are above – some are in the top section of an alcove. You will not need to bushwhack to find them – the are right off the road. When leaving, at I-70 I just went directly across the freeway and turned back to the east on the other side. The median crossing did not have a sign prohibiting that when I was there. Make sure to be careful when doing this as this is an 80 mph freeway.

San Rafael Swell – This huge geologic uplift is traversed by only one paved road – I-70. Starting at the petroglyph turn off above it goes for almost 50 miles (mile markers 147 to 100). Take advantage of stopping at some of the scenic view spots. Note these are on/off exits and not full freeway exits plus it is worth hitting some going both directions on the return trip.

Mom's Café (Salina) – Downtown on the corner of State and Main (about 1.5 hours West of Green River). It is about 2 miles north of the freeway. A standard diner food though service can be iffy. 435.529.3921. About a block west of Mom's on Main Street is **The Hot Spot Drive-In**. I noticed this place but haven't tried it.

Fremont Indian State Park & Museum – The Fremont culture is another old civilization that lived in the region. The park includes pictographs and petroglyphs. You can also climb into a replica pit house. Access via I-70 exit number 17. 435.527.4631

Castle Rock National Forest Campground – It is on the other side of I-70 from Fremont State Park (take exit 17 and follow the well graded dirt road on the south side of the freeway about 2 miles). It was $13/night the time I stayed there (I believe included museum entrance at the state park). No service nearby. Can reserve a site – 435.527.4631. *Noticed the Joe Lott trailhead – haven't hiked it.*

Candy Mountain Express Bicycle Trail - Highway 89 – Just South of I-70 (Highway 89 - exit 23) there is a nice 16 mile paved bike trail that follows the river on an old railroad line. The trail goes by Big Rock Candy Mountain Resort (if you park there, check with the resort before parking if you are not staying there). FYI – the resort caters to the off road crowd since there is a large off-road trail system in the area. Large parking lot with not very clean outhouses.

> **Eastbound Trail to Central Valley** – From the same trailhead, the trail also goes east through Joseph, Elsinore (bike lane for section in front of town hall), and ends in Central Valley at Central Blvd and Main Street (an odd intersection near the LDS church that also has Center Street and East Sevier River Road merging). Main Street and Center Street both connect to State Route 118 that heads up to Richfield. The route basically parallels I-70. This section goes through a pretty rural agricultural area with limited use of the bike trail from what I can see so people may not be used to bicycles. There is a gas station in Joseph and Elsinore. If parking in a town (e.g., Elsinore, might be good to check where to park).

> **Clear Creek Canyon Road** – This starts across from the parking lot. It is the back road into the park from exit 23. I have not ridden it but it appears to also be good for bicycling and continues through the park and on past the park (instead of getting on the freeway at the main entrance to the park) and is the old highway the freeway replaced and it terminates at I-70 exit 7. *Feedback appreciated if it is a good route..*

ANCIENT ROCK ART AND RUINS

There are many petroglyphs and ruin sites in Southern Utah.

Wolf Man Petroglyph (near Bluff)- Also very cool petroglyphs is via Butler Wash road (turn at road about a mile west of the junction for Sand Island). The same intersection has an airport symbol to the south. Both sides are dirt roads. Go right (north) – you will have to open/close a gate. Take it about a mile in and turn to the left just before the road crosses a cattle guard/fence and park a bit further up (if you have 4WD you can drive to the rim itself). Walk west to the canyon rim. There is a ruin you can see across the small canyon to the right. Find a trail that follows a natural rock ramp down to the left. Look for an alcove and follow about 100 yards further down to a varnished rock wall with rock art on it. Remember to look and enjoy but don't take objects or destroy artifacts.

Sand Island River Petroglyph Panel (near Bluff) – West of the town of Bluff. Located just east of the intersection of Highway 191 and Highway 163 (at that intersection 191 heads south across a bridge over the San Juan River) is the Sand Island BLM San Juan river launch site. There are some neat petroglyphs from Anasazi, possibly Navajo and 20th Century times (latter one I ignore). They are on the wall that overlooks the campground.

Grand Gulch Primitive Area (near Mexican Hat) – Above the Moki-Dugway is an incredible area to hike in both for its beauty plus its ruin sites and rock art. Very limited services. You need permits (friends handled the trip when I went) and your own water. Many of the ruin sites may be 10 miles round

trip – so you may want to back pack. Bannister House ruins are on one of the trails. *This is now part of the Bears Ears National Monument so not sure in the future how this spot will be designated.*

Hovenweep National Monument – Access via Bluff, Blanding, or Cortez, CO. See notes under Southern Utah National Parks & Recreation Areas.

Edge of the Cedars State Park – Collection of Anasazi artifacts plus restored Puebloan village. See under Blanding.

Newspaper Rock – On the road to the Needles Section of Canyonlands National Park. See notes under Southern Utah National Parks & Recreation Areas.

Temple Wash Petroglyphs – See under Hanksville.

Sego Pictographs & Petroglyphs – See under I-70 Corridor.

Black Dragon Canyon Petroglyphs – See under I-70 West of Green River.

SOUTHERN UTAH NATIONAL PARKS & RECREATION AREAS

The Southcentral area of the state has four wonderful parks - Cedar Breaks, Zion, Bryce Canyon, and Capital Reef. These are near the towns of Cedar City, St. George/Hurricane, Panguitch, and Torrey. It can be tied into a several day tour of the area that should also include the North Rim of the Grand Canyon and possibly a trip on Lake Powell.

The Southeastern area of the state has several wonderful parks - Arches, Canyonlands, and Hovenweep. These are near the towns of Moab, and Bluff.

In recent years visitation has skyrocketed to the parks. I was shocked to see a tour bus in Kanab, Utah mid-February. But it is still much quieter in the winter. So when planning a trip, if possible, consider going during a slower time – October through March. Even with increased winter visitation many services close late fall and reopen around March 1st so December-February can be more challenging to find a good meal.

CEDAR BREAKS NATIONAL MONUMENT

Near Cedar City and Brian Head Ski Resort is a pretty National Monument with similar rock formations to those found in Bryce. I have never made it a destination in itself. However, it works as a perfect spot to visit if going to the Cedar City Shakespeare Festival as a short day outing.

ZION NATIONAL PARK

Beautiful canyons. My personal third favorite National Park in the U.S. (after the Grand Canyon and Yosemite). Plenty of hiking. Very busy in the summer months and relatively quiet in the winter months. The **Subway** is one of my favorite hikes, ever. Springdale is the closest town to the park – literally right at the entrance. The new shuttle system in the summer requires you to park your car and use the shuttle system (more information on the shuttle under Springdale section).

Angel's Landing - A hike from the heart of the main canyon in Zion. It is past the main lodge in Zion Park. The hike is around 5 miles round trip and climbs quickly from the canyon floor. The last section, past the famous Walter's Wiggles (zigzag section of ramps) has chains to help you get up it – you might not like this last section if you have a fear of heights.

Kolob Canyons Section (Exit 40 off of I-15) - The locals call it the Kolob Fingers since it is a set of fingers coming out of the Kolob Plateau. Off of I-15, south of Cedar City is a newer part of the park that takes you into the Kolob section. It is very scenic and less traveled. This section of the park is a dead end road that terminates at a beautiful overlook. *I recommend seeing both this and the main part of the park.*

Taylor Creek Hiking Trail - I first did a wonderful hike there in June of 1997 that since then has become one of my favorite easier hikes. There is a deserted cabin part way up the trail. It ends up at Double Arch Alcove. The parking lot is on the left about 2-3 miles up the road from the park entrance. It would be a good hike to take kids since there is the stream to keep them occupied.

Bicycling – Zion Canyon Scenic Drive - The main canyon road that goes up past Zion Lodge is now closed to most traffic (except open to private vehicles November 30-March 14) and a great ride. You mostly run into shuttle buses and people that can stay at the lodge itself. *Cyclists are required to pull over and stop when approached from behind by a shuttle bus.* About 14 miles round trip and uphill on the way in and of course downhill on the way out. In summer – try going early in the morning or late afternoon. The visitor center is a good place to start (or from your motel in Springdale). The 1.7 mile **Pa'rus** bike/pedestrian trail starts by the visitor center and ends on Zion Canyon Scenic Drive partway up the canyon at Canyon Junction (shuttle stop #3). A couple of places might rent bicycles – one is a bike shop behind Pizza and Noodle.

Horseback Riding – This company offers rides at the North Rim, Zion and Bryce Canyon parks. 435-679-8665 - https://www.canyonrides.com/

BRYCE CANYON NATIONAL PARK

Very pretty canyon with interesting rock formations. Make sure to hike at least 1-2 miles through the rocks. Very popular spot in the summer. Best bet is to do a loop through the: North Rim of the Grand Canyon, Zion, Cedar Breaks (has Bryce type rock formations), and Bryce Canyon. A good family restaurant on the State Highway 12 (about a mile west of turn off to the park) is **Foster's Family Steakhouse.**

Bryce Canyon Shared Path – From the shuttle bus center there is a bike path to Bryce Canyon National Park. There is a connector route for a few blocks that connects this path with the **Red Canyon Shared Path.**

CAPITOL REEF NATIONAL PARK

Another park that was on my list for years – finally visited it a few years back. I have been back many times, trying to get there in the spring after ski season ends in Telluride. The formations and slot canyons plus fewer visitors make it an A-list spot. Like other parks visitation seems to be climbing. Plus Sunset magazine recently did an article on it

Great hiking – Though be aware of flash flood issues in the many canyons and slot canyons.

Chimney Rock Loop – On west end of the park is a 3.5 mile hike that climbs up to Chimney Rock with nice views of the valley below.

Cohab Canyon – Directly across the road from the campground is a trail that climbs up to an upper valley.

Fremont River Trail – Nice short hike from the campground area. The first part is easy then climbs up to vistas.

Grand Wash Trail – Flat trail that bisects the reef. If doing the whole thing, consider shuttling a car to the other end.

Pick Fruit in the Summer - They have cherry, apricot, peach, apple and maybe pear – you can pick what is in season for a very low cost. I picked apricots for $1/pound or $16/bushel.

Gifford Homestead - They have a little store that for sure is open during busier times – 9:00AM - 4:30PM. It is in an old Mormon homestead house between the visitor center and the campground. The store has home-made ice cream and pies – mmmmm!

Fruita School and Petroglyphs – On Highway 24 east of the turn off for the visitor center is the school the pioneers built. A bit further down is a petroglyph rock panel. Other rock art from the Fremont Culture can be found in the park.

Nice National Park Campground - The campground is set amidst orchards. No shower facilities but they do have regular bathrooms and a faucet with drinking water. Deer frequent the orchards and campground.

Bicycling - Two paved roads dead end or diminish to low levels of traffic and are great for a short road bike ride – both are about 10 miles long one way.

Scenic Drive - Starts at the visitor center and goes past the campground.

Notom Road - Is on the east end of the park and the first section is paved. There is a parking area at the intersection of Notom Road and State Route 24. The first bit is a steep 10% grade. Nice views of the Henry Mountains and the east side of the park (nice to do in the morning).

Swimming Hole - *There was a swimming hole that is permanently closed due to dangerous under currents.*

LAKE POWELL

"Boating in the Grand Canyon". Rent a houseboat from Page – see additional notes elsewhere under Page, AZ. Best tributary to explore is the Escalante (to explore - about ½ way to Bullfrog from Page). I may not agree with the destruction the Glen Canyon Dam caused (and the fact it will eventually fill up with silt and become useless), but it is a very beautiful place to boat.

Rainbow Bridge National Monument - It is a must, a spectacular natural bridge. You can rent your own boat or take a tour there.

Davis Gulch - is a wet hike in hot weather (look for pictographs, remnants of a mining camp and bamboo stands).

Glen Canyon Dam - Worth a quick look and walk through of the visitor center.

ARCHES NATIONAL PARK

Take the time to drive through it and if possible, hike up to delicate arch. The visitation level is much lower in the winter and the summer days can get quite hot. This is near the town of Moab. Take the time to hike. There are no food services in either Arches or Canyonlands, so take a picnic lunch as it is worth spending time exploring.

Road Bicycling – With the bike trail connecting the park from Moab, Arches can be another route to ride. You can also park at the park visitor center. Be aware of traffic since during busy times there is no shuttle like at Zion or the Grand Canyon.

Landscape Arch – From the Devil's Garden Trailhead it is a relatively flat 1.6 mile round trip route to large, ribbon arch. You can continue further on this trail but it becomes more difficult.

Delicate Arch – Well maintained trail to a signature spot in the state. This is a 3 mile round trip kike with about 500 vertical feet elevation change – so more strenuous than Landscape Arch. Bring water since there is no shade.

Windows Section – Right after **Balanced Rock** there is a dead end road that goes out to the Windows Section. Nice short strolls to see different arches and great sunset spot. Photo is below.

CANYONLANDS NATIONAL PARK

This is where much of the mountain biking is done, on slick rock. This is near the town of Moab and other sections are between Moab and Monticello. The following comments are for driving towards the Needles section from Moab.

Wilson's Arch – Right off of Highway 191 south of Moab is a nice arch on the east side of the highway.

Blue Mountains (also called the Abajo Mountains) – The mountain range directly West of Monticello has a nice paved road that connects from the Needles section highway (211) directly into Monticello. It has wonderful views of the La Sal Mountains by Moab and Canyonlands. This road is not plowed in the winter!

Newspaper Rock – A wonderful set of petroglyphs off of the road to the Needles section of Canyonlands National Park (Highway 211). It is about 13 miles from Highway 191 (main highway between Moab and Monticello).

Hamburger Rock Campground and Indian Creek area – This is on BLM land, further in on Highway 211 past Newspaper Rock (about another 17 miles) but before you hit Canyonlands National Park. A friend from Telluride said this was a great place to camp – better if you like to rock climb. Website says $6.00/night to camp and NO water.

HOVENWEEP NATIONAL MONUMENT

Hovenweep is a small yet interesting Anasazi ruin site with tower structures built on top of large boulders and cliffs. Try going out to some of the outlying ruins (e.g., Cajon Site which is on the way back out of the main part of the park). This whole area is full of beautiful canyons... The campground is about the only place to stay nearby - may be too hot in the summer if tent camping. It is located between Bluff and Cortez, Colorado. Driving there is not direct. This page has directions: https://www.nps.gov/hove/planyourvisit/directions.htm

SCENIC DRIVES

Scenic Route – State Highway 12 - This drive on State Highway 12 is spectacular – some incredible views. You might want to allow for more than one day to do this. From **Torrey** driving south you go over the shoulder of Boulder mountain and then into **Boulder** then over to Escalante. You can also do a side trip to **Kodachrome Basin State Park.** Then onto Tropic and **Bryce Canyon National Park.** The **Red Canyon** area has some nice photo opportunities too. Then you can head north to **Panguitch** or south to **Kanab** on Highway 89. *I had wanted to do parts of this for years and it was good as I had hoped it would be.* A good loop back would be on US Highway 89 via Panguitch, to I-70 or state highways back to Torrey. Remember that restaurants and many other services in this region tend to be March 1st to mid-October in operation! https://www.scenicbyway12.com/

Grand Tour - A loop through the North Rim of the Grand Canyon, Zion, Cedar Breaks and Zion Parks (make sure to hit the Kolob Section of Zion off of I-15 south of Cedar City). You could start in St. George and head to **Springdale** on State Route 9 to see **Zion National Park.** Then continue on Highway 9 to US 89 and south to **Kanab.** Then to the North Rim via Fredonia, AZ on 89A. Backtrack to Kanab (might be a good hub spot for a night). Then Highway 89 north to State Highway 12 to see **Bryce Canyon National Park** (might be a good spot to spend a night too). Backtrack from Bryce to Highway 89 and down to State Route 14 to see **Cedar Breaks NM** and down to **Cedar City** and the I-15 freeway. A larger loop could include Mesa Verde and Monument Valley. A shorter loop (1 long day) would be Zion, Cedar Breaks, Cedar City and Kolob Section and if adding Bryce Canyon would take an additional day.

Mexican Hat - A wonderful drive is State Highway 261 north from Mexican Hat though it has steep grades with the switch back section unpaved – locals call it the **Moki-dugway**. The town of Mexican hat is on the San Juan River. Then visit **Natural Bridges National Monument** (east on State Highway 95) and drive back to **Blanding** via 95 – there are a couple of ruin sites you can visit along the way. Then back via **Bluff** via Highway 191, seeing the petroglyphs at **Sand Island Put-In** for the San Juan River (this is just before 191 turns south to cross the river and 163 heads towards Mexican Hat). **Mexican Hat Rock** is a few miles before you reach Highway 261. From Blanding you can also drive up to Monticello and drive the loop around the Blue Mountains (they don't plow this side road in the winter) and then connect with State Highway 211 (going left if you want to see Newspaper rock and the Needles section of **Canyonlands National Park**).

Ridgway-Moab - The drive through **Paradox Valley** is really pretty - recommend it someday if you haven't gone that way. When heading west from **Ridgway, CO** on State Highway 62, instead of turning left for Telluride (you could also pop into Telluride for a bit) - stay straight to **Norwood** then **Naurita** (on State Highway 145). Just past Naturita go left which will take you on State Highway 90 through Paradox. When entering Utah the road will change to Utah State Highway 46 and that will eventually 'T' with US Highway 191. Before 191 it climbs up on the foothills of the La Sal mountains with access to that area as well. You can go north on Highway 191 to **Moab** or south to Monticello or the **Needles section of Canyonlands**. On State Highway 90, there is a BLM takeout in at Bedrock which has a nice picnic area and quiet except during high water times (spring run-off). The Bedrock store is cute – if open. *FYI - the towns on this route, once you leave Ridgway are not touristy, which I actually prefer. This route is much less traveled. I wouldn't drive it in a winter storm.*

SALT LAKE CITY

I included a few items in for Salt Lake City – since by accident I went there in fall of 2012. I wanted to see a music group that was sold out in Denver and they had availability in Salt Lake. I have enjoyed recent visits – since often hotels have nice weekend rates and you can walk to many things.

Bicycling - There looks like a nice loop around downtown that I researched but haven't ridden – much on bike trails: http://www.bikeslc.com/WheretoRide/CycletheCity.html

Farmer's Market – Saturdays in the summer and early fall at Pioneer Park. Nice mix of farmers, artisans and other vendors. When we were there September 2016 it ran until 2PM.

Music Venues – All of these downtown venues are walking distance to several hotels that normally have great weekend rates! However, if there is a big conference over a weekend it may cause rates to be higher. **At the Venue** is in an old warehouse and funky with limited seating. **The Depot** is in a renovated part of one of the two old train station buildings downtown. **The Complex** is another venue that has two stages for music. Some great acts come through them.

Rose Wagner Center for the Arts – is composed of several different spaces. There are 3 theatres (Black Box, Studio Theatre, Jeanne Wagner) and an Art Gallery. I saw a performance in the Jeanne Wagner that was great. It looks like a wide variety of groups use the spaces too. This also was walking distance from my hotel (Marriott Residence Inn in this case). The facility is on 138 W 300 South (Broadway)

Restaurants/Bars

Downtown now has some great eateries.

Capo Gelateria – We loved their gelato and they included flavors more typically Italian like pistachio and hazelnut. 262 200 W.

La Barba Coffee – Great place for coffee – very meticulous in pulling espresso. 327 W 200 S (in same building as Finca restaurant).

Oasis Café – Another place I haven't tried but people told me it was good. They are open for breakfast. 151 S 500 E - 801.322.0404

Omar's Rawtopia – One of my friend's is a raw foodie and I like to eat healthy frequently myself. Found this on my 2013 trip (it is not downtown) – a little pricey yet great food. There is a Whole Foods grocery store across the street. 2148 Highland Dr. - 801.486.0332

Valter's Osteria – I haven't eaten here but checking it out – looks like the real deal for Italian-Italian. 173 W. Broadway - 801.521.4563. My friend Douglas and I will check it out the next time I am in town. *In 2016 we got to finally try it – absolutely amazing service with equally good food. Don Giuseppe was a wonderful head waiter. Make sure to get a reservation.*

Zest Kitchen and Bar – Found this place walking around – trendy healthier food with a full bar. I loved its convenience to the hotel plus the quality of my meal was great. Some on-line reviews slammed it – not sure why. Maybe some items on the menu aren't as great (I let the server guide me on the menu). Service was also great. Although on a 2nd visit in 2016 they were super busy due to a big convention - service was impacted (plus they added automatic gratuity to all meals). Still on my list as they have healthier fare that is harder to find. 275 S 200 W - 801.433.0589

SOUTHWESTERN COLORADO

I lived in Colorado for almost seven years and missed its extensive range of huge mountains until I moved back in 2007. It doesn't have the diverse array of scenery that Arizona has, yet it makes up for it in magnificent and rugged peaks. There are few places like it in the world. Although we think of Colorado as the "mountain" state - the eastern third of the state is plains. I have also enjoyed exploring the plains area in my forays out east of Colorado Springs.

Denver is definitely the cultural capital of the state yet there are often interesting things going on in Colorado Springs, Boulder and Pueblo. Aspen for a town its size has a wide range of cultural offerings, especially in the summer with its music tent and other mountain towns like Telluride have weekend festivals going on all summer.

FRONT RANGE

The front range of Colorado is where most of the population lives in Colorado. It also has some of the most temperate weather (along with some very windy days). It is literally a wall of mountains that runs north to south through Fort Collins, Boulder, Denver, Colorado Springs, Pueblo and Walsenburg. To the East are the plains (at 5000 to 6000 feet in elevation) and to the west huge peaks dominate the scenery. The most famous being Pike's Peak in Colorado Springs and Long's Peak to the North of Boulder, both being over 14,000 feet in elevation.

DENVER

Denver just keeps getting better and finally feels like a city versus a grouping of suburbs. They have done a super job of revitalizing the downtown area. Yet traffic can be a nightmare and a lot of people want to play in the nearby mountains so I-70 and other access points can be very busy on weekends.

Denver Art Museum – Went to a wonderful exhibition there. http://denverartmuseum.org/ Across the street is **Clyfford Still Museum** - Beautiful showcase for the Abstract Expressionist's work. www.clyffordstillmuseum.org - 720.354.4880

Denver Botanical Gardens – Has a nice set of gardens to stroll. 1007 York Street. *I enjoyed the special Dale Chihuly show.*

Denver Museum of Nature and Science - Great Dinosaur collection, popular with kids (and adults too). Really some world-class stuff there! 2001 Colorado Blvd - www.dmns.org

16th Street Mall and Larimer Square – Both are downtown Denver and provide shopping/dining activities in a more urban setting. Larimer Square is a block of shops on Larimer starting at 15th street or so. The 16th street mall is many blocks of shops – some major chains and others local.

Tattered Cover Bookstore - One of the best, and not a predictable chain store with multiple stories to browse. Original one is in Cherry Hills and a newer on right downtown near the train station. 1628 16th Street

Meininger's Art Supply - A wonderful and huge art supply store - carrying just about everything you could think of. Most stores only carry one or two lines of paints - they normally have all the major brands from the U.S. and Europe. They are on 499 Broadway (Lincoln/Broadway are one way streets that run between I-25 and downtown - take Lincoln to 5th and go left if coming from I-25).

Velo Swap – For bicycle enthusiasts a great flea market type setting with vendors and people selling bikes – Velo Magazine does several of these across the U.S. with one in Denver. Mostly high end but many mid-priced bikes as well as clothing and accessories. Thousands attend. Late October/early November (only one day) at the National Western Complex (just North of I-70 and a couple of exits East of I-25 - Brighton Blvd. or Coliseum exits. www.veloswapdenver.com

National Western Stock Show, Rodeo and Horse Show – I never went up for this in Denver but it is a <u>big</u> deal in Western circles and good friends went. It is in the middle of January. Facilities are on the north side of I-70 and just East of I-25 by about a mile. http://www.nationalwestern.com/

Red Rocks Amphitheater - If a good band is playing there, it is worth the visit. Probably the most beautiful outdoor concert stage in the country. On the west end of the Denver metro area. I have heard that fewer venues are run there in favor of a more central auditorium.

Rocky Mountain National Park – A day trip up to the park is worth it. The town of Estes Park is touristy but cute.

Driving South to Colorado Springs

A couple of alternatives in getting to Colorado Springs exist if you have extra time.

Highway 83 – You can take this highway from Denver to the north end of Colorado Springs. Haven't driven it in a few years so expect a lot more sub-divisions. But it has some pretty ranch country. *Used to cruise up that road in my restored 1967 Mustang fastback – some nice memories.*

> **Castlewood Canyon State Park** - Between Colorado Springs and Denver (just South of Franktown), on Highway 83, is a pretty State Park that goes through a small, yet scenic canyon. The highway actually crosses the canyon.

We used to hike and paint there before it was designated a state park.

Highway 67 – Get off of I-25 in Castle Rock and take Highway 85 north to Sedalia and go South on Highway 67. This will take you through Deckers and into Woodland Park. From there take Highway 24 back into Colorado Springs. A section of Highway 67 is unpaved (though well graded) and it is a very curvy road. This area is very popular with off road enthusiasts. At Deckers and 1-2 other spots are spots to stop and have a beer/hamburger (though Deckers resort was closed in the winter). There also is a good hike we found to **Devil's Head**. Take Rampart Range road east 9 miles to the trailhead to Devil's Head (left). You will drive through the heart of major off road trails and campsites as well. In the winter you may have to park at the turn off (adds about ½ mile to a 1 ½ mile hike with about 1,000 feet elevation gain). The hike takes you to a forest service lookout tower you can take the stairs up to with some incredible views of the front-range. This trail is closed to motor vehicles.

Restaurants/Bars

Denver has many fine restaurants and I never really sampled many of them when I lived in Colorado Springs, so this list is a list in progress.

Chapultapec Bar - Not to be missed. In the Northern section of Downtown Denver on 20th and Market Street is a bar that attracts a wide group of people with live jazz music (normally with people that just fill in). The people watching along made it worth-while. I have heard it has become more popular so it may have lost some of its charm. It still years later still is what it is – now surrounded by sports bars and nearby **Coors Field** baseball stadium – gladly it hasn't changed. 303.295.9126

DiCicco's Italian Restaurant - In the airport hotel zone on 6701 Tower Road is an interesting family run Italian restaurant that had opera on a projection television in the main dining room. Even if the meal isn't amazing it is an interesting place especially if you are staying nearby for a flight out of DIA the next day. www.diciccoscolorado.com - 303.574.1956

Euclid Hall – I hear their poutines are to die for (fries covered with gravy and other goodies). Larimer Square, 1317 14th St. - www.euclidhall.com - 303.595.4255

Lucile's - Originally in Boulder. A great breakfast place. Now they are also in Denver (275 South Logan St. - 303.282.6258) and other Front Range towns. This was also recommended by Donna. http://www.luciles.com/

Mataam Fez – Moroccan restaurant on 4609 East Colfax 303.399.9282

Pho Duy on 945 S. Federal between Kentucky and Ford (North of Tennessee). Recommended by someone at the airport. I believe they are a franchise and I ate at the one on 6600 W. 120th Ave. in Broomfield 303.438.7194 (that person also owns the one on Federal). Also **New Saigon café** for general Vietnamese. Another person at the art museum recommended **Pho 79** – there is one close to the Pho Duy in Broomfield (and looks like the Federal Blvd location as well).

Snooze – Recommended great breakfast place in Denver. I haven't tried it. Was told there can be a wait any day since popular. They now have several locations, including Ft. Collins and Boulder. Downtown one is Park Ave & Larimer - 303.297.0700. http://www.snoozeeatery.com/

Sonoda's – Has several Japanese restaurants in the Denver area – including a sushi bar. One is downtown on 1620 Market Street – the main part of the restaurant is downstairs. 303.595.9500.

Tay Do Market – one of several good Asian markets in town. This is on Irving and 74th – close to the Federal and Highway

36 exit (south on Federal and right on 74th). Typical cluttered owner-operated store — prefer them to the fancier ones that have shown up in Phoenix and elsewhere. My friend Eric likes **Pacific Ocean Marketplace** on 2200 W. Alameda (303.936.4845) and they have a 2nd store at 6600 W. 120th Ave in Broomfield (303.410.8168) — their Parrot brand butter coconut biscuits are great and cheap. *I went to the one on 120th Ave since it is next door to the Pho Duy I visited. This is a nicer and bigger store than the Tay Do Market though Tay Do feels more like being somewhere foreign.*

Ted's Montana Grill (multiple locations including one near DIA) — I included this since if flying in/out of DIA and staying at a hotel, getting a good meal can be tough since I am on foot. This one is near the group of hotels right off of 40th Avenue and Peña Blvd. Although a chain — it is high quality buffalo meat from Ted Turner's ranch and I feel although pricier a better meal than neighboring spots. 16495 E 40th Cir. - 720.374.7220

Washington Park Grille — Was recommended by a friend that knows I like little urban neighborhood areas. It is on 1096 South Gaylord Street in a neat urban area on Gaylord Street (west of University and between Mississippi and Tennessee avenues). 303.777.0707

In Ft. Collins there is a wonderful music venue called **Jay's Bistro** — *haven't tried it.*

I-76 CORRIDOR (DENVER TO NEBRASKA)

Ft. Morgan (main exit) — Heading into town is **Peppy Coffee Company** on the left, one light past the freeway — easy drive-through refill. Also **Frankie's Place** is another coffee spot downtown on 119. West Beaver Ave (open Mon-Sat). They make smoothies and a few food items — 970.542.0172.

Sedgewick Exit (Highway 59) - On I-76 just a bit in from the state line with Nebraska is a nice little diner – **Lucy's Place**. My friend Kit's brother Greg has been stopping by there for 20 years on his commute from Vail to Kearny. I had their green chili smothered burger and fries – yum. Greg goes for the green chili solo with tortillas. 970.580.1543.

BOULDER

Boulder is a quaint, vibrant, hip city Northwest of Denver. It is a college town with a wonderful downtown area. The Pearl Street mall is a closed off main street that often has artisans performing in the summer evenings. Part of its charm from the 70/80's seems to have been lost due to trendy chains taking the places of older well established "mom & pop" stores. Those that gave the town its uniqueness but on a recent trip I have to admit it was still a lot of fun and was definitely Boulder.

Rocky Mountain National Park – North East of Boulder is a beautiful National Park. You can drive through and come back via Granby.

Hiking – There is a lot of beautiful hiking in the area. Nice walking trails right from town. Below is city website with maps. https://bouldercolorado.gov/osmp/trails-and-maps

St. Julian Hotel – In the past, on Fridays till around 9PM they have music/dancing in the courtyard in the summers. Not sure what they do in the winters. Was salsa/Latin band when I was there.

Farmers Market – On Saturdays in the summer the farmers market is wonderful with live music, produce and vendors of cooked foods.

Bike Paths – Along the river is a great bike path – goes right by the farmers market and the library.

Restaurants

The Kitchen – Wonderful restaurant on the west side of Pearl Street mall area – actually in the block after the mall ends. 303.544.5973 – 1039 Pearl St. - www.thekitchenbistros.com

Lucile's - Originally in Boulder. A great breakfast place. Now they are also in Denver and other Front Range towns. This was also recommended by Donna. www.luciles.com

Papusas Sabor Hispano – In North Boulder on 4450 N. Broadway – have great El Salvadorian food. 303.444.1729. You have to try their Chocoflan – it is a Mexican recipe but who cares if it is good.

Boulder Dushanbe Teahouse – A gift built by hand and shipped to Boulder from Boulder's sister city of Dushanbe, Tajikistan. 1770 13th Street - http://boulderteahouse.com

GOLDEN

Table Mountain Inn – Hotel right downtown, neat rooms and great restaurant. *Haven't been there in many years but enjoyed staying there when I used to do work for Coors.* 1310 Washington Ave - 970.277.9898 www.tablemountaininn.com

Restaurants

Table Mountain Inn - see above.

Briarwood Restaurant - Great restaurant with a continental focus. 1630 8th Street.

Things to Do

Coors Brewery - Worth the tour, plus you get free, fresh beer (mmmm!). Make sure to park in specified tour areas a few blocks from the brewery, since parking at the plant is not available (follow signs for parking).

Colorado Railroad Museum - On the outskirts of Golden. Wonderful collection of trains, including one of the huge steam trains produced earlier in the 20th century, though be aware that many are not in the best condition. http://coloradorailroadmuseum.org/

COLORADO SPRINGS

Air Force Academy - Gawk at the B-52 bomber and explore the chapel. My favorite was to ride my bicycle in a large loop thru the academy (road bike friendly since the route is paved).

Downtown Colorado Springs - Has a quaint park with fun shops in the vicinity. It also had one of last of the old style department stores that is reminiscent of 60-70 years ago – sadly it closed a couple of years ago and is being remodeled for other uses. Downtown in recent years has been going through a renaissance and has a wide range of places to eat and hang out, though it still seems to have its own identity instead of just having tons of chain places.

Old Colorado City - On the west end of town is the other "downtown" that at one point was supposed to be the state capitol. Now mostly tourist shops, it is still a fun place to spend a Saturday afternoon. Afterwards, head up to Manitou Springs (see below).

Manitou Springs - I love walking around this funky old tourist town on the west end of Colorado Springs. It is the first area you come to when driving Highway 24 from the mountains into town. There are plenty of tourist shops that are more trinket and t-shirt oriented than higher end items, though I enjoy checking out the shops and watching the people. It is really busy in the summer.

Penny Arcade - I am normally not a big Nitendo or video game fanatic. However, I do enjoy going to the penny arcade in Manitou. There is one section of it that has old machines that you can play (e.g., pinball machines from the 60's and 70's). It is hands on nostalgia. In the winter it has shorter hours.

Patsy's Saltwater Taffy - Is right next to the arcade area.

Broadmoor Area – The Broadmoor hotel is a classic "grand" hotel. I love to go feed the ducks on their own lake though public access is more limited than before. They have a neat old movie theater. I learned to teach skiing when the hotel still owned and operated the ski hill behind the hotel.

> **Broadmoor World Arena** - The Broadmoor Hotel used to have great ice skating rinks with some public skating. The World Arena has been moved next to I-25. I have been to the newer facility. www.broadmoorworldarena.com

> **Broadmoor Zoo** - Set on the side of Cheyenne Mountain is a nice zoo. However, it doesn't have the fancy pens that the San Diego Zoo has. They have a huge giraffe collection.

> **Cheyenne Canyon/Helen Hunt Falls/High Drive** - Behind the Broadmoor hotel (to the North of it) is Cheyenne Canyon. Drive up it and take in Helen Hunt falls. Then continue via High Drive (a windy but well maintained gravel road that is only open in the summer and is one way). It will eventually connect on the west end of town near Highway 24. There are numerous hiking trails along the route and pretty scenery.

Garden of the Gods - A much photographed site that is actually a city park. I have ridden my bicycle and hiked it many times. I have seen it on national commercials as well. Take Garden of the Gods Road west (from I-25) until it 'T's at 30th street – go left. The park is about 1-2 miles up on the right. Since I was there last it now has a new visitor center and roads are now one-way with a bicycle lane. In front of the park on 30th street is a nice bicycle trail that goes to Garden of the Gods road.

Florissant Fossil Beds National Monument - West of Colorado Springs about an hour is the Florissant Fossil Beds which have interesting fossilized tree stumps. Worth a visit if you are driving through the area.

Hiking

There are many wonderful hiking opportunities in the Front Range foothills. Often with less people than trails you must drive a distance to reach. One thing is the beer cans litter the first ¼ to ½ mile of many trails due to partying people but they usually loose interest in lugging their beer further.

High Drive (only during the summer) - This is a one-way road that starts from the top of Cheyenne Canyon (just North of the Broadmoor) that gives scenic views of the area, yet just minutes from downtown). Several hiking trails - most are after the summit and go to the west.

Horse Thief Park - Take State Route 67 to Cripple Creek (from Divide) and park after the one lane tunnel. Take the trail over the tunnel which will take you up into the area. A hard to find rock pile will lead you to an upper meadow about 1-2 miles in. If you hike up on the boulders, you will get a beautiful view of the collegiate peaks.

Pikes Peak - Beautiful hiking, though very strenuous. Hike up from the Bar Trailhead (go through downtown Manitou to get there) or take the cog railway from the same location.

Restaurants

2 South Wine Bar – in Old Colorado City on 2 South 25th Street (block North of Meadow Muffins). Great patio (since a block from West Colorado Avenue it is a nice spot to sit outside) and friendly staff. 719.351.2806

Adam's Mountain Cafe - in Manitou Springs on 934 Manitou Ave, is a great health oriented restaurant. But, believe me, the food is wonderful. They are in a newer location (post 2014 flood) – just East of the Eastern Hwy 24 exit for Maintou (phone is still the same). 719.685.1430.

El Tesoro - Next to the old train station, behind the Antler's hotel is, per a friend, a wonderful restaurant.

Josh and John's - A homemade ice cream company that started out with a small shop in town and has grown. Always worth a stop if you like ice cream. They are next to the Peak Theater downtown, has great home-made ice cream. They recently moved to a new location that is glitzier, though I prefer the old one better (still the same great ice cream). Also try the **Colorado City Creamery** in Old Colorado City which has good homemade ice cream.

La Baguette – French bakery in Colorado City. The owners now have a wine bar upstairs above the bakery. Menu of charcuterie and fondue. 719.577.4818

Phantom Canyon Brewing Company - right downtown in a neat old building at Two East Pikes Peak (one also on the east end of town). Good food and beer. Similar in format to the Beaver St. Brewery in Flagstaff. 719.635.2800. Last time I was there the beer was still great but the service sporadic.

Oliver's – Off Rockrimmon road – great deli a friend frequented when I lived there and I hear it is still great! 719.599.9411 on 6602 Delmonico Drive.

The Hen House Café – in Simla on 401 Caribou Street on the Highway 24 between Colorado Springs and Limon – nice diner with friendly service and killer baked goods. *It closed fall 2016 and reopening shortly as with new owners and a similar menu.*

Lodging

Broadmoor Hotel - It must be the grandest hotel in the state with its own lake and beautiful grounds. Over the years it has lost a little of its charm since some of its icons such as the ski hill and the World Arena (skating rink) have been removed or no longer owned by the hotel. Yet it still has impact on you as you drive up the hill to the hotel. If there is a movie running in the in-hotel theater that you like, it if fun seeing in the quaint **Little Theater.** *I found out that the current owner of the Broadmoor produces movies and sometimes does an early showing/premiere at the theater.*

PUEBLO

An old steel town South of Denver/Colorado Springs. Their climate is quite a bit warmer in the summer so Pueblo Reservoir is a popular place to cool off. Their downtown has been in the stages of being revitalized and hopefully it will stick as they actually have a pretty cool downtown as there must have been a lot of money there at the heyday of the steel mill. May want to check out the old train station.

CAÑON CITY

This town is known for its prison but also has a cute downtown. It is on Highway 50 that heads west to Salida, Gunnison and eventually Montrose. The Royal Gorge Bridge is about ½ hour west of town and worth seeing. The whole drive between Cañon City and Gunnison is quite scenic – first canyons and then Monarch pass.

Pizza Madness – A local pizza place with fun, loud decorations. 509 Main Street, 276-3088.

Red Canyon Park – Pretty rock formations north of town.

Drive to Victor – I also remember that State Highway 87 going to Victor (next to Cripple Creek) was an interesting and pretty drive. But it has been 25 years since I have driven that route.

WESTCLIFF

The town is turning into a bit of a tourist area and has more trendy things – in the early eighties when they were still trying to keep the ski area alive it was still sleepy. It is situated at the base of the beautiful Sangre de Cristo range.

A beautiful drive is from Walsenburg (on I-25) on Highway 69 to Westcliff. Then head to Silvercliff and less than ¼ mile past a brick pizza place you will see Oak Creek Grade (road 255) to the left – take this dirt road that normally should be easily passable with a passenger vehicle (I did it in a mini-van). Follow signs to Cañon City, when the road T's closer to town (now on pavement), you will go left and curve to the right which is 4th street and will take you to Highway 50. One the way on the left is **Oak Creek Grade General Store** with interesting stuff in it and in the past they served dinners on Fridays and Saturdays – nice people with interesting stories (*not sure of its current status*).

WALSENBURG

This is a crossroads town for me – though I hear that George's Café on the north end of town (I-25 exit) at or near a truck stop is good and the Huerfano Café also might be worth trying. *But I haven't been through in many years so not sure of the current status of this town.*

Central Mountains

Once leaving the Front Range, you enter the area I call the Central Mountains – including Breckenridge, Vail, Aspen, and Crested Butte – the Heart of Colorado. Many areas have large, flat upper valleys, called parks, surrounded by mountains. South Park around Hartsel on Highway 24 is good example – yes there really is a South Park. When traveling in the winter (and even in fall/spring), pay close attention to the weather since mountain passes can be treacherous.

I-70 Corridor – Denver to Tunnel

Downtown Idaho Springs – Nice historic district. Will be busier on weekends with Denver visitors. The area is popular for zip line tours and rafting too. You may also want to visit the **Indian Hot Springs** in town *(one I haven't tried)* – under new ownership. If you like historic towns, also visit Georgetown and Silver Plume. Below is a picture of Silver Plume.

St. Mary's Glacier (Fall River Road) – Up about 8 miles on Fall River Road (exit 238 I-70) is a semi-permanent snow field I skied 30+ years ago since you can go there in the summer (it is a short run — more for bragging rights that you skied in the summer). I would recommend checking on current status if you intend to ski as you might these days need crampons or other gear. Sledding might be possible but risky due to the rocky terrain. It is popular hiking spot too.

Grays & Torreys Peaks (14ers) — 10 mile round-trip hike that lets you nab two 14ers). I would consult a hiking book or National Forest desk in Idaho Springs Visitor Center before tackling this one. Access via Bakerville exit of I-70 (west of Georgetown). Road may be in bad shape, closed in winter.

Mount Evans (via Idaho Springs) — Highest paved road in America. Closed in the winter. www.mountevans.com

Georgetown Loop Railroad — Scenic railroad tours running between Georgetown (Devil's Gate Depot) and Silver Plume. Closed winters. www.georgetownlooprr.com

Bouck Brothers Distilling (Idaho Springs) — They make nice whiskies — their Colorado Coffee Bourbon is award winning. Friendly staff (Matt served tastings when I was there). FYI - charge for tastings. 2731 Colorado Blvd — 303.567.2547

Marion's of the Rockies (Idaho Springs) - Via a local, great breakfast place. 2805 Colorado Blvd

Tommyknocker Brewery & Pub (Idaho Springs) - 1401 Miner St

Smokin Yard's BBQ (Idaho Springs) - Locally recommended BBQ. 2736 Colorado Blvd - 303.567.9273

Vintage Moose (Idaho Springs) - Fun BBQ & bar hangout friend recommended (haven't tried). 123 16th Ave - 303.567.2375

Bread Bar (Silver Plume) — Before the Eisenhower tunnel on I-70 (leaving Denver) is the little mining town of **Silver Plume**. It is a main street that happily time has forgotten. This spot was a go to when it was a bakery that had an honor box to buy bread if they weren't around. It is now repurposed as a bar. 1010 Main Street - www.breadbarsp.com

Post Office (Silver Plume) - I also loved the little post office where I was trying to get change for the bread and ended up enjoying chatting with the clerk managing the quaint PO.

SILVERTHORNE/DILLON/BRECKENRIDGE

This is an area I have spent very little time since living in Colorado Springs in the early 1980's. I try to avoid the ski areas closer to Denver due to crowds (really spoiled working at Telluride – 7+ hours from Denver). Plus it is a very infrequent drive from Montrose (especially since I normally drive Highway 285 into Denver). That doesn't mean there aren't fun things in the area – I've tried to include a few I've found out about.

Outlets at Silverthorne – Some of my friends love shopping here, especially those of us that live far away from a city. Exit 205 of I-70.

Sunshine Café (Silverthorne) - Highly recommended breakfast place. 970.468.6663 - http://www.sunshine-cafe.com/

Arapahoe Basin – A small mountain with some tough expert runs. A favorite place for late spring and sometimes early summer skiing. FYI - the later in the season, the narrower the window of good skiing – too early/too crunchy or too late/too slushy. The **Epic Pass** lets you ski A-Basin, Breckenridge, Keystone, Vail and Beaver Creek.

Loveland Pass – You can actually ski Loveland Pass itself. It has been years since I've done it. You start around summit and ski the direction back towards the tunnel. There is a switchback in the road where you can use a shuttle car or thumb it up for another run. *Check for avalanche conditions.*

Vail

I taught skiing there in the mid-80's. It is an incredible huge ski mountain with varied terrain – now busier with the Epic Pass and more Denver visitors. Still love walking across the covered bridge into Vail Village.

Gerald R Ford Amphitheatre – Over by Gold Peak there is a great venue for summer concerts.

Betty Ford Alpine Garden – Near the amphitheater is a wonderful garden to visit in the summer.

Bicycle Path – Nice flat bike path through golf course to East Vail. Then you can continue over Vail Pass to Copper Mountain. The climb from Vail to summit is much bigger than coming from Copper Mountain. Be prepared for newbies on this ride too – there are those that shuttle people to the top just to ride down. Their bicycle handling skills are often weak.

Vail Library – Next to the hospital is a nice place to chill. The walking path to Lionshead goes right in front of it.

Ice Skating – there is skating at Solaris as well as Lionshead outdoors. Otherwise try **Dobson Arena's** public hours – it is a full sized indoor rink and just West of the hospital.

Christiania Hotel - Helmut Fricker entertains once a week (Thursdays in the past) with a combination of Austrian songs (accordion), jokes and stories of Vails past. It is a hoot!

Sonnenalp Hotel – Kathy Morrow singer/pianist performs Jazz standards in the King's Club lounge, typically once a week during the ski season (can check her web site for a schedule). http://katsjazzmusic.com/

Vail Ski Area Closing Day – Top of four at four I believe is the saying. It wasn't an event I remember when I worked there but it is a big deal now on closing day. They also brought in a great live band that played in town that evening.

Shopping

Bookworm – in Edwards is a nice book store on 285 Main Street. That shopping are backs onto the river with some restaurants having nice decks over it. www.bookwormofedwards.com

Holy Toledo – couple of female friends love this high end consignment store in Minturn. You can even find new winter coats! 970.827.4299.

Solaris – The replacement for the Crossroads shopping center is done and although pretty upscale is a happy addition to the village. The **Bol** bowling alley although expensive is a fun place to go bowling with great food (and watching women's league night was a plus). It also has an upscale movie theatre (with $10 before 4PM or after 10PM movies.

Restaurants

As with any ski town, check for off-season specials in the newspaper. Also ask locals about what is good. You tend to pay the same $$ for a good restaurant as a not so good one.

Sweet Basils – In the 1980's this was my favorite spot when teaching skiing in Vail. It was always consistently good for years. *On a recent trip to Vail, we skipped eating there due to some negative feedback. I left it on the list since on-line reviews are hit/miss which sadly happens in many ski towns since it is hard to get consistently good staff.*

The Left Bank – Still great as well though in my years at Vail in the mid-80's their service would almost be too formal and sometimes cater to the obvious high rollers.

May Palace – In West Vail on frontage road. This was a staple for me when it was in Vail Village years ago. Still good and handy if traveling through. Last time we got take out and ate it in Glenwood Canyon when heading back to Montrose (the rest stops in Glenwood Canyon are really nice with picnic tables along the Colorado river). 970.476.1657.

Pazzo's Pizzeria – In front of Solaris is an affordable pizza & sandwich place. Check for coupons in the paper too. I prefer eating at the bar where they make the pizzas.

Avon/Eagle Vail – **Blue Plate Bistro** is located at the Christie Lodge in Avon is a great locals spot. 970.845.2252. **Route 6 Café** is a great breakfast and lunch spot on the North frontage road (gas station in front). 41290 Highway 6. 970.949.6393. They are busy on weekend mornings! *They I believe have moved.* **Foods of Vail** is a nice deli I checked out – 150 E. Beaver Creek Blvd. 970.949.0282

Minturn – Minturn has always been a place to go if you want to *'slum it'* for an evening. The well-known **Saloon** is still there with great memorabilia pictures on the wall but I feel it is kinda pricey. Try instead the **Minturn Country Club** for grill your own steak/seafood (and look for specials they run in the newspaper). Plus there is a great Greek place **Nicky's Quickie** that makes things from scratch and has affordable prices in a deli like atmosphere (you order at the counter) 970.827.5616 – this is one place I plan on frequenting in the future.

GLENWOOD SPRINGS

Home of the well-known Glenwood Hot springs that in years past was a popular honeymoon spot (guessing since it was right on a major train line). It also is a great jumping off point to Aspen. It is a quaint mountain tourist town.

Glenwood Springs Hot Springs - The hot springs have a 100 meter hot mineral pool that is a blast for kids and adults. A water slide is available in the summer and a smaller, hotter pool is available for major soaking. A nice break from a Vail or Aspen ski vacation (about an hour from both resorts). It is just North of I-70 and downtown Glenwood Springs.

Yampa Spa & Vapor Caves (Glenwood Springs) – Also try the vapor caves, a separate business just east of the Glenwood Springs hot springs pool 970.945.0667. They have natural steam baths in underground caverns (not probably as much fun for kids as the hot springs pools). It is also a bit more off beat than the often packed hot springs pools down the street. *I prefer wearing sandals as the steamy environment is a little funky.*

Bicycling

Glenwood Canyon Bicycle Trail – A wonderful bike/walking trail through Glenwood Canyon that doesn't have any steep climbs (starts directly to the east of town just past Yampah Spa & Salon and follows the I-70 corridor).

> **East Trailhead** – Exit I-70 at Dotsero (exit 133) and take the I-70 Frontage Road west till it terminates.

> **I-70 Rest Areas Access** - You can get off at several canyon rest areas on I-70 and park and ride or walk on the path. Most rest areas include river access. Many have picnic tables right along the river. If not going long distances I would recommend Grizzly Creek (skipping Bair Ranch on the east of the canyon or the one at No Name) since you are in the heart of the canyon so those that just want to stroll will have great views immediately. *Last summer driving home from Vail, we got take out at May Palace in West Vail next to City Market (called the order in en route) and then ate our meal at one of the rest stops.*

Aspen – Basalt Trail System - Also consider riding up to Aspen on that trail system – not sure where you can connect to get to Glenwood Springs as I've only ridden down form Aspen to the Basalt/El Jebel area. Basalt is a nice destination for breakfast if in the Aspen area or further down valley. You can also put your bike on a bus to get back (uphill). Just be prepared that others like to do that too so the racks can be full. A new trail follows the road up to Snowmass Village too plus there has been one on Owl Creek road for a while now (that road goes up behind the airport and hits the highway at the north end of Buttermilk Ski Area.

Shopping

Artist's Mercantile & Gallery – On 720 Cooper Ave – is a nice gallery and art supply store. They carry a lot of nice art supplies. 970.947.0947.

Food

Tequilas - Is a wonderful chain Mexican restaurant 970.384.1588. They have some of the best Mexican food I've ever had. *Though I notice lately it is a chain popping up in other towns so not sure if they are maintaining quality.*

Glenwood Canyon Brewery - across from the train station in the Hotel Denver.

ASPEN

Although this is known as an upscale ski town of the rich and famous, it is an amazing inexpensive place to kick around in the summer, especially if you can find inexpensive lodging or camp. Downtown has the famous Hotel Jerome and the Wheeler Opera House and the Music School is nearby the round-a-bout as you enter town.

Things To Do

Aspen Center for Physics – Is a focal point for physics in aspen (in the same area as the music tent and Aspen Institute campuses). They have free lectures to the general public on current topics in Physics that can be quite interesting. They have summer lectures as well as a winter series. www.aspenphys.org

Aspen Music Festival & School – Founded in 1949, it is a summer classic music festival running late June till late August. Many events are free, including the ability to enjoy some of the concerts from the lawn outside the performance tent as well as student recitals. www.aspenmusicfestival.com

> **Sunday Symphony Concerts** - During the festival, there typically is a concert at 4PM every Sunday at the music tent – I prefer sitting on the lawn outside but you can also buy tickets. If on the lawn, bring rain gear as rain is not uncommon. A friend likes to go to the Noon rehearsals.

> **Student Recitals** – These are frequently at the Aspen Community (Methodist) Church on Bleeker Street (though in 2013 due to renovations, it was moved to the Aspen Chapel at the roundabout). Every recital I went to was free and the variety of composers selected and quality of the recitals makes it top on my list.

Aspen Institute – This is a big think tank that in the summer often run free lectures on science geared towards us lay people. They are wonderful – check out the local newspaper for schedules. They also run an annual **Idea Festival** in early July that brings in some heavy hitter people to discuss current topics in the world. www.aspeninstitute.org

Aspen Center for Environmental Studies – It is just behind the post office and has ponds and other things to explore. 970.925.5756 - www.aspennature.org

Aspen Shorts Fest – A short film festival run at the end of the ski season. This has really high quality films – have been to other things like this and been disappointed but not this. A single ticket for one screening is $15. 970.325.6882 or www.aspenfilm.org

Doc Eason Magic Show – for at least a couple of decades Doc has been doing fun magic shows in Snowmass Village. Currently he is at the **Stonebridge Hotel** in Snowmass Village on Thursday and Friday evenings. Although it is in the bar, it is kid friendly. During the off-season he may not be performing so I'd call to verify.

Towns of Carbondale, Basalt and **El Jebel** – These outlying 'down valley' communities have neat downtowns serving people that work in Aspen but live elsewhere. Carbondale had a super bicycle shop and a nice coffee house – but last time I went through the bike shop has moved out to the strip. Very good restaurants have moved down valley and I'd recommend taking a trip to Basalt for dinner or lunch one day.

Better yet, bicycle down on the bike path and either ride back or take the bus back (be aware the bus can only take 4 bicycles at a time so prime time is mid to late afternoon for bus access). The trail from Aspen to Woody Creek Tavern is graded dirt so a mountain or hybrid bike would be best.

Art Mecca

Aspen has some wonderful galleries, selling original art of artists often seen elsewhere in poster form. Not all galleries were to my liking though since some seemed to sell overly expensive examples (in my opinion) of impressionism or cubism type work by contemporary artists. Plus the Aspen Art Museum and Anderson Ranch are local gems.

Aspen Art Museum – their new building (August 2014) is stunning. Though sadly I wasn't impressed with the show I saw there. Though will go back as it their focus is contemporary art. Plus have the **So Rooftop** Café with a nice lunch menu and après ski specials (during ski season) from 3-6PM. 637 East Hyman Avenue - https://www.aspenartmuseum.org/

Anderson Ranch Arts Center (Snowmass Village) – Wonderful campus providing art classes you can sign up for. They also bring in top instructors that give free public talks plus the occasional artist showcased just to give a talk (most of this is in the summer and free!). I really enjoy the talks – typically on Tuesday evenings in the summer and infrequently a guest lecture on Thursdays. They also have a gallery with rotating shows. Plus early August is their annual action and picnic – a lot of fun even if you don't bid on something. 5263 Owl Creek Road – www.andersonranch.org.

Art-Aspen – Early August the Aspen Ice Garden is turned into a gallery with exhibitors from all over the world. www.art-aspen.com (the host company has other events in the US).

Red Brick Council for the Arts (110 East Hallam Street) has an opening every month (Thursdays). Their gallery is the hallway of an old school building where many of the classrooms are now artist studios or meeting spaces. The art was quite good when I was in there and much less expensive than the downtown galleries. I try to stop when walking through that neighborhood from downtown to the music tent.

CCAH (Carbondale Council on Arts and Humanities) – recently moved to the Launchpad downtown on 76 S. 4th Street and has a gallery. There is a monthly art walk in Carbondale too.

Raven Gallery – 433 E. Cooper has a nice art glass gallery. There was a wonderful art glass gallery in the same spot for years but the owner retired.

Crystal Glass Studio (Carbondale) – Another nice art glass gallery is in Carbondale on 50 Weant Blvd. They make custom functional pieces for houses plus have several local artists represented.

Aspen Restaurants

The recent economy has hit Aspen with a lot of turnover on restaurants and shops. So be prepared for changes. Though many restaurants have great bar menus to explore if you are one a tighter budget – but you may need to ask for them and it is on a space available basis.

Butcher's Block Deli - 970.925.7554 - 415 S Spring St. Near City Market and close to the gondola. Upscale meat/cheese deli but also serve great soups, salads and sandwiches you can eat at a small counter by the window or outside at tables. *I still like popping in here for a light picnic type meal that has good ingredients.*

Cache Cache – Downtown Aspen – eat in the bar for a much more reasonably priced meal at one of the better restaurants in town – the food is superb. I seem to get stuck with the Coq au Vin which has been on the menu each time I've been there. During season get there early as it gets busy quickly.

Explore Booksellers & Bistro – This is a nice bookstore that has an upstairs café. One of my local friends loves the place. It is also a nice spot for an afternoon tea or coffee (along with a sweet if so desired). 970.925.9318. *They recently were closed off-season so not sure if there will be a new reincarnation or the same food when winter season resumes.*

Jimmy's – Downtown Aspen – eat in the bar for a much more reasonably priced meal – have super hamburgers. If your name is Jim, they let you write your name on the wall – I took advantage of that!

L'Hostaria - <u>Great</u> bar menu. My friend Annie loves this place and my current one too! 620 East Hyman Avenue - 970.925.9022

Limelight Hotel – On 355 S. Monarch Street might have the best happy hour with a great deal on pizzas, beer and their house wine.

Little Ollie's – On 308 S. Hunter has good Chinese food at really fair prices for Aspen. *This used to be my go to for a low key meal but lately prefer bar menus at other restaurants.*

Meat & Cheese – this deli based from a local cheese and I believe sausage produce in Paonia also serves lunch/dinner. 970.710.7120.

New York Pizza – Great place to get an affordable slice of pizza. 409 E Hyman Ave (upstairs) - 970.920.3088

Peaches Corner Cafe - Great lunch spot with a wide range of dishes (including vegan!). 121 S Galena St - 970.544.9866

Pinons – Across the street from the Hotel Jerome is a local recommended eatery I'll try on my next trip. 105 S Mill St. - 970.920.2021

Victoria's Espresso and Wine Bar – my favorite place for coffee! 510 E Durant Ave. – close to the bus station in town.

Woody Creek Tavern – North of Aspen in Woody Creek – known for its great burgers and occasional celebrities that visit the funky watering hole. A very nice bike ride (mountain bike) from Aspen for lunch!

A bit out of town is **Ashcroft Pine Creek Cookhouse** – 970.925.1044 – This is in Ashcroft (take the Ashcroft turn-off from the roundabout for Aspen/Ashcroft and the Maroon Bells. In the winter you must ski there or take a sleigh ride and reservations are pretty much a must. There are remnants of the Ashcroft ghost town too that you can see.

Down Valley Restaurants

There are also several <u>very</u> good restaurants in Basalt – in fact I'd venture some would hold their own with Aspen. I always like to eat down valley in Basalt 1-2 times a trip because of that and I like the town – still historic but quieter and more relaxed.

Café Bernard – Great for dinner but I like going in the morning and having croissants and fresh orange juice (note they often run out of them by 10AM but you can order the day ahead) 970.927.4292

Riverside Grille – Behind the grocery store along the river – has great salads and lunch fare. Haven't eaten there for dinner. Great for summer lunch if you can get a table on the deck.

Tempranillo – A Spanish restaurant with wonderful food with Aspen quality and also price. I enjoyed my meal there and would eat there again when looking for a nicer evening out – though noticed a couple of recent reviews that weren't as good so not sure if it was super picky people or they have lost their edge. 970.927.3342

In Carbondale there are several good places as well though Basalt seems to have better high-end food.

Tortilleria La Roca – 780 Highway 133 on south side of road, past 2nd gas station (if turning from State Route 82) and before you get to Main Street. Great fresh tortillas, salsa (homemade hot sauce style), chicharones, and baked stuff. Next door is **Valley Meats** a Mexican carniceria (786 Highway 133) that makes great, affordable burritos – probably the best tacos and burros in the area. There is another Mexican market/café on State Route 133 just as you turn from State Route 82. Also **Wine Time** next door is a nice shop with good value for the region and very knowledgeable owners (doing wine tastings on Friday afternoons too).

Red Rock Diner - Right at the intersection of 82 and 133 that has reasonably priced meals (open pretty early for breakfast too). 970.963.4111. I haven't been back to the Red Rock diner lately and now prefer going to downtown Carbondale.

Redstone Inn and **Crystal Club Café in Redstone** – Two local recommendations in Redstone (on the road to Paonia over McClure Pass). 970.963.9515 for Crystal Club Café.

Town – This is my new favorite place down valley. Right in downtown Carbondale. Counter service for breakfast and lunch. Dinner has a wait staff. 348 Main Street - http://www.towncarbondale.com/

Village Smithy – downtown Carbondale with a front lawn area. This might be the best breakfast place down valley. 970.963.9990 – they are busy on weekend mornings/lunch!! Kiddy corner to the restaurant is a great thrift shop. They have great pie too – got an amazing piece of pecan pie to go last trip through. Kiddy corner to the Village Smithy is the **Miser's Mercantile** which is a good 2nd hand store and place to wander if waiting for a table (though I hear it was amazing years ago when they got more 'stuff' from Aspen). Also try **Back Door Consignment**.

Lodging and Transportation

Public Transportation – The RFTA (925.8484) provides transport between Glenwood Springs and Aspen/Snowmass as well as Aspen Airport. There is a fee and it stops in towns along the way along with express buses. Also there are day-time free buses between the four Aspen ski areas during the ski season. The buses typically can take bicycles which can be handy (e.g., you rode to Basalt and don't want to climb back up the hill on a bicycle to Aspen). Be aware the bus bike racks can fill up and there is a priority system at some locations for who gets to use them first.

Lodging – Aspen/Snowmass has tons of high-end places to stay. Some more reasonable ones are **Pokolodi** in Snowmass (close walk to the lifts and right below the mall) 800.666.4556, **Little Red Ski Haus** right in Aspen (don't know how affordable it is lately).

Camping – There are campgrounds in the area, some on the road up to the Maroon Belles (this also allows you to drive up the road to the Maroon Belles rather than take a bus or ride a bike up). 877.444.6777 is the National Recreation Reservation Service that can book the campground sites (or ReserveUSA.com).

Hiking

There are many neato places to hike in the area.

Maroon Bells - Take the bus to the Maroon Bells and hike up from there to the lake above it (or all the way to Crested Butte).

Cathedral Lake – This is an incredible hike. Take the road to Ashcroft (one of the spurs at the round-a-bout before entering Aspen) and drive about ½ mile past the Ashcroft Nordic center and town site. Then take the dirt road up about ¾ a mile to the trail head. It is a 7 mile total round trip and 2,000 feet elevation gain to a beautiful lake above tree line.

Photo above shot on a rainy/misty day.

American Lakes - The trailhead is about ½ mile before the Ashcroft Nordic Center. It is about a 2,000 vertical elevation gain hike, though a bit lower than Cathedral Lake nearby.

Lost Man Loop —This is an easy-to-access trail that gets you high immediately – wonderful to get newbie hikers into beautiful high meadows without a long uphill ascent. The upper and lower trailheads are directly on Highway 82 near the summit of Independence Pass. Driving up from Aspen, the lower trailhead is clearly marked with a big sign (this section of the trail is still in the trees). Before the highway traverses a big cliff is a parking area on a big corner to the left (a sharp right turn as you are heading up the pass). This is the upper trailhead and where I like to hike since you start right at tree-line. If you shuttle cars, you can hike down to the lower trailhead. There is another trail up to **Linkins Lake** that I haven't tried but hear it is steeper. If you stay on Lost Man, it climbs at a gentler pitch to a minor summit before dropping back down to the lower trailhead. I haven't gone past the summit and just turn around when I feel like it.

Snowmass – Right from the bus station at the mall, you can hike up behind and get into a nice trail system with nice views about 2 miles out of town. First it is the Nature Trail then becomes the Ditch Trail – you will walk up a short section of dirt road as the Nature Trail ends then at an intersection of two paved roads the Ditch Trail starts.

Bicycling

On one of my first trips to Aspen, I rented bikes from **Ajax Bike and Sports** 970.925.7662 downtown Aspen. They had a good selection and fair prices. The bicycle path system in the area is incredible. You can ride from Aspen over to Snowmass and then down valley to Basalt and Carbondale. Parts are paved and some are dirt. Getting from Snowmass Intercept

Bus Lot directly to Aspen is either a dirt section or the trail or steep climbs through Snowmass or Cemetery Lane.

Maroon Bells Road - is one great ride though a pretty fair climb – make sure to have better bike for this trip.

Rio Grande Down Valley Bicycle Trail From Aspen - Another is Woody Creek Tavern for lunch via the Rio Grande bike path – great place to visit for lunch and famous too. The hill coming back up from Woody Creek (about ½ mile climb) is steep but the rest is a gentle grade since the trail follows an old railroad line. A key part of this is a graded dirt trail so you would want a hybrid or mountain bike (the other formal bike trails in the valley floor are paved). Here is a link for the Rio Grande Trail: http://www.rfta.com/trailmap.pdf

Ashcroft - Also it is popular now to ride up to Ashcroft which is a dead end paved road (about 22 miles round-trip from the round-a-bout).

Skiing

Aspen is most known for its downhill skiing – of which Aspen has some very good expert skiing along with wonderful family environments at Snowmass or Buttermilk. Highlands is my favorite for expert skiing.

X-C Skiing - For an 'anti-Aspen' experience, try the **Ashcroft Ski Touring** 970.925.1971. Last time I was there it was $30 to rent skis and use the trails. In the winter, it is at the end of the road. They provide ski rentals and passes to their groomed trails. You can also ski up the road for free and just rent skis. For a fun experience, book lunch at the Ashcroft Pine Creek Cookhouse. At the round-about, coming from Glenwood Springs, take the second right (the first goes to Aspen Highlands). It is about 11 miles down a pretty valley. As a bit of trivia – this is where they originally were going to put the Aspen ski area rather than Ajax.

Night Clubs

Sadly several of the great evening venues have closed – Aspen's legendary night life isn't what it used to be. Though **Belly Up** is a super place to see a well range of music venues, including national level acts. Tickets seem to be in the $35-55 range – but worth it if you like the group since it is such a great venue for music. If you are not going to reserve a seat (higher than base ticket price), get there early, as non-reserved seats tend to go quickly.

The night crowds in Aspen will vary. There are several private clubs but you will need to be a member or know someone that is to get in. NOTE: Also Latin dancing at **Jimmy's** restaurant (currently just one Saturday a month so best to check). Jimmy's also has a great bar menu besides food in the main restaurant.

Après Ski – Sadly many ski towns après ski doesn't rock any more. *My favorite après ski spot in Snowmass, a Chinese restaurant is gone.* However the **Sky Hotel** in Aspen has a pretty good one though they are closing summer 2017 I hear. http://www.theskyhotel.com/ Also the **Limelight Hotel** has a nice lounge.

LEADVILLE

A real mining town with recently active mines. Main street looks a little more real too as it isn't all foo-foo-ed out.

Cookies With Altitude – On717 ½ Harrison Avenue (main drag) is a great place for a cookie or cup of coffee. 719.486.1026.

Ski Cooper – Another one of the smaller areas in the state that I haven't tried.

SALIDA

Until 2009, I had driven through this town many times but since downtown was bypassed many years ago – never went there. The highway strip has the community hot springs pool and a few good restaurants but it feels like any other strip mall by-pass – empty. Downtown is really nice! It may be the nicest historic main street in Colorado. *Every visit the town continues to grow on me – and downtown seems to keep evolving into something better. Also if you are coming in from Buena Vista, take the 291 cut-off right into downtown.*

Monarch Ski Area – Heading up Monarch Pass is a day area that caters to the Colorado Springs/Pueblo crowd.

Mt. Princeton Hot Springs Resort (Salida)- They have beautiful scenery and is between the towns of Buena Vista and Salida. But they don't stay on top of little things – guessing the endless families coming over from the Front Range will show up regardless. 1.888.395.7799

> *I hear locals prefer* **Cottonwood Hot Springs** *5.5 miles west of Buena Vistsa on Cottonwood Pass road – 719.395.6434 (which I haven't tried). They also have lodging. There are also other private hot springs sites up the road past Mt. Princeton Hot Springs – you may even be able to rent a house (I haven't researched this yet).*

Second Saturday Gallery Tour – This probably works better for people that may come in from the Front Range versus a Friday night event. There also is an annual multi-day **Salida Art Walk** in June. www.salidaartwalk.org

The Book Haven – 138 F. Street – nice bookstore. A variety of stores in the area – **Beadsong** is another right across the street (107 F. Street).

Highway 50 - On Highway 50 heading towards Cañon City is a neat art gallery in Coaldale – the **Artpost Gallery** with Robert

Parker the key artist and his wife Kay runs the gallery 719.942.4389. I also checked out the **Riverside Café** in Howard (719.942.3942) that looked good (just had lunch so wasn't hungry).

Restaurants

Café Dawn – 203 West 1st – Great coffee plus snacks. Nice people too. 719.539.5105. If *you are coming into town on 291 from the North, it is on your right at the intersection of G Street.*

Amicas – On 136 East 2nd Street – great pizza, salad and related fair joint. They also sell micro beers. The owner makes up an amazing squash soup. 719.539.5219

The Fritz – On Sackett across from the park on the river and one door in from F Street. A great lunch and dinner spot with a long list of appetizers (tapas-esque).

These two restaurants are not tested but recommended by a local: **El Reynaldo** a taco stand on the main drag and **Twisted Cork** (potentially poor service but the food makes up for it).

GUNNISON

A college town on Highway 50 between Montrose and Salida and the junction to Crested Butte. I really like this town and have stopped many times and just walked around.

Gunnison Art Center – Gallery and music events. 102 Main Street – 970.641.4029 – www.gunnisonartscenter.org

Gunnison Pioneer Museum – Worth a visit if you have the time. On Highway 50. Has cool old steam engine. 970.641.4530

The Bookworm – Nice bookstore with good stock of maps/books for the region. 970.641.3693

Boom-a-Rang – Clothing consignment store and furniture. 225 North Main Street. Also try **Paws Abilities Thrift Store**.

The Bean – Coffee shop on 120 North Main Street about 3 doors north of the crossroad with Highway 50. *I normally stop there for coffee when blazing through town.* Has a nice college feel to it and they have a pretty good range of lighter food too.

Blackstock Bistro – Upscale. Dinner only. Happy hours 5-6:30 and 10PM-Midnight. Taco Tuesdays. 122 W. Tomichi – 970.641.4394

High Alpine – Brew pub and killer pizza. Nice bar. 111 N. Main St. – 970.642.4500.

Twisted Fork – Asian fusion and burgers. New owners were very friendly. 206 N. Main Street – 970.641.1488.

CRESTED BUTTE

It is a quaint mining town that has some of the best extreme skiing in Colorado. Be aware it can be a cold mountain to ski too! I would say it is the last of the 'real' ski towns in Colorado with Telluride being 2nd. It has its upscale places but hasn't lost its funkiness or charm.

Camp4Coffee – my local friends say this is the best place for morning coffee.

Brick Oven Pizzeria & Pub – Fun place to have a beer and pizza and sometimes live music. Also try the **Secret Stash** which may have even better pizza.

The Eldo – Upstairs bar (215 Elk Ave) that is a popular hangout. What is really cool is mid-week they sometimes get really good bands there. *Noticed the Radiators playing there April 1, 2014 – the cook happily talked about the great music, saying the bands play much bigger venues on the weekends and they like playing in CB.*

Saturday Farmer's Market – Summers

Mountain Earth Whole Foods – Nice local organic food store.

Ginger Café – recommended by my friends – haven't tried it.

SAN LUIS VALLEY

South of Salida when Highway 285 clears Poncha Pass, you enter the huge San Luis Valley. They grow a lot of potatoes here. Highway 160 crosses the bottom of the valley. From Alamosa heading west you go through towns of Monte Vista, then Del Norte. From South Fork you can head north to Creede or Lake City or continue west on 160 over Wolf Creek Pass to Pagosa Springs and then Durango. Heading east from Alamosa on 160 you go over La Veta pass into Walsenburg.

ALAMOSA

This is another crossroads town for me as I travel the Southwest and have good friends that grew up there. The area has some tourism though to me towns in the area still primarily serve the local mining, agricultural and ranching communities. I like the downtown area since it still feels like a real downtown and has seen a rennaisance. South on 395 in Antonito is where the **Cumbres and Toltec Scenic Railroad** starts.

Great Sand Dunes National Monument - Colorado's beach. There are several hundred foot high dunes that can be hiked, sledded on (cardboard type sleds), played on or even skied (I actually skied it years ago – skis don't move fast on sand!).

Bird Watching - A few miles north of town there are a lot of wetland areas that are stop over points for the Sandhill cranes (with a few Whooping cranes the time I got to see it) and other birds on their migratory flybys.

Movie Manor Motel – In nearby Monte Vista is a drive-in movie theatre that has a Best Western motel where you can watch the drive-in movies in your room! Clean, well run place.

Locavores – Restaurant with locally sourced focus. 2209 Main St.- 719.589.2157 - www.eatlocavores.com

The Rubi Slipper – Great burger joint and bar. Lots of beer on tap. 506 State Ave.

For coffee try **Roast Café** at 420 San Juan or **Milagros Coffee House** at 529 Main Street. If you prefer espresso Roast Café may be a better bet.

G6 Hamburger Stand – Open seasonally in Antonito on south side of town (right on Highway 285 on east side of 285).

CRESTONE

Interesting spiritual center in Colorado. I was told a woman donated a large tract of land – dividing it out to different spiritual groups. This includes a Zen Center complete with a Japanese style Zendo meditation room and a Hindu temple.

Bliss Café - Great eatery in town. Draws an eclectic mix of people. Lunch and dinner only. 719.256.6400

Coffee/Art Gallery – In Moffat where the turn off to Creston is, there is a cute artist gallery and coffee place just North of that turn-off on the west side of the road.

Joyful Journey Hot Springs – North of Crestone on State Route 17 (just south of where it merges with US 285) is an oasis in the valley. Lodging too. http://joyfuljourneyhotsprings.com/

SAGUACHE

On Highway 285. Community market and thrift shop (404 N. Main Street downtown). Same building will house a coffee shop. **Cozy Castle Cinema** across the street shows a variety of flicks. Next trip I want to try the **Saguache 4th Street Diner & Bakery** as is a popular breakfast/lunch place (719.655.6411).

SOUTHWEST MOUNTAINS

This region includes the beautiful San Juan Mountains. Highway 550 cuts through the heart of this region and is covered in the next section.

TELLURIDE

Neat old mining town, now a ritzy ski town set in an absolutely incredible mountainous valley. Though I do miss some of the hippie charm it had in the late 1970's. Great skiing - if you are an expert skier yet has great Green/Blue terrain for families. Plus a couple of fun on-mountain restaurants (**Alpino Vino** and **Le Bon Vivant**). I have taught skiing there now for 12 seasons. The picture below is from the top of Chair 9 where

some of the famous runs from the 70's are accessible (the Plunge and Spiral Stairs). It has a wide range of fun summer festivals (Bluegrass in June and the Film Festival on Labor Day Weekend are probably the best known). The drive over Lizard Head pass to Rico is spectacular.

Noel Night – Early December (generally the first Wednesday), the shops are open later and everyone comes out to shop and get together. Similar feel to the art walks of other towns like Flagstaff, but a bit more festive.

New Year's Torchlight – An annual event. Ski School skis down on both Mountain Village and town sides (with bright car type flares) and fireworks finish it off. Last year it started at 6:30PM. Do a smaller event on Xmas as well.

Fire Festival – January has a festival celebrating fire – just finishing its 3rd season. http://telluridefirefestival.org/

Art Walk – First Thursdays from 5-8PM – 19 venues. 970.728.3930 is the Telluride Arts District office. May want to check if they have them during the off season.

Summer Festivals – Telluride hosts a variety of wonderful summer festivals that attract very distinct crowds. Most famous are **Bluegrass** the end of June and **Telluride Film Festival** on Labor Day weekend. I like **Mountain Film Festival** on Memorial Day weekend that focuses on outdoor topics – adventure and informational. The **Wine Festival** the end of June has great wines and food. **Blues and Brews in September** was a favorite of my neighbors from Flagstaff. And others love **Jazz Festival**. So many wonderful choices! *Many festivals let you volunteer for passes – of course the best spots are taken up by long-time locals. But if you have the time it is a great way to experience a festival that needs volunteers (best to sign up way ahead of time).*

Summer Wednesday Concerts in Mountain Village – These generally run all summer and are from 6-8PM but may end early. In 2009 they were at the top of Chair 1. If in town you can take the gondola over and then a short walk to the top of chair 1.

Free Gondola – The gondola is free and connects the town and mountain village. Really spectacular views both at day and night. Don't need skis to ride it either – just shoes or boots. *It is closed during the off-season - late fall and in the spring after the ski area closes.*

Sheridan Opera House – It has many events, including locally produced plays. Core theatre is old with newer areas connected to it. Have a bar upstairs and was able to bring drinks into the theatre too. Bigger events may end up at the Mountain Village conference center or the Palm Theater which is in the high school complex at the roundabout when you enter town.

Ah Haa School for the Arts – At 300 S. Townsend Street in the old train station is a wonderful place to take art classes. They have an annual art auction in the summer that is a fun event. 970.728.3886 - www.ahhaa.org

Telluride Historical Museum – It is in the old hospital. An option for those visiting that aren't skiers or hikers and are history buffs. 201 W Gregory Ave - 970.728.3344 - http://www.telluridemuseum.org/

Wilkenson Library – An amazing resource for the town. They also rent movies, often have lectures/talks in their meeting room, and a great children's section. 100 W Pacific Ave.

Telluride Thrift Shop – A nonprofit shop that donates all proceeds to the Telluride Animal Foundation. 335 W Colorado Ave

Zia Sun - Great gift shop with a neat selection of toys. 214 W Colorado Ave

Over the Moon Fine Foods – a nice deli and small specialty grocery on 200 W. Colorado. 970.728.2079

Sawpit Mercantile – Heading down valley from Telluride on Hwy 145 in Sawpit is a gas station and store. The store has interesting foods from Europe and a great chocolate selection. They have a connected liquor store with separate entrance so popular for people post-ski/work. Not open in the mornings early. *Summer 2012 they have new owners – added sandwiches to their offerings.*

Hiking & Walks

There is tons of hiking in the area. These are just a couple.

Bear Creek Trail – This is a favorite is since you can access it right from town from the end of South Pine Street. It goes up to Bear Creek Falls (2.5 miles one way).

San Miguel River Trail - The 4+ mile trail weaves through town is a fun walk as well! Many places to connect to it, including Town Park. Photo above.

X-C skiing

Though Telluride is known for its alpine skiing, there is Nordic skiing up at the ski area and some of the slopes surrounding the lift 10 area (in fact that lift can be used to gain access). Ski school also has trained instructors in Nordic for private lessons and occasional events up at the area.

Valley Floor – The open space before you get to town is also great for x-c skiing.

Trout Lake - Also, don't miss the Trout Lake area – go to end of Trout Lake road and look for a parking area. Trout Lake is just below the summit of Lizard Head pass (State Route 145 that goes to Cortez) on the Telluride side of the pass. Normally a track is set, that goes up to Lizard Head summit. Donation recommended to pay for trail grooming.

Matterhorn - Or just below Trout Lake park at Matterhorn National Forest camp just below Trout lake. It is on the east side of the highway - opposite side of Matterhorn drive that goes into the housing community of San Bernardo. They have up to 4.5 miles of trails there that circle through Priest Lake. Donation recommended to pay for trail grooming.

Restaurants

An up-front comment on Telluride eateries – service can be amazingly up/down in many of the establishments compared to other major resorts like Vail or Aspen. The same fun hippie type nature of the town seems to bring a different energy to people serving.

Argentine Grille - In Rico in the hotel, open with variable schedule so best to call. 970.967.3000 or 800.365.1971 – the hotel is now housing for Telluride employees. *In the past they have had an early-bird menu with discounted entrees. They were closed for a season and reopened winter 2016.*

Baked in Telluride – It is a local icon that burned down and was rebuilt better than the original. The food, in my opinion, is good but not great. They have an amazing baked goods selection plus pizza and other entrees. For many this is a morning tradition.

Bon Vivant – This is a mountain restaurant at the top of chair 5 with stunning views. On a sunny/calm day it is a great place for a break or lunch. Menu is a bit pricey so if on a budget split a crepe and just get drinks. Get there well before noon if you don't want to wait or catch them in the afternoon before they close.

Cindybread – In Lawson Hill area on 168 Society Drive has good bread and baked goods plus sandwich/burrito fare for breakfast and lunch (open M-F). Two doors down is **Telluride Coffee Roasters** (also generally open M-F) where you can pick up fresh roasted coffee (they also sell under the Steaming Bean label in City Markets). They also can make you a coffee. If timing is right, a good stop en route to your condo in Telluride.

Cosmopolitan – Right across from the gondola in town. Upscale restaurant and can eat in the bar. Reservations would probably be better in busy times. During slow times, they have an early bird special – verify if available and what time it is valid (often 5:30-6:30) and off-season have other specials. 970.728.1292

Cornerhouse Grille – 131 N Fir Street – block off the main drag. Good light fare and good prices. 970.728.6207

221 South Oak – great little restaurant in an old house. They have had Wednesday bar specials (mussels or gumbo and a glass of wine for a fair price). *Though I'd check since during high season they may not offer this.*

La Cocina de Luz – Next door to Telluride liquors (where coffee cart is). Great healthy style Mexican food – trying to include organic ingredients when possible. 728.9355 or www.lacocinatelluride.com. *There also is* **Caravan,** *a cart outside the restaurant that serves up Middle Eastern food (you can eat inside at Cocina if you want).*

La Piazza – It is in the plaza right at the top of Chair 1. The best place for a relaxed sit down lunch on the mountain (they take lunch reservations). Gnocchis & Petto di Pollo are my favorites. They also own **La Pizzeria** next door which is much more informal and has casual menu that includes homemade gelato (kid's love it) as well as **Rustico Ristorante** in town. Also on the same plaza is **Poachers** which is a good place for simpler fare like burgers or sandwiches.

La Marmotte – Great French restaurant. I do hear they can be a little inconsistent but this is where I probably had the best meal in town of Telluride. They also at the bar have special pricing for a glass of wine/appetizer (nice if you just want to get out). 970.728.6232

Telluride Coffee Company – Right on the main plaza (big yellow awning) in Mountain Village is where I go for morning coffee. Convenient location with cooked to order breakfasts.

There – is a place I want to try, a friend loved it. Be aware there is not a lot of space and it can be busy. Noted a review where a reservation was not honored and given to someone else – so be flexible as their service may not be reliable (and is an issue with Telluride anyways – restaurant service is not up to par with other key ski resorts) 627 W Pacific Ave (closer to Coonskin chair 7).

Village Table – Winter of 2017 had in my opinion the best happy hour value in Mountain Village, including half price tapas. They also have a nice Mediterranean inspired dinner menu. If you want a busier happy hour, go to **Tomboy Tavern** right at the base of Chair 4. It is on the plaza that the conference center is also on. 970.728.1117

NORWOOD

A small ranch town that is also a bedroom community for people that work in Telluride. The volcanic peak Lone Cone dominates the area – the last peak leaving the mountains to the west in Colorado. *There were a couple of additional nice places to stop and eat at in town, sadly they have closed.*

Happy Belly Deli – Another place recommended by locals that I haven't tried. Open for breakfast/lunch – Mon-Sat.

BEDROCK

Near Paradox and West of Ridgway and Norwood. There is a BLM takeout which has a nice picnic area and quiet except during high water times (spring run-off). The parking lot can get full at the river running times. But it has several picnic tables and from what I know can be used for camping. It is right on the Dolores River, nestled in the mouth of a canyon. The **Bedrock store** is cute and sells basic supplies — though it is for sale (and still for sale 2 years later!).

CORTEZ AREA – MESA VERDE GATEWAY

Cortez is at the crossroads of Highway 160, 491 and State Route 145. It is the gateway to Mesa Verde. The drive up State Route 145 through Dolores and Rico over Lizard Head pass is beautiful — especially when the Aspens are changing (picture on next page). Sleeping Ute Mountain dominates the landscape around Cortez. **Mesa Verde National Park** along with nearby **Hovenweep National Monument** are really interesting places to explore (and if you like those sorts of historic sites – go to **Chaco Culture National Historic Park** as well). Hovenweep boarders Utah so it is in the Utah section of this guide. It is a smaller park but the tower ruins sites are mesmerizing.

Mesa Verde National Park - The most famous of the Southwest Native American ruin sites. It is really worth a visit. It is a bit of a drive from Highway 160 – so it really isn't a pop in and out sort of thing. It also deserves two days to explore. I also like the book **"Ancient Ruins and Rock Art of the Southwest: An Archaeological Guide"** - David Grant Noble – it is a pedestrian book to the ruins of this region. *I went back in fall of 2012, staying at Far View lodge (closed in the winter). It was sure handy to be right there in the park. Though breakfast and lunch choices were not very good at neighboring cafeterias (hotel restaurant was great but pricey for dinner). Make sure to book tours when you first go to the visitor center for Cliff Palace and Balcony House – those are AMAZING to see. The short hike to Spruce Tree house is a must – add on the 2+ mile hike on the Petroglyph trail for a better feel of the park. Cliff Palace can be seen as part of a $40 tour that actually was very good – or you can book that tour yourself with the park & save quite a bit of money.*

Sand Canyon Trail (Canyon of the Ancients National Monument) – South of Cortez turn off Highway 491 south (also Highway 160 West) for the airport (County Road G). Drive 12.4 miles on County Road G to the trailhead (stay on the road – don't go into the airport itself). Parking lot is a flat area of slickrock to the right. Trail 6+ miles one way if you do the entire thing – last section is steep (I didn't hike that far). Goes past ancestral Puebloan ruins. There is a north trailhead as well. If you get to Sutcliff Vineyards, you've passed the trailhead. You may also want to visit **Sutcliff Vineyards** which is on the left side about a mile further down the road from the trailhead. Open Noon-5PM daily. Might be good to book an appointment. They do charge for wine tasting. 970.565.0825 - https://sutcliffewines.com/

Anasazi Heritage Center – Off of State Route 184 near Dolores. I went there many years ago and is worth a visit if making a tour of the area. One web site about the center is http://www.mesaverdecountry.com/tourism/archaeology/ahc.html and phone is 970.882.5600

Books Used Bookstore –I love this store as it has a better selection than most and low key. It is on 124 Pinon Drive just NE of where Highway 491 to Dove Creek spurs off of Highway 160 on the west side of downtown (in fact only really a block or so from either road in that triangle area).

Sutcliff Vineyards – See notes under **Sand Canyon Trail**.

Cliffrose Garden Center – There is a really nice garden center about ½ mile east of town on the north side of Highway 160 to Durango. 970.565.8994

Food

Spruce Tree Coffeehouse – A few doors West of City Market in Cortez is a small coffeehouse in a house. Have pretty good sandwiches. The staff is friendly and a good place to hang out and get some work done if on the road. Hours are seven days a week, 7AM-7PM. 970.565-6789

Ute Coffee Shop – At the intersection of the highways to Shiprock, Dove Creek and Durango. Great little diner. Love their huevos rancheros. 970.565.2650.

Absolute Bakery & Cafe – In downtown Mancos (110 South Main Street) is a <u>great</u> bakery and breakfast/lunch place. It is a few blocks south of Highway 160 through town. Mancos is between Cortez and Durango and you also go through it if going the back way from Dolores to Durango. Open Sundays until Noon. 970.533.1200

Riverfront Pizza and Subs – In Dolores. Annie's friend loved this place. 1919 Railroad Ave - 970.882.4007

Lodging

Tomahawk Lodge – On Highway 491/160 on south end of Cortez heading to Shiprock. Looked like an affordable old motel – planned to stay there once but travel plans shifted. 800.643.7705 (reservations only) or 970.565.8521

Dolores Mountain Inn – Basic clean motel in Dolores. 970.882.7203, www.dminn.com

PAGOSA SPRINGS – HOT SPRINGS

Cute hot springs town between Durango and Alamosa on Highway 160. Just east of town is Highway 64 that winds down to Chama and Taos, NM.

Wolf Creek Ski Area - Is nearby as well at the top of Wolf Creek Pass. It is legendary for its snow. Sadly it is one resort I haven't skied in Colorado.

Pagosa Springs Center for the Arts – This includes the Thingamajig Theatre Co. http://pagosacenter.org

Healing Waters Hot Springs – More affordable hot springs spot. 317 Hot Springs Blvd.

Pagosa Hot Springs – Deepest geothermal hot spring in the world. www.pagosahotsprings.com

Restaurants

Pagosa Baking Company – Breakfast, lunch plus coffee and pastries! Nice place to stop for coffee and a snack when going through town. 238 Pagosa Street.

Riff Raff Brewing – Brew pub in a Victorian house. Geothermally heated. 274 Pagosa Street – 970.264.4677

Alley House Grille –Fine Dining. Close Sundays. 214 Pagosa Street. - 970.264.0999

Kip's Grill – Tacos and enchiladas. 121 E. Pagosa Street.

Hiking

Plenty of hiking here. Sadly a place I haven't played in yet. These notes come from an outdoor group I ran into while on an outing in Utah. http://pagosa.com/pagosa-hiking/

Piedra River Trail – To get to the trailhead, on the west end of Pagosa Springs, take Piedra Road north from Highway 160 16 miles (mostly a dirt road). After crossing the Piedra River, park in the parking area. Cross Piedra Road and hike up the hill to the trail – about 6 miles one way and 500 feet elevation gain.

Piedra Falls – A shorter hike with a longer drive out Piedra Road 17 miles and continuing further a few miles. I would recommend getting local advice on this one, especially since on dirt roads.

Four Mile Falls – 6+ mile hike. From Hwy 160 downtown, turn north onto Lewis St. and an immediate left onto 5th St. Stay right onto Four Mile Road (CR400 - this becomes FS #645) driving north 8 miles from Pagosa Springs. Turn right at the junction for four more miles to the trailhead.

Highway 550 – Million Dollar Highway

Highway 550 runs through the heart of the **San Juan Mountains**. It starts in Montrose and heads through Ouray, Silverton, Durango and onto Bernalillo, New Mexico. The section from Ouray to Silverton is called the "Million Dollar Highway" which I was told is due to the incredible cost to build the road during the 19th century mining era. The section of Highway 550 from Ridgway to Durango is also part of the **San Juan Skyway Scenic Byway** which is a loop through the region.

Montrose

The largest town in the region. It has grown on the south end with a lot of strip-mall developments. Though downtown is surviving. **Black Canyon of the Gunnison National Park** is to the East on Highway 50. Nearby is the town of Olathe – famous for its sweet corn – good as anything in the Midwest.

Black Canyon of the Gunnison National Park – This is northeast of town (go on Highway 50 east till the signs then drive up to the park). Worth a peek. In the winter it is a great place to X-C ski – though you want to do it after a recent storm as at this is when they generally groom. Photo on previous page.

Museum of the Mountain West – A great collection of Western memorabilia from 1880-1930's with a collection of buildings from that period. It is on the east side of town at the intersection of Highway 50 and Miami Road (entrance is on Miami Road). Adults $10 - M-Sat 8:30-4:30 - 970.240.3400

Ute Indian Museum – On the south side of town just off of Highway 550 is a museum dedicated to the Ute people. *FYI – Under renovations and reopening summer 2017.* 17253 Chipeta Rd. - 970.249.3098

Shavano Valley Rock Art – this was really cool to see and much more than I expected. It is a mix of eras – most recently Ute. The picture to the left is a large boulder with a variety of images. Another interesting one is of a horse. You need someone to take you can call the Ute Museum and see when a tour is scheduled.

I found out about the rock art at a meeting of the **Chipeta Chapter of the Colorado Archeological Club** that meets the 3rd Wednesday of each month (currently at the Methodist church fellowship hall on the corner of Park and South 1st). They don't meet in the summers.

River Bottom Park – This park has a nice skateboard park and a new water park with several rapids designed for people using kayaks or other water sports platforms. **Montrose Kayak & Surf** on 302 W Main St is open seasonally to rent stuff for the park or other rivers/lakes in the area - 970.249.8730

Montrose Summer Music Series – Once a month on the first Friday of the month is a free live music event at the Black Canyon Golf Course (1310 Birch Street just east of Hillcrest Dr). http://www.montrosesummermusic.com/

Fox Cinema Center - I love the upstairs Penthouse theater! 4PM weekend matinee and Wednesday night specials. Friendly staff. 27 S Cascade Ave. **Second Sunday Cinema** – the 2nd Sunday of every month at 1PM they run an art or foreign flick. 970.249.8211 - http://montrosemovies.com

Star Drive In Theatre – Nice family run drive in right in town. Movies weekends late spring and early fall and generally 7 days a week during the summer. 970.249.6170. Usually run a double feature. They have the best French fries in town and also sell hamburgers and hot dogs. Delta also has the **Tru-View** drive in right on State Route 92 to Hotchkiss/Paonia too.

Canyon Creek Bed and Breakfast – Looks like a nice place to stay too. Kendra the owner has had summer music in the past on her lawn. 820 E. Main Street. 970.249.2886.

Montrose in Motion – At one point this was a Thursday night event through the summer. It has gone through some growing pains as on a hiatus. If it restarts, it is a great expression of community.

Olathe Sweet Corn Festival – This feels more like a single day county fair. It has recently gone through some changes, they used bring in a major musical act for the evening. Currently it is a bit smaller event than in the past. Be prepared for a hot day or rainy day. Normally the first Saturday of August. www.olathesweetcornfest.com

Shopping

D'Medici Footwear - Great shoe store in downtown Montrose. I like the walking shoes she sells. Several of my female friends have gone nuts there as the selection of shoes is incredible for women (might beat any store on the Front Range). 316 E Main St - 970.249.3668

Fabula – Eclectic gift and kitchen store. 317 E Main St - 970.765.2274

Hypoxia – 300 E Main Street has outdoors oriented clothing. Also **Great Outdoors Company** on 10 S. Selig.

SheShe Botique – Nice, trendy woman's clothing shop on 340 East Main. **Pollux** is another fun shop the next block down across the street (also a Pollux in downtown Grand Junction).

Straw Hat Farm Market & Kitchen Store – One of the key vendors at the farmer's market now runs a permanent store in the building that is part of the farmer's market - 514 S. 1st. They have fresh baked goods daily. Though, Saturdays is the day where there is the best variety (and things sell fast so get there early). Ryan or his mother Karen are usually at the helm. Tues-Fri 10:00-6:00 and Sat 10:00-3:00 970.417.4744

The Vine Market and Bistro – See under Restaurants

Farmer's Market – Downtown Saturdays in the summer and indoors at 514 S 1st every other Saturday in the winter.

Kinikin Processing – Is a local meet processor that opened recently a retail store on 1032 64.50 road just south of the San Juan Bypass (that road south of the bypass is also called Park) - http://www.kinikin.com.

Bicycling

The road bicycling opportunities in Montrose just keep getting better and better. http://www.visitmontrose.com/128/Biking

Olathe Via 6450 Road – A nice route is to take Park Ave. north in Montrose and cross the bypass (it then changes into 6450 Road). This road will head north and dog-leg a few times – eventually becoming Falcon Road as it goes left (at that intersection going right would be a dirt road). Follow this to Highway 50. Carefully cross the highway and it will take you into town.

County Roads – There are many other secondary county roads that are paved providing great routes through farming areas. *Tip: Going west requires climbing up onto the mesas west of Montrose. I like to go west out of town on Oak Grove but climb up 6300 road to Ohlm Road (go right) then right on 6250 Road and then left on Oak Grove. This skips a windy narrow section of Oak Grove that can be iffy with traffic. Coming back in from the west I like to go downhill on Highway 348 (Olathe) or LaSalle (returning to town on Marine Raod). I recommend paying attention to trucks and maybe letting them pass before you make your descent. I do not recommend using Spring Creek Road to get in/out of town.*

Grin and Barrett Charity Ride – This end of July ride has 33, 50, 75 and 112 mile routes that support a local charity. There also is a 155 mile Gran Fondo team-based challenge. The 112 and 155 mile route go through on the highway on the

North Rim of the Black Canyon (the 112 mile route is shuttled to Blue Mesa dam and the 155 mile route rides to the dam from Montrose). The post ride food is the best I've ever seen. http://www.gbbiketour.com/

Black Canyon of the Gunnison – From town take Miami Road east till it merges with Highway 50. Go right and stay on the shoulder till the left turn for Black Canyon of the Gunnison National Park (Highway 347). Now climb up to the park entrance (5.5 miles and about 2500 vertical feet of climbing) – to continue further you will need a National Park Pass. You can go about another 7 miles to High Point in the park.

Mission to Ride – This is a May ride that has several routes that all start/finish in Montrose.

Restaurants

Camp Robber – On the south side of town on the main road, on the east side, before you get to Wal-Mart is a great local restaurant. They also have a full bar. My sister Janet when visiting liked it enough to go the 2nd day without even checking in for other eating options.

Colorado Boy on 320 E. Main St. is a brew pub with yummy pizza and popular with many of my friends (GF pizza too).

Daily Bread – Classic old-school bakery on the corner of Main Street and Cascade downtown. I like to go there for their breakfasts – huevos rancheros unless a special catches my eye. Open Mon-Fri.

El Jimador – Great mainstream Mexican restaurant on the corner of Townsend and South 12th. Full bar. 970.249.8990

Guru's Nepal Restaurant – Two blocks east on 448 E. Main Street from intersection of 50/550 where 50 becomes Main Street. Provides nice variety to Montrose area. Lunch buffet weekdays (quality can vary a bit – sometimes great and sometimes tired). 970.252.8777. **Himalayan Pun Hill Kitchen** – a new Nepali restaurant on 710 North Townsend Ave. that on my visits to their lunch buffet has consistently fresher food than Guru's.

Lobby Grille - Montrose Memorial Hospital – The food at the hospital is actually good and affordable.

Pollo Azado – On the NE corner of Townsend and South 7th street is an affordable eatery that serves up yummy grilled chicken.

Two Rascals - Is a brew pub on North 1st Street in an old warehouse. A food truck outside serves up bar food.

Stonehouse – On the south side of town on Highway 550 across from Walmart. Popular spot for people from Telluride getting something to eat while doing weekly shopping. Having a burger and a beer at the bar (or glass of wine) is a nice way to have lunch. 970.249.8899 – take reservations.

The Vine Market and Bistro – On 347 East Main Street (corner Main Street and Cascade Avenue) is a great specialty market and restaurant. The market specializes in local offerings from vendors and farmers. It includes a nice deli. *The Bistro Restaurant moved here January 2017 joining forces with the people running the market.* 970.812.7977

Coffee

Buckhorn Coffee – Charlie serves up great brewed coffee and iced nitro coffee or chai plus espresso drinks. You can't beat the "Buck a Cup" for a small brewed coffee. 1048 S. Townsend Ave. - 970.901.8916

Cimarron Coffee Roasters – My favorite for a European style espresso with a nice sitting area. Eric is meticulous in roasting coffee. Open M-F 7AM-Noon on Grand and South 1st.

Coffee Trader - Is a good local coffee house near downtown on East Main. In the summer you can sit in the nice garden.

Looney Bean - Is in the same shopping complex as Target on the south side of town is another good coffee place with in-house baked goods and nice espresso drinks.

La Zona Colona Coffee – 10 minutes south of Montrose on Highway 550 is a wonderful coffee shop that also has great doughnuts. It is right off of Highway 550 in Colona where Ouray County Road 1 (Hotchkiss Ave) spurs off to the west so an easy stop if traveling through. 970.249.5124

RIDGWAY

On the Highway 550 between Ouray and Montrose is a mountain town that has grown into its own. Hippies moved in kept the place alive but it has shifted to include people that commute to Telluride, some trust-funders along with some hold outs from the ranching/mining era. And ranching still exists in the area – though some ranches are now owned by some pretty wealthy folks.

Sherbino Theater – A great place for live events. https://sherbino.org

Ridgway Music Series – Thursday evenings in July there is live music in the town park (right off of Highway 62). The same type of event is run in Paonia since both are sponsored by the Paonia-based public radio station KVNF.

Chipeta Solar Springs Resort & Spa – This is a nice place to stay! If there is live music on the upstairs patio bar – a really wonderful place to hang out! They also have a restaurant below the bar that a well-known chef from Telluride, Honga, took over as **Lotus Root** serving Asian Fusion cuisine. Food is great, though service can be slow on busy days. May be closed in the off season. *They also own a sister resort Koro Sun Resort in Fiji.*

Lupita's Bizarre Bazaar – Great funky gift shop! 380 Sherman St - 970.626.5050

Second Chance Thrift Store – On 309 Sherman St (between Town Park and the river). Packed to the gills with fun stuff.

Hiking/Walking

Uncompahgre River Way Trail – This trail system eventually will link Delta, Montrose, Ridgway and Ouray via a 65-mile route along the Uncompahgre River. The section that starts in Ridgway and goes north to the Dallas Creek area of Ridgway State Park is paved. This section of the trail runs primarily on the former Denver & Rio Grande Western Railroad corridor. I often walk this if needing a little exercise and not enough time for a formal hike. It starts in town but I usually park in the small parking area where North Railroad Street ends (this road connects to Sherman Street which is the main road through town). From the parking area, you can see the old railroad trestle bridge that the trail crosses. The trail also goes by **Dennis Weaver Park** which has a very nice eagle sculpture (you have to cross the river where the road crosses the trail to get to the park – the park is also accessible from Highway 550).

Blue Lakes – This wonderful hike is about a ½ hour drive from town to the trailhead (picture on next page). The trip includes wonderful meadows of wildflowers (end-July usually the best time). I normally hike up to the lower lake which is nestled at the base of Mt. Sneffles (6.5 miles round-trip and an elevation gain of about 1500 feet). From Ridgway take State Highway, towards Telluride, about 5 miles west and turn left (brown sign identifies the road) onto East Dallas Road (CR-7). Drive another 9-miles on East Dallas Road to the trailhead (I have driven this in my convertible). It is a popular hike so parking could be more difficult on a popular day. Bring rain gear!

Orvis Hot Springs - In Ridgway is another option for a soak. They are just South of the intersection of that highway with Ridgway. It is has several pools, two larger ones but none the size of Ouray or Glenwood (which are huge swimming pools) – so Orvis is a bit more intimate. Note they are clothing optional. They have a few rooms (shared bathrooms) and you can camp there as well. With the latter options, you have access to the facilities after hours! Nice walk up the county dirt road in front of the property (gets away from the main highway in about ¼ mile. 970.626.5324. www.orvishotsprings.com.

A person at Orvis recommended a spot in the Pacific Northwest – **Bagby Hot springs** *P.O. Box 15116 Portland, Or, 97215 – FS 63-FS 70 near Pegleg campground.*

*I also found the spot I loved in Washington – **Goldmeyer Hot Springs** – 202 N. 85ᵗʰ. St. #106, Seattle, WA 98103 206.789.5631. Both require reservations and the addresses are in the city but they are not!*

Food and Coffee

Adobe Inn – Really great Mexican restaurant with some healthier options as well. If turning from the Ouray/Montrose Highway 550 into Ridgway, cross the river and turn left at the first real street. It is up on your right about 2 blocks. It is only open for dinner at 5:30PM though the bar opens about ½ hour earlier. Reservations recommended on busier nights. 970.626.5939 Also have lodging – hostel type with shared bathroom. *The bar at sunset is a wonderful place to have a drink!*

Cimarron Books and Coffeehouse - They serve coffee, tea and smoothies and have many places to plop. It is in the building next to the grocery store. Eric, the owner, really makes an incredible cup of espresso. 970.626.5858 Also a Montrose location. If you are traveling north to Montrose, also in Colona is **La Zona Colona Coffee** (see item under Montrose).

Colorado Boy Brewing Company – Next to the Sherbino Theatre (one block off of the main drag). Great place for a barley pop. Friend Ursula works there once in a while. Have great pizza! Nice to sit at picnic tables summer afternoons.

Eatery 66 - Seasonal outdoor eatery friends rave about. 566 Sherman St

Kate's Place – great for breakfast on 615 Clinton – *maybe the best breakfast in the region.* 970.626.9800. Was previously Sandy's Kitchen.

Lotus Root – In the **Chipeta Solar Springs Resort & Spa.**

Melry's Lunchbox – New place I haven't tried that got positive input. 631 Sherman St. - 970.216.8208

Provisions – New fall 2015 – a place I haven't tried except for a nice glass of wine but comes recommended. Also sell items to go like a European deli. 616 Clinton - 970.626.9861.

Taco Del Gnar - On 630 Sherman Street is a <u>very</u> popular spot with my friends. Serves up creative tacos in a fun atmosphere. They have a sister location in Telluride. http://gnarlytacos.com/

True Grit – Small town restaurant across from town park. Worth going in to see the wall of Dennis Weaver photos.

Thai Paradise – great Thai restaurant – name just changed (used to be Siam). The place has grown on me and the owners are from Thailand. Their Drunken Noodles are a good alternative to always getting Pad Thai. Sit at the bar and yak with the kitchen staff if on your own.

OURAY

A wonderful mining town with neat shops and restaurants nestled in a narrow mountain valley. The shops are more the classic tourist shops rather than the upscale ones you'll find in nearby Telluride. The famous hot springs are fun to visit (on the north end of town). A nice hike from the SW edge of town takes you up over the town for some incredible views.

Wright Opera House – Although not as ornate as some of neighboring mining town's show houses, the Wright Opera house has lots of character. It was built so the owner's daughter could attend cultural events in Ouray's heyday. Now used for a variety of events.

Ouray Ice Festival – End of January. It is the main fundraiser for the Ouray Ice Park. http://ourayicepark.com/ouray-ice-festival/ Also the **Chix with Pix** event is in January.

Mountain Air Music Series – Thursdays, 6PM in June there is free music in Sellin Park (next to hot springs pools). Similar in format to the July concerts in Ridgway. *Please check as I recently heard this series was cancelled for 2017.*

4th July – Great small town feel and in such a beautiful spot. The 4th of July parade is fun to watch. My favorite event is the fire hose water fight put on by the fire department (photo is above). Fire station puts on an annual dance the night before. Fireworks at night are great but sometimes cancelled due to fire danger (and if you drive into town for them, expect a slow drive home).

Ouray Hot Springs Pool and Fitness Center - Run by the city in Ouray and next to the Ouray Visitor Center. 1220 Main St - 970.325.7073- http://ourayhotsprings.com

Wiesbaden Hot Springs Spa & Lodgings (Ouray) – You can just pay to use the hot springs. 625 5th St - 970.325.4347 Plus ones at **Box Canyon Inn** where you must stay there to use them.

Shopping

The Blue Pear – Michelle has a fun, unique gift shop on the corner Main Street and 7th Ave.   970.325.0440 or www.thebluepear.net

Buckskin Booksellers – This is a wonderful bookstore in Beaumont Hotel building.   The selection of books is well thought out. I love that the owner, Robert, deep knowledge of books includes Sci-Fi and Fantasy.   His book advice is appreciated! http://www.buckskinbooksellers.com/

Khristopher's Culinaire - Nice kitchen store with a really nice selection of real chef's knives. 545 Main St - 970.325.7311

Mouse's Chocolates – Love their homemade chocolates, milk shakes, and their scrap cookies! If you bring in your own coffee mug, they let you roll the dice for a prize for not wasting a paper cup – cute idea.

Outdoor Activities

There is so much to do here. Jeeping is popular as there are a lot of dirt roads/tracks that are only open in the summer.

Bear Creek Trail – As you head south on Highway 550 towards Silverton, you will go through a small tunnel. The parking for the trail is just after the tunnel and you cross the highway and hike over the tunnel.

Cascade Falls Park – At the end of 8th Avenue is a park with trails up to the Lower Cascade Falls. The Perimeter Trail also passes through this area.

Ouray Perimeter Trail – This trail circuits around the entire town. On easy spot to start is across from the visitor center that is just north of the hot springs on the highway. You cross the highway and head up a wood edged path next to some condos. www.ouraytrails.org/city-ouray-trails/perimeter-trail

Ice Climbing – Not something I'd do but for those with interest there is a world class ice climbing area in Ouray. http://ourayicepark.com/

Ironton Nordic Area – South on Highway 50 about ¾ way up Red Mountain pass is a small Nordic area that has a couple miles of groomed trails. Not tons of parking (used to have a plowed parking area but that hasn't been done this season). Ironton is actually a deserted town so fun to see the buildings. Also you can skin up and back country ski above the area or other areas nearby – but best to know the area well since there are avalanche issues.

Lodging

Box Canyon Lodge & Hot Springs – 45 Third Avenue. They have their own hot springs (several big wooden tubs for about four people). Nice rooms – upgraded motel. They have simple continental breakfast but with great coffee. Have discounted mid-week rates and a plan if you stay one night a month during the winter (can skip one month and share between friends). Talked with Karen (she and her husband own it) – nice people and love skiing. 970.325.4981

Spangler House B&B – Stayed here as well. Very comfortable B&B with large common area. Steve cooks up a great breakfast. Hot tub and discount coupons to hot springs pools. They really try to make their guests happy. 970.325.4944

Food

Bon Tons – Downstairs is a good Italian/American restaurant that might have specials during the week (was Pizza one night and Pasta another). 970.325.4951. The chicken picatta is amazing - consistently good food in Ouray. You also may want reservations as they can get busy. This is one of my favorite places to eat.

Maggie's Kitchen – I somehow overlooked this wonderful place for a burger for years, thinking it was too touristy. Well it isn't. I had their signature 420 Burger and it was massive and yummy. Friendly service too! 970.325.0259 – Closed April & November plus Monday/Tuesdays in the winter months.

Ourale House (Mr. Grumpy Pants Brewing Company) – Next door to Maggie's. Hutch (owner) serves up great beer. http://www.ouraylehouse.com/

Outlaw – Some friends tried it and liked it. More American fare but tasty they told me.

Roast and Toast Café – New to Ouray in 2015. They pull a great shot of espresso and also have breakfast and lunch. They have their coffee roasting operation in Ridgway that also serves up coffee with limited hours. 636 Main Street.

SILVERTON

It is located in a high mountain valley between Durango and Cortez. It has a small ski area renowned for its back country feel and tough terrain. A great place to visit in the summer though can get tons of snow in the winter and brrrrrrrrr. To the right is a shot of Silverton as coming down  Molas pass. It is also the end point of the Durango-Silverton railroad.

There are a couple of places to eat in town – had a good burger at one but need to get a card the next time I go.

DURANGO

This popular tourist spot can get really busy in the summer months. The wonderful downtown area worth a visit. Fort Lewis College gives it a college town feel plus it has many outdoor opportunities nearby

so it draws in people living the outdoor life.

Durango & Silverton Narrow Gauge (DSNG) Railroad - A popular option is to take the steam narrow gauge train to Silverton (though pricey) - 888-872-4607. The depot for the train is downtown on Main Avenue. I hear that you can take the train to a mid-way stopping point that takes you into some neat hiking areas (there are no roads to that area). There is a **DSNG Railroad Museum** that sits behind the depot.

Farmers Market – On summer Saturdays on the bypass directly west of downtown is a great farmers market.

Music in the Mountains – Mid-July to early-August. I haven't tried it but looked interesting. www.musicinthe mountains.com 970.385.6820

Trimble Hot Springs – North of town a bit on Highway 550. Nice place to soak with large garden area.

River Trail – There is a nice walking/biking trail along the river that goes through downtown all the way up to 31st street.

Road Bicycling – Popular road bicycling spot. Also the **Iron Horse Bicycle Classic** 50-mile ride to Silverton end of May

3ʳᵈ Avenue – this section of town (2 blocks to the east of the Main Avenue) has a nice boulevard and nice old historic houses.

Durango Mountain Resort – This was previously called Purgatory ski area and is about 30 minutes north of town and is a good family mountain with lots of intermediate trails (its expert terrain is a bit weak and Telluride, Taos or Crested Butte are much better options for expert skiers). Pretty much directly across from the turn off to the resort (east side of Highway 550) from the highway is a hiking trailhead that takes you into a wonderful trail hiking system – can even hike to viewpoints where the Durango-Silverton railroad is following the river in a pretty valley. *June 2010 I went by the trailhead and it appears to have been moved into a newly created subdivision. It does mention the trailhead on the sign.*

Shopping

Downtown Durango is a really fun town to explore with lots of interesting shops. Not the typical very upscale shops of the more well-known ski towns. Yet plenty of galleries and places to get a 'find'.

Backcountry Experience – Great outdoor store with some of the best shoe/boot fitting you'll find. Have gone there (from

Montrose) a couple of times to get hiking/walking shoes. 1205 Camino Del Rio - 970.247.5830.

Bread – Great bread and also cookies, pastries, sandwiches, and coffee (even do hand pulled espresso but don't focus on fancier drinks). 42 County Road 250 (at Florida Road). http://breaddurango.com/

& Gallery – It is a gallery formed by several artists with an eclectic mix of art. 1027 Main Avenue. http://anddurango.com/

Lodging

Rochester Hotel – On 721 East 2nd Avenue – next to Cyprus Café. Friend Denise stayed there and liked it. *"Lovely but not too expensive"* was their comment. They also enjoyed the Cyprus Café's food.

Restaurants

Cyprus Café – On 725 East 2nd Avenue – one block east of Main Avenue. Had a great lunch there. 970.385.6884.

Guido's Favorite Foods – Great deli and restaurant. Have the best Castelvetrano olives! 1201 Main Avenue – 259.5028. info@guidosfavoritefoods.com *Still good on a recent visit and got some of the great Castelvetrano olives from the deli!*

Highway 3 Roadhouse & Oyster Bar – Friends Frank and Ursula found this gem. Open Wed-Fri (4-8PM) – yes! Those are the hours. 955 Colorado Highway 3 (south of downtown and east of Highway 550 and the river) - 970.385.7444

Oscar's – A diner on the north end of the strip mall City Market is in downtown on Camino del Rio. Good breakfasts. There may be better places now but it has a local's feel that I liked.

Kennebec – It is actually between Mancos and Durango on Highway 160 (west of Highway 550 in Durango by about 12 miles). It is a wonderful restaurant that would hold its own in any ski town but in the middle of no-where. 970.247.5674 – reservations recommended. *They do a Sunday brunch too!* www.kennebeccafe.com

Real Texas BBQ – They have two locations, on is on the main drag on the north end of town (west side of the street). Great for BBQ.

Taco Delite - Small taco stand recommended by locals.

Grand Mesa Country

This arid region lies west of the Continental Divide and is dominated by huge uplift called Grand Mesa which is a wonderful winter playground. The largest city is Grand Junction and has its own charm. Much of the area is agricultural so look for farm stands open in the summer selling peaches, sweet corn, vegetables and other fresh foods.

I-70 Corridor Grand Junction to Glenwood Springs

I have typically blazed through this section of road, skipping communities along the way – coffee mug in hand. There are several cute smaller towns along the way – Rifle, Silt, and New Castle.

Highway 6 – I-70 follows much of the old Highway 6 in this part of the state. In places it still exists, also working as a frontage road for the interstate. From just west of Rifle (exit 87) it runs to east of New Castle (exit 109). It becomes the Main Street in Silt and New Castle.

Rifle Falls State Park (Rifle) – About 12 miles north of Rifle on Highway 325 is a popular stopping spot to view the falls. Though it isn't recommended if your focus is to hike – I'd recommend other spots like Hanging Lake for that. Park pass or fee required. *In 1972 in Rifle Gap (7 miles north of Rifle en route to Rifle Falls SP on Highway 325) the "Valley Curtain" was a huge temporary art installation spanning the gap by artists Christo and Jeanne-Claude caused controversy and media attention. Christo had plans to do a similar scale project over the Arkansas River east of Salida but cancelled it in 2017.*

Midland Arts Company (Rifle) – Nice cooperative art gallery downtown on 101 East 3rd St.

Whistle Pig Catering (Rifle) – Nice coffee place with baked goods, breakfast and lunch options – even gluten free ones. Service was friendly yet a little slow the time I was there (yet worth the wait). 121 East 3rd. 970.456.3199

Miner's Claim Restaurant (Silt) – *This is one I really want to dine at with very high marks from locals.* Christian the owner, has deep restaurant experience, working at the Pine Creek Cookhouse in Aspen before landing here. Open for lunch (M-F) and dinner (Sun-Sat) – closed between lunch/dinner. Happy hour specials too! Also wonderful summer outdoor seating. 740 Main Street - 970.876.5372 - www.theminersclaim.com

Misty's Coffee Shop (Silt) – Cute coffee shop with sweet owner. Closed Saturdays. 704 Main Street - 970.876.2035

Burning Mountain Bakery & Deli (New Castle) – Great coffee & bakery plus a nice breakfast or lunch stop. FYI – they may be moving locations in 2017. 316 W Main Street.

Maria's Cake House (New Castle) – Cute Mexican bakery specializing in cakes that they will sell by the slice plus some other baked goods. In alcove to behind Lazy Bear Restaurant. 970.319.4614

Sunshine Farm – Between Silt and New Castle on Highway 6 is a cute garden center that does garlic classes 1-2 Saturdays in October. FYI – it is a very low key place. 970.984.3320

GRAND JUNCTION

Just inside the Colorado boarder from Utah is Grand Junction – where the Gunnison and Colorado Rivers meet. North/south county roads are miles to the state line (e.g. 24 Road is 24 miles to Utah). It has a really nice downtown that you might miss from the strip mall lined I-70 corridor. Couple of friends liked the clothing consignment stores as well.

Things to Do

Colorado National Monument – This has wonderful red rock landscapes and is just on the edge of town. Great hikes are right past the east entrance (such as No Thoroughfare Canyon that goes to seasonal waterfalls). Also a popular spot for bicycling – though beware of big climbs and a mix of tourist/local traffic on the east end of the park (cyclists need front/rear lights). If you have the time, driving through the monument is also really worth it. You can enter the Monument from Fruita (west entrance) or from Redlands Mesa (east entrance).

Art Center – This is a public gallery with rotating exhibits/shows. Nice gallery store too. *First Friday evening of the month is usually an opening with food/cash bar.* On the corner of Orchard and 7th (just south of the hospital). Closed Sunday/Monday.

Colorado Mesa University Downtown Gallery – Recently the university opened a downtown student art gallery. It is fun to see a nice mix of passionate art. They are open Monday – Saturday from Noon-4PM (though sometimes I have found them closed during scheduled hours). They normally participate in the First Friday evening art walk.

Avalon Theatre – Right downtown on 7th and Main (at the roundabout), has performing events along with movies. Finally got to see a movie there – they have run more art type flicks. Great venue that just had a major upgrade fall of 2014. http://www.tworiversconvention.com/avalon/index.php

Summer Thursday Evening Farmers Market (summer through mid-September) – They close off main street in downtown (including side streets!). Great place to go and get produce and wander around. 5-8PM through the end of September.

Downtown Music Festival & Grand Junction Off-Road Mountain Bike Event – Mid-May is a nice festival with free live music (at nights they have a pretty good act on the main stage). In recent years it has been tied to the Grand Junction Off Road mountain bicycle event with the finish line downtown.

Country Jam - Mid-June is at Jam Ranch in Mack (west of Grand Junction). It brings in some good acts! http://countryjam.com/ **Loud Wire Music Festival** – Was end of June rock music event at Jam Ranch that has not run past two years. http://loudwiremusicfestival.com/

Wineries – Many wineries in the Junction as well as Palisade and Hotchkiss/Paonia areas (separate info in those sections). There is a huge variability in quality, yet I still enjoy visiting them since many do not charge for tasting.

> **Two Rivers Winery and Chateau** - One we like up on Redlands Mesa. They have good wines, nice tasting room, and a great venue for music events in the summer (the "Jazz Among the Grapevines" is worth going to if you see something playing there and it also supports the Art Center).

> **GVWA Barrel Into Spring** – Two weekends in the spring you tour a selected list of vineyards that includes food pairing. These can sell out so if interested, sign-up early. The Grand Valley Winery Association (GVWA) site has information on that and other events: https://grandvalleywine.com/

Jet Boat Colorado – This probably isn't my cup of tea but will be a lot of fun for many. Colorado River boat tour agency in De Beque, Colorado (easth of Grand Junction) - 970.644.1121 - https://jetboatcolorado.com/

Lodging – There are several chain hotels right downtown that serve the convention center – handy to walk everywhere downtown but they tend to be a bit pricier. Horizon Drive off of I-70 has many places to stay.

Shopping

Enstrom Candies – Local candy maker known for their toffee (and it is good!). They have a downtown store with an area to watch the factory too – and free samples. 701 Colorado Ave. (on 7th street a block south of the downtown roundabout).

Grand Valley Books – very nice independent bookstore at 350 Main Street, 970.424.5437. They have a sister store **Twice Upon a Time** at 2885 North Avenue just west of Morning Glory road, 970.242.3911.

Heirlooms for Hospice – Nice thrift store that supports local hospice. Just couple doors west of the Avalon Theater. Montrose also has a nice one.

Loki Outdoor Shop – This is the company store for a local outdoor clothing company that makes unique twists to parkas, jackets and other outdoors wear. 445 Colorado Ave.

Willow Creek Herbs and Teas – Interesting herb shop at 411 Main Street. Debora the owner really knows spices and herbs. 970.241.1126

Bicycling

Between Junction and Fruita are wonderful farm roads to ride on plus you can ride into the Colorado National Monument. Winds come from the East so it is better to ride to the East first if you are doing a longer ride – higher chance of a tail wind.

Mountain Biking - Is very good in the area – check with the locals (haven't had a chance to ride there 'yet' as I have been more into road bicycling lately). Fruita is the hub for the Grand Junction area with a couple of bike shops catering to mountain biking downtown. The **Kokopelli's Trail** starts off of I-

70 at Loma Exit #15. A regional mountain biking organization has maps on their site: http://copmoba.org.

Colorado National Monument – Amazing routes for road biking though a pretty good climb (you will need headlight and taillight to ride the monument due to several tunnels). The Fruita side has less traffic than the Grand Junction side.

Collegiate & Para-Cycling Road Racing National Championships – These have been held several times in April-May with routes through downtown. Fun to see high caliber riders.

Rose Hill Rally - an annual event sponsored by St. Mary's hospital in early May (in the past was the first Sunday). There are 50K and 100K rides. The ride is easy to get to on 24 Road at I-70 where the big park with ball fields is located - http://www.stmarygj.org – note the hospital doesn't post the event till about a month out.

Tour of the Valley – A century ride in late summer sponsored by Community Hospital. Also 30, 55, and 75 mile rides. Two of the routes go over Colorado National Monument (I chose the 50 mile ride over the monument – luckily they had headlights for sale at check in since I didn't realize one was needed). Nice post ride meal with local beer/wine and live music when I did the ride.

Colorado Riverfront Trail System – A great bicycle and pedestrian trail that goes from Fruita almost to Palisade along the Colorado River (the last bit into Palisade can be done on farm roads). I access either in Clifton (D road just East of Highway 141 is the trailhead – past water treatment facility) or at the Botanical Gardens downtown Grand Junction (7th Street dead ends going south at the Botanical Gardens). http://riverfrontproject.org/

Restaurants

626 on Rood – Downtown – Rood Avenue is 1 block North of Main street. A wonderful find that friends Frank and Ursula turned me onto years ago and is my favorite stop when doing errands in Junction. Owners Theo and Brenda do a superb job. It is upscale and has a great 'Social hour' from 3-5:30 with wine, cocktail, and food specials in the bar area. French fries with truffle oil are a great twist to an American favorite (*I am addicted to them*). Their macaroni and cheese is also to die for. 970.257.7663

Ale House – on 2531 N. 12th Street on the SW corner of Patterson. Have Breckinridge Brewery beer and good grille type food. They also have several billiard tables and a ton of TVs in the bar (though you can eat in areas that don't have TVs if you want) - 970.242.7253. I was less impressed the last time I was there so tried **Kannah Creek Brewing** – they have great beer and brick oven pizzas (they also have a location in Fruita in the strip mall area south of the freeway exit). They are on 12th just north of Orchard – 970.263.0111

Edgwater Brewing - Part of the Kannah Creek Brewing family in South Downtown just off the Colorado River bicycle trail (you can park and ride from here) serves beer and pub food. Live music too - go online for their schedule. 905 Struthers Ave. - 970.243.3659

Bin 707 Food Bar – In the Alpine bank building down town – great upscale eatery with a nice happy hour (2PM-6PM Mon-Fri and 6PM-Cl Sundays). It is a popular spot and can get a little noisy so not best for a quiet meal. www.bin707.com

Bistro Italiano. Friends Karen and Mike found this spot and I finally tried (and liked it) it and several others strongly recommended it too.

Blue Moon – weekends on Main street downtown is a good spot. Note that live music is something harder to find in Grand Junction, at least the night we were in town. Also haven't been in there in a while.

eC's Asian Station – Nice Chinese restaurant with a more varied menu. Believe they make all their own sauces. 200 West Grand Avenue – this is in the Clock Tower strip mall at the intersection of Highway 50 and Grand (NW corner). Just had dinner again recently and *Susan was very helpful in picking out a dish (she had her own restaurant elsewhere and now works waiting tables).* 241.7219

Juice Stop – 200 W. Grand (same strip mall as eC's Asian Station) – they make pretty good smoothies and juice type stuff. Nice place to stop on a hot day when you want something healthier yet tasty and cold. Staff has always been friendly too. 970.243.5082

Kamal's Kitchen – Friend in Grand Junction cooks up some amazing East Indian food for friends – sadly he doesn't have a formal restaurant at this point.

Kuniko's Teriyaki Grill – Great, simple Japanese food. Looks family run. 1133 Paterson Road – 970.241.9245.

Lois' Place – Great downtown diner with locals having breakfast. 241 Grand Avenue

Nepal Restaurant – Also downtown has good food from a friend's recommendation. 970.242.2233 – 356 Main Street.

Randy's Southside Diner - On Highway 50 just a bit South of downtown (on the left about 2 miles after crossing the river). Good for basic breakfast. Have one in Clifton too.

Suehiro – 541 Main Street has wonderful and affordable Japanese food. The Salmon Teriyaki was great (and $9 the time I was there – and big enough to split) as was their sushi (their sushi is really good but they don't go as crazy with presentation as some other places I've been). 970.245.9548. If you want a more modern, trendy spot – try **No Coast Sushi** on 1st and North.

Thai Chili and Pho – Recommended – the only Vietnamese pho restaurant in the area. The women serving there are a hoot – they have fun with their regular customers. Rimrock Marketplace, 2536 Rimrock Ave #700 Grand Junction, Colorado 81505 - 970.242.3299.

FRUITA

A cute town on the west side of the valley that has quickly become a mountain biking capital, plus a good entry point for road biking Colorado National Monument – see more on bicycling under the Grand Junction section.

Museums of Western Colorado: Dinosaur Journey (Fruita) – Just off of I-70 at the Fruita exit (exit # 19). Fun interactive place for kids. 550 Jurassic Ct - www.museumofwesternco.com - 970.858.7282

The Vintage Common – Next to Hot Tomato Café is a sweet little vintage shop that includes books, vinyl, clothes, eclectic items plus handbags and clothes that the owner Michelle makes. 951.741.6113

Copper Club Brewing Company – Nice local brewery that has live music some nights. 233 E. Aspen.

Hot Tomato Cafe – in downtown Fruita. Recommended by a friend as a GREAT lunch spot (open lunch-time till late – closed Sunday/Monday). I agree! They have pizza and strombolis by the slice too. 124 N Mulberry St., 970.858.1117, http://hottomatocafe.com/

Camilla's Kaffe – in downtown Fruita is probably the best place for breakfast in Fruita. It is open for lunch/dinner too. 206 E. Aspen Ave. If you want a traditional diner, try **Judy's Family Restaurant** - 435 Highway 6 and 50

PALISADE – PEACH & WINE CAPITAL

The fruit capital of the state. If driving through stop by and buy fresh peaches and other types of fruit. Tree ripened. The shop I stopped at was **Herman Produce** 970.464.0420. FYI – prices in farm stands are almost twice the supermarket but it is worth it if you truly love fresh fruit. Vineyards also have begun dominating the area – a more durable crop considering occasional harsh weather.

Blue Pig Gallery – On 101 W. 3rd Street (right on the SW corner of the main intersection downtown is a nice gallery with local artist. 970.464.4819.

Sprigs & Sprouts – On Highway 6 (G-Road) just west of town is a lavender farm with a store that specializes in products using lavender. 970.234.1261.

Wedel Pottery – Just out of downtown on 3813 North River Road is a nice pottery workshop and studio. The owner lives next door and may be in/out on slower days so might be best to call to make sure he is around. 970.464.7795

Coffee, Food, & Spirits

Inari's A Palisade Bistro – On 336 Main is an upscale restaurant in downtown Palisade. My friends really liked the place as it is the only nice restaurant for an evening meal on that side of town. However our service was a bit spotty.

Slice O Life Bakery – On 105 W 3rd is a wonderful bakery with pastries and lunch items plus good coffee. Open morning thru lunch (Tues-Sat and closed mid-winter). 970.464.0577

Peach Street Distillers – Across the tracks from downtown is a spot with wonderful libations. They have a bar, nice outside patio and food truck. They also do tastings several days a week. I loved their Five Year Bourbon and want to try their flavored brandies next time (peach, apricot and pear). 970.464.1128 - 144 South Kluge

Lodging

Wine Country Inn – Right on I-70 at the Palisade exit. The people were really nice and the breakfast (included) a bit better than the average. 970.464.5777 or their website www.coloradowinecountryinn.com

Wine Tasting

You could spend a couple days hitting wineries in the area. Remember to check hours if visiting in the winter. Also if you like hard cider there are producers in the region as well   Plus **Meadery of the Rockies** is just west of town on Highway 6 (G-Road) - 970.464.7899.

CAVE – Non-profit serving Colorado wineries, providing education for their members. The Winefest below is a key fundraising event. Their office is a good stopping point to get winery information. 124 W. 3rd St.

Colorado Mountain Winefest — Annual event in September draws over 6,000 people. Saturday is the main event in Riverbend Park — which includes a VIP tent and tons of tasting opportunities from wineries all over the state. There is also a shuttle service Saturday to hotels in Grand Junction. They love volunteers. http://coloradowinefest.com/

> **Tour de Vineyards** — On the same Saturday as Winefest is a bicycle tour of vineyards in the area with 23 and 58 mile routes. It supports local non-profits. http://tourdevineyards.com/

Carlson Vineyards — On East Orchard Mesa — 461 35 Road. They make traditional grape wines as well as fruit based wines. Open daily except holidays. www.carlsonvineyards.com Nearby is **Avant Vineyards** on 3840 E Road. Tastings by appointment. 970.216.9908 - www.avantvineyards.com

Colterris Winery Tasting Room — This local winery grows and produces all their wines — with plots scattered over the valley to take advantage of different growing conditions. Just a bit east of town - 3907 North River Road is their year-round tasting room. If you are looking for Cabernet Sauvignon or Cab Franc wines — this is probably your spot. I also liked the White Cabernet Sauvignon that drank like a nice summer rosé. The tasting room is nice and Olivia was a great hostess. They have a sister tasting room and **High Country Orchards** out on East Orchard Mesa that is open in the summer. There they sell fruit in season too. They do charge for the tasting. https://www.colterris.com/

Graystone Winery — Right off of Highway 6 at F Road is a winery that specialized in ports. I enjoyed their Port V and Lipizzan (latter chilled). www.graystonewine.com

Red Fox Cellars — West of town on 695 36 Road between Highway 6 (Front St.) and G Road is another winery whose wines I like (Bourbon Barrel Merlot is one). They also have hard ciders to taste. Will sell wine/cider by the glass plus they make wine cocktails. Includes a patio designed for lingering. Rachel did a wonderful job serving the tasting I had. http://www.redfoxcellars.com/

Maison La Belle Vie Winery – On 3575 G Road a little west of 36 Road is a French inspired winery with a selection of wines that includes a nice Syrah and a wonderful **Vin de Noix** dessert wine. www.maisonlabellevie.com

Varaison Vineyards and Winery – On 405 W. 1st Street has a nice wine tasting set up. Plus during the summer they have had a Friday night event out on their patio. 970.464.4928

CEDAREDGE & GRAND MESA

This is the large flat top mountain east of Grand Junction. Grand Mesa is a great place for winter sports and in the summer there are tons of lakes (though mid-summer it can be buggy so better to go later in August when they have had their first freeze). Cedaredge is the town on the southern flank of the mesa on the State Route 65 that transverses it to the ski area and then down to I-70.

Powderhorn Ski Area - Is on the north side of Grand Mesa on State Route 65 – about 40 miles from Grand Junction via I-70 East then State Route 65. It is a very nice day ski area (with some nice gladed runs). The bar in the day lodge is fun to have a beer on a slower day. They recently put in a high speed quad lift on their main intermediate terrain.

Sledding on Grand Mesa – A bit south of the turn off for Powderhorn on State Route 65 is a large parking area and outhouses with a sign that says Mesa Creek. This is the old Powderhorn Ski area slops and a popular area for sledding. Before turning the kids loose, I would assess the current conditions, crowds, and obstacles so your kids stay safe. You can also hike/skin up the old runs – here make sure you are prepared for backcountry conditions and skiing.

Cross Country Skiing on Grand Mesa

Between Powderhorn ski area and Cedaredge are three places to cross country ski that have differing levels of groomed trails. FYI - I have noticed that in the middle of winter it can get cold quickly on the Mesa so be prepared – and if you skiing on County Line trails you are at summit of the highway which is around 10,800. The non-profit **Grand Mesa Nordic Council** maintains the trails http://gmnc.org/.

> **Ward Lake** - Is closest to Cedaredge and has rolled tracks and allows dogs. The grooming here is a bit more sporadic and they don't have the full grooming machine that County Line and Skyway have.
>
> **County Line** (my favorite)- In the middle is at the summit of State Route 65 (10,800 feet). It also is connected to the Skyway trail system.
>
> **Skyway** - To the North before dropping back down off of the mesa. This is the closest spot to Grand Junction. They also do not want dogs on this trail system. If you have a dog please go to Ward Lake or County line.

Sandhill Crane Spring Migration (Eckert) – The same cranes that stay North of Alamosa during spring migration spend one night traveling to the reservoir East of Eckert. Groups travel through for several weeks – mid-March to early April. There can be a handful, 200-300 a night, and upwards of 2-3 thousand. Take North Street from Colorado 65 to the east about 2 miles to an area that overlooks Fruit Growers Reservoir. They tend to take off around 9:30 AM (but varies with weather). These large birds take a while to gain elevation and circle overhead while climbing – it is quite a site! Crane counts that landed the night before are currently posted on: http://www.eckertcranedays.com/.

AppleShed (Cedaredge) – Interesting gift shop, gallery, furniture, restaurant, plus wine/hard cider tasting in an old apple shed. The owners also have apples for sale from their orchard in the fall. I love to stop there for a piece of pie and wander. On State Route 65 just south of Main Street. 970.856.7007

Stacy's On Main (Cedaredge) – On 260 West Main Street is a cute gallery and coffee shop that was recently taken over by new owners. 970.656.6070.

Drost Chocolates (Eckert) – Just south of Cedaredge is a nice chocolate shop that also sells ice cream. They have a great display of antique cash registers too! I believe they are open spring through Christmas and only Wed-Sun.

Fritchman Orchards (Eckert) – Just north of Eckert on Highway 65 is a great fruit stand that is open during cherry season and then peach through apple. I always learn a lot about "orcharding" from the owners and they have a lot of fun memorabilia on the walls.

Living Waters Greenhouse – Cute family run garden center out in the country off of 2100 Road which goes between Eckert and Austin. Open April 1st to end of June – Mon-Sat. http://livingwatersgreenhouse.com/

Route 65 Burgers (Eckert) – Just south of North Road in Eckert, is an auto repair shop – tied to it is a new burger joint that shares the lobby for the repair shop. Burgers are from local meat and fresh cut fries cooked in peanut oil. Can call ahead to order -970.835.4910 – 12912 Highway 65.

Lodging

Cedaredge Lodge – Have never stayed there but it always is a bustling place. On the highway as you head north out of town. They recently went through renovations and added some new rooms. http://www.thecedaredgelodge.com/

PAONIA/HOTCHKISS

This area has tons of orchards and fruit/vegetable stands. Paonia has a large hippie contingency from what I can tell – so you find organic orchards and related offerings which I love.

Kebler Pass Road (CR12) – Just East of Paonia (via Colorado 133) is Kebler pass road which is a summer seasonal road that goes to Crested Butte. A beautiful drive on a well graded dirt road (can take a normal car).

Creamery Art Gallery (Hotchkiss) - A nice local coop gallery. If they have an art opening it is fun as the locals all turn out and the times I have been they have a pretty good spread of yummy things too! You must check out the bath rooms as they were both given to artists to create so they are pretty cool - cool bathrooms in Hotchkiss - go figure. Recently trying to have live music at least once a month (often last Saturday of the month). 970.872.4848

The Used Book Store (Hotchkiss) – on Bridge Street (main drag) is a neat used book store in an old house on the South Side of the road.

Rose (Hotchkiss) – Consignment shop for clothing and other items. 130 W Bridge St - 970.872.1144

Bristlecone Books – Antiques (Austin) – New bookstore by friends that ran one for years in Ridgway. On 22036 Main Street in Austin (off of State Route 92 driving from Delta to Hotchkiss). 970.209.7426

North Rim Glass Studio (Crawford) – in nearby Crawford is a nice glass blowing studio, right on the highway on the south side of town. 970.921.4527 – www.northrimglassstudio.com.

Paradise Theatre – This downtown Paonia theatre has some interesting offerings (live music and movies). *It is a great venue and you can get a glass of wine and organic popcorn!* 970.527.6610 www.paradiseofpaonia.com

Blue Sage Center for the Arts (Paonia) – Gallery & live music venue (generally classical or world music). www.bluesage.org

Paonia Community Supported Art Library – What a great concept – an art library in Paonia. You have to pay a monthly fee but can check out art for your house. 970.527.7243

KVNF Radio – This locally grown radio station has some NPR news but mainly plays a broad range of music (90.9 in Paonia, 89.1 Delta/Montrose, and 99.1 Grand Junction - http://www.kvnf.org/).

The station also sponsors free **Pickin' in the Park** concerts in June in Ridgway and August in Paonia on Thursdays at 6:30PM in each town's park. Check the web site for the current year's schedule. They bring in some pretty good talent and it makes for a nice evening. The photo on the right is of an event in Paonia.

Delicious Orchards – They are between Hotchkiss and Paonia and are open for a longer season than most stands. They make the local apple cider that is popular in stores plus now produce hard ciders (and have a tasting room). There is also a restaurant. 970.972.3065. Another regional orchard is **Sowell Orchards** in Palisade. 970.208.7079 Plus **Fritchman Orchards** in Eckert.

Vineyards

There are several in the region. Generally they are open seasonally from late May till sometime in October. Check if they are open if you are trying to visit late-fall into early spring. Also check out **Delicious Orchards** for hard cider.

Leroux Creek Inn and Vineyards – Joanna and Ivon are wonderfully eccentric hosts. They have wine tasting and have re-opened their B&B in a wonderful house overlooking the vineyards. 970.872.4746

Azura – The owners are artists/architects. So you not only can taste wine but look at wonderful art in a tastefully designed space. It has to be the prettiest winery in the state. They also have model boat races in the summer once a week. Honestly, it isn't my favorite winery but buying a glass or bottle of wine and sitting on their veranda is a must for the view. 970.390.4251

Stone Cottage – I also like their wines and a fun thing to do is hang there and buy a glass of wine. I think theirs is the best value to do that. Better to go up the way past Azura then the other route further to the East. 970.527.3444

Terror Creek Winery – this is above Stone Cottage and it has a nice lawn area with two tables – perfect for a picnic. 970.527.3484

Restaurants

Back Country Bistro (Paonia) – Downtown on 210 3rd street. I like going there for coffee. Also great for Saturday breakfast. 970.527.5080 I liked their description of a bistro:

> *"Bistros likely developed out of the basement kitchens of Parisian apartments where tenants paid for both room and board. Landlords could supplement their income by opening their kitchen to the paying public. Menus were built around foods that were simple, could be prepared in quantity and would keep over time. Wine and coffee were also served. The limited space for diners in these cramped corners prompted the tradition of adding table service to the footpath."*

Coaltrain Coffeehouse (Hotchkiss) – 328 W. Bridge Street (on left as entering town from the west). 970.872.JAVA – nice comfortable coffee house with lunch items. Open Mon-Sat till 2PM. www.coaltraincoffee.com

Delicious Orchards (Paonia) – Besides their store they have a nice cafe. Closed winters. On south side of highway just west side of town where speed limit drops to 45.

Flying Fork (Paonia) – 1 block from the main part of downtown (corner 3rd and Main Street) is the restaurant locals consistently recommend. I agree (though prices were closer to Telluride than I'd expected). It serves up Italian fare. *Sadly the past couple of years, their hours can vary and may close in the winters, so best to check before your visit.* 970.527.3203 www.flyingforkcafe.com

High Tower Café (Paonia) – Right downtown on 201 Grand Avenue (same block as Paradise Theater) is a pretty good diner. Fresh cut French fries and strudel are things that come to mind. If you want something simpler and less pricey – a good call. They are also open late which is a plus. *The recently opened up a 2nd location in Hotchkiss near City Market.*

Living Farm Café (Paonia) – Downtown on 120 Grand Avenue. This is one of the new generation of "farm to table" restaurants. They do ½ orders for dinner – nice! Whether breakfast or dinner a sweet place to have a meal. Its only weakness is the ambiance if the indoor restaurant – could use a little attention though the patio is great in the summer. 970.527.3779 – is the phone number for the inn that is connected to the restaurant. The inn is nice & affordable too.

Old River Trading Post (Paonia) – They have a vegetarian lunch Mondays and Sunday lunch by donation. I hear for lunch it is less expensive if you bring your own utensils (sounds strange but I think they also cater to people that work there). On 15495 Black Bridge Road – 970.527.4740.

PJ's Neighborhood Pub (Hotchkiss) – A newer place that is pricey for Hotchkiss but has really good food. Right in center of town on Bridge Street. Dinner only. Do some monthly specials like sushi night – those nights the regular menu is limited. 970.872.4582

Taco Hut (Hotchkiss) – Cute, friendly, little low key Mexican eatery – more Colorado-Mex than real Mexican or Tex-Mex. 301 East Bridge Street – 970.872.2100.

DELTA

Small farming town between Montrose and Grand Junction.

Confluence Park (behind City Market) - Spot where the Gunnison and Uncompahgre Rivers meet. There is a small fort that is open summers for tours. The park is a good spot for a short walk – often take my girlfriend's dogs there if they need a break when running errands. **Bill Heddles Recreation Center** is in the park with nice facilities including a great aquatic center - 970.874.0923

Westwinds Airpark – Off of Highway 50, just east of mile marker 66, on the right side as you are leaving town, heading to Grand Junction is a wonderful rose garden behind the sales office (the sell fly-in-out homes).

Escalante State Wildlife Area - Hamilton Tract – North of Delta, off of Highway 50 on G50 Road is access to wetlands – there are two signed parking areas (the first about ½ mile from Highway 50). It also is open to hunting so be aware of that during hunting season.Public access is prohibited on the Hamilton and Lower Roubideau tracts from March 15 through July 31. http://coloradobirdingtrail.com/

Dominguez Canyon Wilderness (25 minutes north of Delta) – Great place for spring, fall and winter (if mild) hiking. *This is part of the **Dominguez-Escalante National Conservation Area** – I plan on adding more items from this area in future editions.* To get to the trailhead, drive north from Delta on Highway 50, just past the sign for entering Mesa County (mile marker 52) is Bridgeport Road. Take that west until it dead ends at the Gunnison River and railroad (there is a parking lot on the left before the road dead ends – only use that if there isn't parking at the end of the road). Do not take the road labeled Dominguez Canyon from Highway 50. You will hike on the road next to the railroad for about a mile – there are no trespassing signs but also other signs saying it is OK to go there. *Do not walk or play on the railroad tracks and keep clear of trains.* Cross the railroad at the obvious spot. You will see two bridges crossing the river, cross on the second (more modern) bridge. Then follow the river for about ½ a mile and water baby planted cottonwoods if you want (with buckets near them). Now the canyon heads west away from the Gunnison River. The trail will dogleg to the left and then later the valley splits, one leg to the right and one straight – the main trail goes to the right. It follows a stream with nice wading pools and about ½ mile up is a rock with petroglyphs.

Egyptian Theatre - They have a great restored movie theatre (built in 1928 I believe designed by the same architect that created the Mayan in Denver), normally with main stream films at 7 and 9PM – but schedules can change. Sound system is the place's only weakness. Recently upgraded to a digital projection system so can see new 3D movies there.

Shopping

Clubbs Variety - Ben Franklin – Great "five and dime" store on 502 Main Street (SE corner of main street and 5th). Includes a huge jigsaw puzzle selection, homemade fudge, art supplies, plastic flowers and craft stuff. Easy parking behind the store.

Ryan's Finishing Touch – Funky gift shop with art supplies in the back in the old J.C. Penney building. Was looking for a bear item for my sister's lake place and they had a small section just for bears. 435 Main Street. Closed Sun/Mon. Also **4 & Main Exchange** on 365 Main Street is another spot to check out.

Davis Clothing – On 410 Main Street (SW corner of 4th and Main Street). A 100 year old dry goods store with a good selection of Western clothing. I buy my jeans there since they also hem pants for free! 970.874.4370.

Good Vibrations Books & Gifts – 326 Main Street (Wed-Sat). Unique, upbeat spiritual gift shop.

Homestead Meats – on 741 W. 5th Street 970.874.1145 – past the grain elevator. Great locally raised meats for sale (frozen) and their slaughter house is behind the store. www.homesteadranches.com

Restaurants

CB's Tavern – Friendly, great place for a burger, fresh cut fries, and a beer. Thursdays they have had live music (though earlier than most bars). Closed Tuesdays. 334 Main St. - 970.399.3292

Daveto's Italian Restaurant - Best sit down restaurant in Delta. 520 Main St - 970.874.8277

Doghouse Espresso – Across from the Egyptian Theater (449 Main Street). I love this place. Cassie and the rest of the staff are always great. They have consistently good espresso. Also have pastries and quiche. Closed Sundays.

Kenell's Valley View Bakery – A from scratch bakery that is on 8th and Main (on the east side of the highway). I like their cowboy cookies. 970.874.1937. They are closed Sunday and Monday and close weekdays at 5:30PM and Sat at 1PM.

El Tapatio Restaurant – Good Mexican restaurant. Their sandwiches are really good – smothered. Some of their food can be spicy so carefully check if you can't handle spicy food before ordering. 353 Main Street - 970.874.4100

OLATHE

A small unassuming farm town between Delta and Montrose (downtown is about ½ mile west of Highway 50). Best known for its sweet corn and the one-day **Sweet Corn Festival** – usually the first weekend in August. You can volunteer for the event and recently they have been trying to add other activities to make the event more than a single day activity.

Busy Corner White Kitchen – Classic small-town diner. I frequently have lunch there on my bicycle rides through the area. Definitely a locals place and they tend to get a bit better service than a newcomer. 318 Main Street - 970.323.6215

Hottie Coffee – Olathe finally has a nice place to stop for coffee. Steevi the owner offers up great service. M-Sat 6:30-4PM. It is on the frontage road to Highway 50 so easiest access if traveling through is to turn on the north turn into Olathe (Family Dollar store is just up the street). 970.323.5621

Primitos Bakery – Mexican bakery. If you have never had "Pan Dulce" – it is great with coffee. I have run into better bakeries in Mexico and a few American towns but this one isn't bad and they bake everything there. Right downtown across from the hardware store. What I am recently hooked on are their Tortas – Mexican sandwiches with rolls they make there.

Rocking W Cheese and Milk – Just a few miles West of Olathe on Highway 348 is a dairy that has way better than average milk plus they make their own cheese – including cheese curds (though slightly different from the 'real' cheese curds of the

Midwest). 870.323.9322. Homemade ice cream is hopefully to follow – right now they sell regular soft serve ice cream that I still like to stop for. They also now make half and half – wonderful for coffee!

Wineries

Three wineries are west of Olathe on Hwy 348:

Mountain View - Is first which also has an orchard and a fall corn maze (their Apple Chardonnay and Apricot wines are delightfully unusual). It is open seasonally. It is a handy stopping point bicycling too. 970.323.6816

Cottonwood Cellars – Is further west. Sadly on recent visits just didn't seem to have great wines.

Garrett Estate Cellars - Is also nearby on 53582 Falcon Road. They only do infrequent open houses (and they do have a wine club). So you need to check ahead for their schedule. 970.901.5919

GATEWAY

A beautiful drive is from Naturita to Whitewater via Gateway. Up to Gateway you will be in killer red rock canyons. Check out **Hanging Flume Overlook** near Uravan. At Gateway that river heads west and then the rest of the way towards Grand Junction is more granite type rock formations. This would be a great road to get out on either a motorcycle or road bicycle.

Gateway Canyons Resort – An unexpected oasis at Gateway. A great place for a romantic getaway though it is pricey to stay there. If you are a car buff, the automobile museum is a must. Don't expect a large collection – however all of the cars are top shelf. This includes the famous Oldsmobile concept car as well as a couple of Auburns and Duesenbergs. http://www.gatewaycanyons.com/

SCENIC DRIVES

Colorado has some of the most spectacular scenery in the world. I never tire from driving through its mountains. However, be aware of winter storms that can hit from October through April and could make driving treacherous.

Cortez to Telluride to Durango - Either the drive from Cortez to Telluride (Lizard Head Pass – State Route 145) or Durango to Ouray (Million Dollar Highway 550 - which includes Red Mountain, Molas and Coalbank Passes) are both spectacular. You can make a loop out of it as well – there is a back way from Dolores to Mancos that allows you to skip Cortez if you want. Above is shot from the top of Molas Pass parking area.

Delta to Carbondale – Pretty drive over McClure Pass that is less traveled. In the summer you can also drive over Kebler Pass into Crested Butte (the turn off is just below Paonia reservoir). Start in Delta on Highway 92 and then take 133 in Hotchkiss. Lots of farm stands – one is **Delicious Orchards** just west of Paonia on the right side (970.527.1110). Paonia is a cute town to visit on the way. You will go through some small mining communities as well – one is a spur road to Marble (where the marble for the Lincoln monument was mined).

Make sure to drive into Redstone as the town is not on the main highway. There are historic coke ovens in front of the turn off for Redstone. Plus there is a neat old mansion on the south side of the highway about where the speed limit changes from 40 to 50mph just west of Redstone. In Carbondale you can get a cup of coffee and lunch at **Town**.

Ridgway-Moab – See notes under Utah.

Glenwood Canyon - I-70 between Glenwood Springs and Gypsum, Colorado is incredible. I liked it better when it was just a two lane road (yes I can remember back that far - it was actually still two lane in the middle 1980's) but it is still an incredible drive. Better yet ride a bike on the separated bike path! Hanging lake is a nice hike.

Independence Pass - From near Buena Vista, State Route 82 goes into Aspen over a pass that hits slightly over 12,000 feet in elevation with incredible scenery. Be careful if there are heavy summer storms on the pass as it can easily hail at that elevation. Closed in the winter and has very windy curves and narrow stretches (may not be suitable for larger motor homes).

Denver to Vail to Colorado Springs - Try driving a loop from Denver to Vail on I-70, then past Vail to Minturn and Highway 24 to Leadville. In Sliver Plume or Georgetown during May-Oct you can take the **Georgetown Loop Railroad** – reservations recommended at busy times – www.georgetownlooprr.com. From Leadville continue on 24 to Colorado Springs, and then back to Denver via Highway 83. You can also take Highway 285 back via South Park and Fairplay. You could stop at downtown Salida, Florissant Fossil Beds National Monument, Cripple Creek, Castlewood Canyon State Park and other spots along the way.

Guenella Pass – I have not tried this route but looks nice. Paved route from Georgetown (I-70) to Grand (US 285). Closed in winter. Info line: 303-679-2422 ext 2

NORTHERN & SOUTHWESTERN NEW MEXICO

I fell in love with New Mexico the first time I visited it. It is a unique blend of three cultures: Latin, Native American and Anglo. Sometimes I feel like I am in a time warp. Driving some of the two-lane highways takes me through towns little changed in over 40 years. *What I have noticed is that it is a place you either fall in love with or you don't.*

I feel that Santa Fe is the cultural center of New Mexico, though Albuquerque has a wide range of activities as well. Taos is another interesting community worth exploring; though some of its charm has been lost due to the impact of tourism (Santa Fe is feeling this impact as well).

I love the mix of Anglo, Native American, and Spanish (no not Mexican - most immigrants in this area came directly from Spain and consider their heritage to be Spanish) cultures. Be careful if you adventure out into smaller communities in

Northern New Mexico. Some are not very open to outsiders. This is especially true in some areas if you are going to backpack and leave your car unattended - my advice is ask before you go. The main areas such as Santa Fe, Taos, Las Vegas, Los Alamos or the National Forest north of Pecos should be no problem.

Bandelier National Monument - Near Los Alamos is an Ancestral Puebloan ruin site with cave dwellings, cliff-side houses, and a valley town with its massive kiva. It is of a later era than Mesa Verde.

Chaco Culture National Historic Park - This is south of Farmington. Worth a visit since it is one of the best sites for Anasazi ruins. It is a bit of a trip since part of it is by dirt road (come in from the North since the road is in much better shape than from the South). I have driven both with my passenger vehicle. There is a campground at the park and no other facilities except a visitor center.

Cumbres and Toltec Scenic Railroad – A narrow gauge steam train ride from Antonito, Colorado or Chama, New Mexico - Late-May to Mid-October. You ride the train from Antonito to Chama (or the reverse). They bus you back to your starting point. 800.724.5428 – www.cumbrestoltec.com *I haven't ridden this one - had a colleague who used to manage the business and run the trains.*

El Morro National Monument – See under Gallup. Also nearby Malpais NM is worth a visit.

Blake's Lotaburger – I know it is fast-food but it is a chain unique to New Mexico. You can find them in virtually any community. I like their burger with green chile and cheese. www.lotaburger.com

ROUTE 66 (I-40)

GALLUP

Crossroads to the Navajo Nation, Colorado and Zuni. I skipped this adorable historic downtown for many years. My mistake. The historic **El Morro Theater** has movies/events. Also a visit to the **El Rancho Hotel's** lobby is worth it and a drink in their bar (I have not stayed there).

Gallup Inter-Tribal Ceremonial – Early August – over a week of activities. http://gallupceremonial.com

Summer Evening Dances – Performed in plaza in front of the court house (8PM). Check at visitor center for current schedule.

New Mexico State Route 602 & 53 – This drive visits Zuni, El Morro NM, and Malpais NM and ends up in Grants.

El Morro National Monument – 55 miles SE of Gallup on State Routes 602 & 53. Ancestral Puebloans, Spanish and American travelers carved over 2000 symbols/names into this sandstone promontory. Historians can trace various Spanish and American expeditions from their signatures here. Nice 2 mile hike to pueblo ruins. Campground first come first served.

Zuni Pueblo – South of Gallup on State Route 602. Check with Zuni Visitor Center if the pueblo is open as they close for summer/winter solstices and other times. www.zunitourism.com

Shopping

Many downtown shops sell Native American artwork and handcrafts. **Richardson's** is the largest vendor in town.

Indian Arts & Crafts – 117 W Coal.

Perry Null Trading – 1710 N. 2nd St. - 505.863.5249 www.perrynulltrading.com

Inscription Rock Trading & Coffee – Wonderful gift shop & coffee/smoothies. Next to Ancient Way Café. 505.783.4706

Restaurants

Ancient Way Café – A few miles east of El Morro NM on Highway 53 is a wonderful eatery with pies and baked items to die for. FYI – Friday/Saturday evenings is a special plated dinner by the chef (reservation recommended). 505.783.4612 Also RV hookups and cabins to rent.

Don Diego's Restaurant – Great New Mexican diner. 801 Rte 66. Also want to try **Maria's Restaurant** on 110 West Coal.

Gallup Coffee Company – Tiffany and her husband roast their own coffee and make their bakery items in this sweet coffee shop. 203 W Coal Ave - 505.410.2505

GRANTS

On I-40 between Albuquerque and Gallup. The **West Theatre** on 118 W Santa Fe has a nice neon light façade.

Malpais National Monument – Sandstone formations and an enormous volcanic field of fractured basalt flows, sink holes, and cinder cones. Hiking and if you get a caving pass at the visitor center you can explore the caves as well. 27 miles SW of Grants on New Mexico 53 (you can tie it into a visit to El Morro too).

Cafecito – Via a local recommendation I tried out this local eatery (820 E. Santa Fe Avenue) and liked it! Clean with friendly service and classic New Mexican fare. Though looking at reviews, some were pretty negative – if you are looking for super fancy "Mexican" versus a good small town "New Mexican" restaurant you might be disappointed. They are closed on Sundays.

ALBUQUERQUE

In the past I blazed through Albuquerque on I-25 or I-40 and never stopped. Lately have been setting time aside to explore it and have found it has some gems.

Things to Do

Tramway - The tramway that goes to the top of Sandia Peak is worth it. It has dining opportunities too - very romantic. Went there about 30 years ago for dinner and still remember it though can't speak for current service/food.

Old Town - Popular tourist area though the old church and plaza are worth exploring. We ate at **La Placita** restaurant when I was in Junior High and it is still there many years later (505.247.2204). South of I-40 near Rio Grande & Central.

The KIMO Theatre - Downtown on Central - didn't see inside but seems to be a really neat place for special events. 505-848-1370 or http://www.cabq.gov/kimo

Tamarind Institute – Lithography studio & workshop with a nice gallery. Affiliated with the University of New Mexico but with its own program. Open M-F 9AM-5PM. Entrance is on Stanford Street and you must buzz to get them to unlock the door. You can also park in their lot behind the building – get a parking permit after getting buzzed in. 2500 Central Ave SE.

Alphaville - Video store downtown specialized in art films – they closed but keep a website: http://www.alphavillevideo.com/

Talin Market – on the SE corner of Central and Louisiana is a good Asian market with some European & Arabic items. This is something I look for since on the Western Slope of Colorado, we have only one small nice Asian market that just can't stock all the weird things the bigger stores have. Comments say service can be iffy and check expiry dates on cans you buy – I didn't find that when there. They are a bit pricier than the ones in Phoenix/Tucson/Denver too. FYI – the neighborhood is a little funky so may not want to go after dark. Also a location in Santa Fe. http://www.talinmarket.com/

Paseo del Bosque Trail – 16 mile paved trail follows the Rio Grande River. When staying at the Marriott Pyramid hotel (Printers Way area - I-25 & Paseo del Norte), I accessed it by first riding the **Paseo del Norte Trail** west towards the river (that trail goes almost to I-25). The Paseo del Norte Trail connects directly to the Paseo del Bosque Trail. FYI - there are several places to park and use the trail. All types of cyclists and walkers/runners/skaters use the trail and it is nice to see the big cottonwoods. The trail has underpasses for major roads. A bicycle shop that is reasonably close to the trail (I stay in the Printers Way area frequently) on the north end of town is **High Desert Bicycles** on 8110 Louisiana NE 505.842.8260 – on Paseo del Norte a couple of lights East of I-25. Also I have accessed the trail from the downtown area (see **Golden Crown Panaderia** listing).

Restaurants

Annapurna's® World Vegetarian Café – Wonderful Indian and non-Indian food. 5939 4th St NW - 505.254.2424 (two other locations – one in Nob Hill – the 4th St. location has easy parking). Also one in Santa Fe.

Barelas Coffee House – Recommended by locals for breakfast. 1502 4th St SW - 505.843.7577. Looks like accessible from the Paseo del Bosque bicycle trail going east at Bridge Blvd.

El Bruno's Restaurante y Cantina – I have fallen love with this place for the bar and the friendly locals that hang out there. They have great weekday happy hour specials and good drinks. Honestly their food isn't as good – but what a great place to spend an afternoon. 8806 4th, NW 87114 (you will want to look up this address as it is a little convoluted to get there from Paseo Del Norte). They have a sister restaurant in Cuba, NM. 505-897-0444

Capo's Italian Restaurant - Traditional American style Italian food downtown. *Getting recent mixed reviews since my visit few years back. Though its location alone may make it worth it.* 722 Central Ave SW – 505.242.2006.

El Patio – Off of East Central at 142 Harvard Street is a wonderful New Mexican café – 505.268.4245. 11-9PM most days except Noon on Sundays. *Spring of 2014 they changed and now are open for breakfast as well (didn't confirm the time) – still great food! Probably my favorite spot for green chile.*

Flying Star Café – Have a wonderful bakery case and you order up front and take a number. Setting is trendy. One spot is: 3416 Central SE in **Nob Hill Area** (West of I-25) – 505.255.6633. That area of Albuquerque also has neat shops – many close by the restaurant. There are also other locations - one is on the SE corner of Paseo del Norte and Wyoming plus Santa Fe. *When there on recent visit, I get a sense with so many locations that the quality is not what it used to be, though still worth a visit and I felt Mezza appetizer was a bit pricey.* www.flyingstarcafe.com

Frontier Restaurant – Right on 2400 Central Ave. SE. Haven't been there but green chili and burritos are local favorite.

Garcia's – There are several run by the same family in town – one of the first is 1732 Central SW and I'm told their Chili Rellenos (though a friend wasn't as impressed) are the best (only on Friday and one other night), 505.842.0273. They also charge for every extra thing such as pico de gallo – so be aware of that. Take I-40 to Rio Grande and then go south to Central – go left on Central several blocks (it is on your right). This is also the old town area of the city.

Golden Crown Panaderia - Friendly owner Pratt Morales has traditional Mexican pan dulce and empanadas along with a great green chile bread. 1103 Mountain Rd. N.W. - 505-243-2424. http://goldencrown.biz *Also Mountain Road is a designated bicycle route that we took west to the Paseo del Bosque Trail (follows Rio Grande river). That route takes you through a museum district and Albuquerque's Old Town. The botanical gardens are just off of the trail if you head south.*

Limonata – on 3222 Silver Ave SE (in Nob Hill area one block South of Central between Wellesley and Bryn Mawr) has really great hand-pulled Italian espresso and breakfast/lunch fare.

P'tit Louis Bistro - French restaurant specializing in mussels & oysters. Also lunch Tues-Fri - closed Mondays. 3218 Silver Ave SE - 505.314.1110

Thai Vegan – Great vegetarian Thai food. 5505 Osuna Rd. NE. Also Nob Hill (3804 Central) and Santa Fe locations.

Vibrance – <u>Wonderful</u> vegetarian restaurant. Fri-Sun (Sunday brunch buffet). When we went for brunch they also had live music. 505.639.3401 4500 Silver SE (actually enter off of Jefferson).

TURQUOISE TRAIL – NEW MEXICO 14

If driving to Santa Fe, consider taking New Mexico State Highway 14. You can start from I-25 east of Albuquerque (exit 175) heading north on the eastern side of the Sandia Mountains. When you get to Santa Fe NM 14 becomes Cerrillos Road. www.turquoisetrail.org

MADRID

Madrid is a funky old mining town that is popular with bikers (probably partly due to it being in the movie "Wild Hogs") and people popping up from Albuquerque. Listen to Madrid's local radio station - KMRD 96.9.

The Hollar – Local's favorite to eat with a varied menu. Outdoor patio. 505.471.4821

Java Junction – Good place for cup of coffee with friendly staff but nasty restroom (porta-pottie).

Galleries & Gift Shops

Cowgirl Red – Fun shop, friend Mary Ann bought boots there.

Moonbow Herbs & Gifts – Healing herbs in back.

Range West – Water sculpture and nice indoor gallery. 505.474.0925

Trading Bird – Nice Native American and other finds. 505.438.6144. **Gypsy Gem** – Sister gallery to Trading Bird. Nice jewelry and artwork.

SANTA FE – ART & CULTURE MECCA

I love Santa Fe! It is expensive, but worth it with its charm, history, art galleries, shopping, and wonderful dining opportunities. I just love wandering around the streets in the core of the city. Check out the main plaza as well as some of the old churches and buildings downtown. Parking can be difficult, the best bet is to stay an evening with a hotel walking distance to the plaza to really take it all in.

Palace of the Governors - Is right on the main plaza and is an interesting museum with lots of historical pieces. Native Americans normally sell jewelry in front of the museum, year round. The **New Mexico History Museum** is now part of the same campus that includes the Palace of the Governors http://www.nmhistorymuseum.org/

Lensic Performing Arts Center – Is a wonderful Spanish styled theater on 211 W San Francisco Street. I had wanted to see a show there for years and finally saw "Fiddler on the Roof" performed by a talented local theater troupe.

Loretto Chapel – Worth seeing is the Miraculous Staircase – a wooden spiral staircase that was hand-made by a mysterious mystical carpenter. Today we could only build it with the aid of a computer designing it *(hint: the lack of a central support would normally make the spiral collapse on itself)*. It is a short walk from the main plaza. http://www.lorettochapel.com/

Santa Fe Opera – Three miles north of town on US 285. Want to go some day. I hear the tailgating event must not be missed. 800.280.4654

Santa Fe Motel - Walking distance from downtown, ask for the casitas (old pueblo houses that have been remodeled into rooms). Not fancy but clean and accessible. 510 Cerrillos Road - 505.982.1039 – *it may not be as nice as in the past but haven't personally checked it out though when checking recent reviews it still rates well, I think my friend that wasn't excited about it didn't realize that Santa Fe is very pricey and affordable and clean plus walking distance to the plaza is rare.*

Art Museums & Galleries

Santa Fe is a mecca for art both in museums and galleries that sell art.

Canyon Road – Spurs off of Paseo de Peralta and is where many art galleries are located. Just wander up the street and explore the wide range of art being sold in these galleries. In fact, there are so many galleries, don't wear yourself out and try to see all of them in one day! I like the kinetic wind sculptures of the **Mark White Gallery** – 414 Canyon Rd.

Downtown – Some nice galleries on Galisteo Street including **Santa Fe Art Collector** on 217 Galisteo Street – the owners Darrell & Phyllis are nice hosts. I also like **Andrea Fisher Fine Pottery** on corner San Francisco Street and Don Gaspar.

Meow Wolf – An amazing collaboration (did I say amazing?) between a group of Santa Fe artists that is in an old bowling alley that opened spring 2016. **Prepare to be surprised.** It also was quickly "found" so it can be a line getting in and noisier on the weekends. Very kid friendly (just stick with them as they can disappear quickly in this huge artist inspired playground). They also have concerts. 1352 Rufina Circle - www.meowwolf.com

Museum Hill – Several museums (including the **Museum of International Folk Art**) plus the **Santa Fe Botanical Garden** are located in one spot on Camino Lejo just off of Old Santa Fe Trail. There is enough to see here, that you might want to hit a different museum each day or each trip depending on how museum focused you are.

New Mexico Museum of Art – Just of the Plaza (next to the Palace of the Governors) is a wonderful regional museum in a beautiful early 20th century Pueblo Revival building.

Buffalo Thunder Casino – North of Santa Fe on Highway 285, the hotel/restaurant level of the casino has a large collection of amazing Native American artwork scattered throughout that level (even two paintings from Shonto Begay).

SITE Santa Fe – This art gallery with rotating exhibits also stands out as different – in fact exhibit I saw was very modern and intense. Since they are kinda on the edge some shows may not resonate as well as others. *They are closed until Fall 2017 for renovations/expansion. Sometimes Fridays are also free.* 1606 Paseo De Peralta – 505.989.1199

Indian Market (August) - One weekend each year during August; there is the famous Indian Market where Native Americans sell some absolutely incredible artwork. Most is around the main plaza. I would recommend checking current mass transit options since parking is at a premium – they do run a shuttle to the Rail Runner train station and city buses may be free on the Indian Market weekend. Hotels are also at a premium so book way in advance. https://www.swaia.org/

Ski Area Road

Fall Colors – Drive up to the ski area – several great overlooks and mountainsides of Aspens. The dirt road to the radio towers from one of the overlooks is easy to hike or mountain bike.

Hyde State Park – On the road to the ski area (take Washington to Artist's road in town and later Hyde Park road). Great campground facility and $10/vehicle. Some good single track mountain biking that starts just above the RV campground area – Dale Ball North.

Ten Thousand Waves - A friend recommended this place. It has nine open air hot tubs in a very nice garden setting. FYI – it is not a real hot springs resort. 3451 Hyde Park Rd – take Artist Road that turns in to Hyde Park road (about 7-10 minutes out of town). 505.982.9304 - make reservations! They do have a public tub ($14/person) and private tubs (best value seems to be the Ichiban at $24/person).

Restaurants

Café Fina – Great bakery/coffee/café. Have Southwestern style fare plus other options. 624 Old Las Vegas Highway (I-25 exit 290 for US 295 south Fe - there is nothing else at this intersection). *This has become my "go-to" when I want something in town but not venture downtown.*

Café Pasqual - Near the plaza on 121 Don Caspar Avenue. *Very well run and perfectly prepared New Mexican food though it is a little pricey. For dinner reservations are needed! It may be easier to get in for breakfast.* 505.983.9340

Chez Mamou French Bakery & Cafe – This place has a local recommendation. 217 E Palace Ave - 505.216.1845

Cowgirl Santa Fe – Was told by locals to go here for margaritas! Near the train station on 319 S Guadalupe St. - http://www.cowgirlsantafe.com/

El Farol – Great night spot on Canyon road (where tons of galleries are situated). Locals say the food has slipped a bit bit still a good night spot.

Geronimo – On Canyon road – very upscale but very good. A place to be 'seen'. 505.982.1500

Harry's Roadhouse – Popular eatery with a fun bar. Can be very busy. 96 Old Las Vegas Hwy (I-25 frontage road).

Iconik Coffee Roasters – Amazing coffee spot! They also are downtown but I prefer this location. 1600 Lena Street (can access from 2nd Street from Cerrillos). **La Lecheria** across the street looks like good spot for ice cream (open afternoons).

The Kitchen Window – In Design Center. Like their breakfast items. Rachel, the owner, was helpful when I was in. Drive up window too. And easy parking in their lot. Morning hours can vary so call ahead. 418 Cerrillos Rd - 505.982.0048

El Meson Restaurant & Tapas Bar - Tapas bar with live music (jazz Friday/Saturday). *Recommended by Lois who grew up in New Mexico. Will visit my on my next trip.* 213 Washington Ave - 505.983.6756 - www.elmeson-santafe.com

Original Pantry Restaurant – Great New Mexican diner serving up food since 1948. Also a handy spot if you want breakfast but don't want to venture to the plaza area. 1820 Cerrillos Rd - 505.986.0022 – www.pantrysantafe.com

PC's Restaurant Lounge – This was across from my hotel (used hotel points that trip) which was closer to the freeway. It is a great basic New Mexican restaurant. You will probably get more upscale food downtown but sometimes there isn't the energy to drive all over the place or wait in line and pay high prices. This was the hotel manager's favorite place – so it also might be a bit more authentic. 4220 Airport Rd (just west of Airport and Cerrillos Road also Airport turns into Rodeo when it crosses Cerrillos), 505.473.7164

Plaza Cafe - We almost skipped this fun restaurant by, since it is right on the plaza. We thought it would be too touristy. Per Joy the best coconut cream pie she ever had (I liked it too – and still good in 2015). Pleasant staff and prices seemed pretty fair too, though they are strict on substitutions and less pleasant when busy. 502.982.1664, 54 Lincoln Ave.

Rasa Kitchen & Juice – Great vegetarian spot with very helpful/friendly staff. Organic pressed juices and smoothies. 815 Early St - 505.989.1288. Other vegetarian spots are **Thai Vegan** on 1710 Cerrillos Rd (parking in back off of 2nd Street) and **Annapurna** on 1620 St. Michaels Dr. – both of these are Albuquerque based restaurants.

Secreto Lounge - St. Francis Hotel – The lobby bar is great for an end of day drink! Also have happy hour prices on their expensive but well-made cocktails.

Tecolote Cafe – On Cerrillos Road near the Indian School and Deaf school. Good family run eatery.

Tia Sophia's – Well-known local eatery for breakfast and lunch right down town (couple blocks from the plaza). Good basic New Mexican food and not pricey. 210 W San Francisco St, 505.983.9880.

Tomasita's – Well known eatery at the train station (500 South Guadalupe). *I had heard the food had gone downhill but have to admit my chicken enchiladas with green chile and an egg on top were great.* And not too pricey. Open at 11AM. That area of town is seeing a renaissance with new mixed with old (including an REI store). The **Rail Runner train** comes into town here as well. Another reason I like Tomasita's is that you can often get parking in their parking lot – something that can be tougher in other areas of Santa Fe.

Tune-Up Cafe - Favorite breakfast spot for friends Andy and Jane - 1115 Hickox S - 505.983.7060

NORTH OF SANTA FE

PECOS

The mountains north of Pecos (south end of the Sangre de Cristos) are really neat; it is mostly National Forest with lots of camping and backpacking opportunities.

Pecos National Monument - Interesting ruins of a large Spanish Missionary post with plenty of history (the Pueblo Revolt of 1680 pushed out the Spaniards for several decades).

OJO CALIENTE – HOT SPRINGS

These are smaller communities on U.S. 285 between Espanola and Antonito. In Antonito you can take the **Cumbres and Toltec Railroad** over Chamas pass in the summer months. The drive from Chama on Highway 84 then 64 from Tierra Amarilla to Tres Piedras is pretty. Also Highway 84 from Pagosa Springs to Chama is a nice drive.

Ojo Caliente Mineral Springs - North of Santa Fe on U.S. 285 are very nice. It was a quaint, rustic spot that has been increasingly spiffed up over the last 20 years. Now there are four public pools open and a very upscale lobby/shop area. It is a very relaxing spot and you can get massages/facials. Winter is the best time, since even fewer people. *Recent years have seen soaking fees increase dramatically.* 505.583.2233 or 800.222.9162 - http://ojospa.com/

Mesa Vista Café – This is a local eatery that has been there forever but I had never tried till spring 2016. Since my other favorite places in town on the highway serving New Mexican fare are now closed I finally tried it and loved it. Great New

Mexican fare and a friendly staff! However it is not fancy, just good basic diner fare. 505.583.2245. Closed Tuesdays.

Hiking - You can hike behind the Ojo Caliente hot springs up on to the mesa behind it. Going to the left (South) is a pueblo ruin site about 1/3 mile down from where the trails "Y" left and right at the top of the mesa. Lots of pottery shards and caved in roofs. Nice views into the Sangre de Cristo Mountains to the east too. Remember to not remove artifacts.

TAOS

Neat artist community. Surprisingly less gentrified than Santa Fe, yet you can find nice places to stay and eat.

Mabel Dodge Luhan House — A historic inn and they run various workshops there, including writers workshops by Natalie Goldberg. Nice little shop with books by a range of authors including those that run workshops there. It is off of Kit Carson road just east of the Plaza on Highway 64. 505.751.9686 or http://www.mabeldodgeluhan.com/

Plaza — Although a bit touristy, it is fun to walk around the plaza and check out the shops. Lots of art galleries and jewelry shops. The bookstore on the plaza isn't huge but has a pretty tasteful selection of books. If eating lunch — a lot of restaurants seem to close sometime between 2-3PM — just be aware of that.

Rio Grande Gorge — If heading to Tres Piedras — the bridge crossing the Rio Grande is a pretty spot.

Taos Pueblo - A very old community that does allow tours. It is one of the more famous pueblos and the subject or many paintings. Please respect their requests for no photographs.

Taos Ski Valley - One of my favorites, though make sure they have enough snow as they need a good base to be open.

There are many other ski areas in the area to explore, that are less known then Taos (though they also do not have the level of expert terrain that Taos has).

LAS VEGAS

North of Santa Fe on I-25 is Las Vegas. A town in the foothills and has two plaza or town centers separated by about ½ a mile. The architecture is predominantly Victorian, instead of adobe, since it was a railroad town.

Carnegie Library - Like many small towns of its age, it has a Carnegie Library (Colorado City in Colorado Springs also has one). It is an attractive building and can be seen if walking around downtown.

El Rialto - A good New Mexican restaurant, on the street between the new and old plazas (454-0037).

La Galleria de los Artesanos – really, really cool Western bookstore that is on the plaza in the old section of town. *I hear they closed – sad as a special place.*

RATON

Just South of Trinidad, Colorado (another interesting town to explore) on I-25. I had passed by their downtown many times. On the last trip, I stopped through and found some of the downtown architecture interesting (including the county court house).

Shuler Theater - Brings in entertainment en route from Denver/Colorado Springs to Santa Fe.

Highway 550

Highway 550 starts in Montrose, CO going through Durango en route to Bernalillo, NM (just north of Albuquerque). Part of the Colorado section is called the "Million Dollar Highway" due to the cost to connect to mountain mining towns.

Aztec

Also on Highway 550 but pretty close to Durango. I am starting to like this town after I dove into some side streets – interesting neighborhood.

Aztec Ruins National Monument – Just outside of Aztec, is a small ruin site with a well preserved set of rooms (pueblo style that were built out in the open) as well as a reconstructed great kiva which I found very interesting, it was a <u>big</u> building.

The Bistro (it used to be called the Atomic Bistro) - On 122 N. Main is open for breakfast and lunch and is a nice place to stop. Open 7AM-2PM Monday-Friday & 8AM-Noon Saturdays. 505.334.0109 – _www.aztecmainstreetbistro.com_.

Farmington

Southeast of Aztec is the biggest town in the region. I had only driven through town and didn't have a high opinion of it. Actually they have a downtown that is kinda cute and a nice shopping mall. It is also a good crossroads town for exploring the region. I stayed at the **Marriott Courtyard** (505.325.5111) on Scott Avenue, just east of downtown. If you get a room there facing the river, you don't even feel like you're in town. In fact there is a boardwalk along the river there and that specific hotel really has leveraged its landscaping to take advantage of it. I also enjoyed a nice meal at a well-run family restaurant **Si Señor** at 4015 E. 30ᵗʰ Street – 505.325.9050. They served up good New Mexican fare that wasn't pricey and very popular with the locals.

Chaco Culture National Historic Park – Make sure to visit this wonderful place. See start of Southern New Mexico section for more information.

CUBA

On Highway 550 about 1 hour NW of Albuquerque. It is at about 6000 feet elevation so it has cooler weather than I'd expected.

Prescilianos Restaurant - I liked this. On the west side of town. They had great home style food – had the blue corn flat (stacked) enchiladas with green chile. 505.289.3177

El Bruno's Restaurante y Cantina - Is across the street and down a bit – have only been to their Albuquerque location where I love sitting in their bar for a margarita.

JEMEZ PUEBLO

Walatowa Visitor Center (Jemez Pueblo) - North of Highway 550 on New Mexico State Highway 4 is Jemez Pueblo. Their visitor center is worth a visit with a nice museum. www.jemezpueblo.com – I'd recommend taking a look at **Visitor Etiquette** under Visitor Information on the website if planning on visiting the pueblo.

New Mexico State Highway 4 – This pretty mountain drive comprises most of the Jemez Mountain Trail National Scenic Byway. I bicycled it a while back starting in Bernalillo, taking NM 501 into Los Alamos. **Jemez Springs** is about the only spot to stop for food until Los Alamos. You also go by **Valles Caldera**. www.jemezmountaintrail.org

SOUTHWESTERN NEW MEXICO

QUEMADO

Small town south of I-40 on the pretty scenic drive between Silver City and Grants or Gallup on I-40 (if going to Grants you go by the east side of **Malpais National Monument** on NM 117). It goes through small towns like Glenwood on the way. Glenwood looked like a nice town and the **White Water Motel** looked affordable and clean - 505.539.2581. From Silver City, Highway 180 hits an intersection where you head towards Reserve on NM 12 and later head north to Quemado on NM 32, then NM 36 to intersection where NM 36 heads towards Gallup or NM 117 towards Grants.

Largo Café (Largo Motel and Café) - Wonderful diner style New Mexican restaurant with great enchiladas (I prefer stacked with an egg on top). Also have homemade pies – mmmm. Motel number is 505.773.4846 (haven't tried motel).

Very Large Array - Cool spot I want to visit some day between Quemado & Socorro on US 60. www.vla.nrao.edu I also want to try **Pie Town Café** – further NW on US 60. 575.772.2700

SILVER CITY

Beautiful historic downtown worth walking around. Sadly have not kicked around here as much as I would have liked since usually mid-point on a long travel day. www.visitsilvercity.org

Gila Cliff Dwellings National Monument – Cool cliff dwelling from the Mogollon Culture (late 1200's). About 45 miles north of Silver City on State Route 15 – windy road.

New Mexico 152 – This state highway heads east towards Hillsboro and eventually I-25. Another secondary scenic route.

Highway 180 – Heading north out of Silver City is a pretty drive up western New Mexico. It eventually heads to Alpine, AZ. The time I drove it I took New Mexico 12 then New Mexico 32 towards the town of Quemado.

HILLSBORO

A cute little town on State Route 152, a by-way from I-25 to Silver City. This road is very slow in places but worth it (lots of 15 mph corners up in the mountains). In Hillsboro I ran into a sweet garden run by Ellen Tafoya – she has a sign up calling it **Happy Flats Iris Gardens** (she has 100's of varieties of irises). She is retired and if out in the yard likes to show her garden off.

I-25 ALBUQUERQUE TO LAS CRUCES

TRUTH OR CONSEQUENCES

T or C used to be called **Hot Springs, New Mexico** but renamed itself after the popular radio (1940-1957) and later TV show. The radio show host Ralph Edwards in 1950 had a contest for the first town changing their name to Truth or Consequences would get the show hosted in their town. He fell in love with the town, visiting it the first week in May for the next 50 years – the event was called Fiesta and continues today. **Elephant Butte** is the neighboring town that serves the Elephant Butte reservoir – including several RV parks.

T or C is on the Rio Grande River – though can be dry since the river also fills up the Elephant Butte reservoir. Some of the town is a bit rough on the edges but it has charm. **Hatch, NM** is just down the freeway and a famous spot for chiles.

Ivory Tusk Restaurant – Over in Elephant Butte at the Elephant Butte Inn & Spa is a good eatery for Mexican food. We didn't expect it but they do a great job. Fun place to have a drink at the bar!

Passion Pie Café – In downtown T or C on 406 Main Ave. They are open for lunch and breakfast and have great coffee plus baked goods.

Pacific Grill – A nice seafood restaurant that Brenda likes. Closed Mondays. 800 N Date St - 575.894.7687

Sacred Rose Gift Shop – Dee the owner imports a variety of things from Nepal with good prices.

Studio de la Luz – Great space that has yoga, spiritual gatherings and other activities. 308 South Pershing St. 575-740-3680

Hot Springs

As its original name implies T or C has hot springs! In fact there are many places in the core part of town that have plumbed hot springs water.

Sierra Grande Lodge and Spa – A wonderful place to stay. From what I can tell a bit more expensive than other spots in town but worth it. Home baked goodies for breakfast. 505.894.6976 or www.sierragrandelodge.com.

Riverbend Hot Springs - Is a place on the Rio Grande river that Brenda likes (575.894.SOAK - 100 Austin St). They also have lodging.

La Paloma Hot Springs and Spa - Try if wanting even less pricey (311 Marr St).

Blackstone Hotsprings - Eclectic 1930s hotel with courtyard offers hot spring baths. 410 Austin St. - 575.894.0894 - www.blackstonehotsprings.com

Mesilla

This is a wonderful old town on the Western side of the Las Cruces metro area. It has an old plaza with a quaint church and fun shops and eateries.

Fountain Theater – The Mesilla Film Society shows films in this wonderful old theater. The films are more indie and international in nature. http://www.mesillavalleyfilm.org/

Chopes Bar & Café – About ½ hour south of Mesilla on State Highway 28 with a pretty drive through pecan orchards is a wonderful eatery. You can choose the converted house or the bar. The bar definitely attracts locals with affordably priced 40 oz. beers. The food here is closer to Mexican since way south of Albuquerque. The chile relleno was the best I've ever had and the red sauce was yummy (saying a lot since I go for green normally). 16145 NM-28, La Mesa, NM 88044 – 575.233.3420

SOME THINGS TO DO BY CATEGORY

This section of the book breaks out activities by category rather than by city or state. It is not meant to be as inclusive as the previous sections were. Rather it is a list of some of my most favorite things. Most of them will have more extensive information in its section under that state and a few are only listed here.

MUSEUMS/TOURS

Aspen Art Museum – New modern building with rotating shows (no permanent collection) plus a nice upstairs café for lunch.

Arizona Sonora Desert Museum (Tucson) - Incredible zoo of native animals as well as other exhibits on plants and minerals related to the area.

Bird Cage Theatre (Tombstone, AZ) – This is one place I really felt the west was still alive. It sure isn't fancy or renovated, but that is the charm.

Clyfford Still Museum (Downtown Denver) - Across from the Denver Art Museum. Wonderful showcase for the Abstract Expressionist's work.

Colorado Railroad Museum (Golden, CO) - Has an excellent collection of trains, though many are not in the best condition.

Coors Brewery Tour (Golden) – Still love doing the tour of the brewery – though it has been a few years (and I once had an inside connection that let me even do the cooler VIP tour).

Heard Museum (Downtown Phoenix) - <u>Excellent</u> Native American collections. This really is a unique, special museum and worth the visit. If you have access to light rail, there is a stop near the museum.

Hubbell Trading Post National Historic Site (Ganado, AZ) – Historic trading post managed by the National Park Service.

Karchner Caverns Tour (Sierra Vista, AZ) – Beautiful cave. On State Route 90 between Benson and Sierra Vista. 520.586.2283

Kitt Peak National Observatory Tour (Tucson Area) – SW of Tucson, the impressive collection of huge telescopes is worth the visit. For more hands on viewing – I recommend Lowell Observatory (though they don't have any instruments of the size at Kitt).

Lowell Observatory Tour (Flagstaff) - Excellent hands on exhibits and night viewing sessions. The observatory discovered Pluto.

Museum of Northern Arizona (Flagstaff) – Good collection of artifacts from the area as well as exhibitions. The summer weekend sales of Native American work are especially good and the museum shop has neato stuff. They recently built a new collections complex and it would be worth a tour if you can arrange it (you may need to be a member).

Denver Museum of Nature and Science - Excellent dinosaur collections.

Phoenix Art Museum – Their art museum is maturing into a nice space. The **Phoenix Main Library** (walking distance from the art museum) also has a good collection of hand-made art books – by appointment only. Also **Arizona Science Center** is nearby.

Santa Fe, NM – It has many wonderful museums (many on Museum Hill). Also wonderful art to see in galleries on Canyon road and downtown.   Don't miss **Meow Wolf** which is an <u>amazing</u> artist collaborative that opened spring 2016.

Tamarind Institute (Albuquerque) – This is on Central Avenue across from the University of New Mexico in the Nob Hill District. They have a nice gallery upstairs. You need to buzz at the door to get into the building.

SHOPPING

Durango, CO – This mountain town has vibrant, fun downtown shopping.

Flagstaff, AZ – Downtown has outdoors stuff, galleries, Native American artwork and retro clothing.

Phoenix, AZ - Biltmore Fashion Park- High end "power" shopping.

Santa Fe, NM - High end Southwest shopping, especially so during Indian Market (one weekend in August). Canyon Road is the hub for Santa Fe's art galleries and studios. **Taos** also has nice shopping around the Plaza.

Sedona, AZ – Uptown has tourist trinkets, Native American artwork, and art galleries. Tlaquepaque shopping area, just south of the intersection of 179 and 89 is a wonderful set of shops and restaurants (next to Los Abrigados resort).

Scottsdale, AZ - High end "power" shopping at **Fashion Square Mall** and Southwestern and fine art are in the downtown Scottsdale area. **El Pedregal** - At the intersection of Scottsdale road and the Carefree Highway in Carefree, AZ is a nice high end shopping area. If you like it, also try **Tlaquepaque** in Sedeona.

Ski Resorts - Vail and **Aspen** both have wonderful high end shopping, though don't expect any bargains. **Telluride** and **Crested Butte** still have the feel of being real ski towns – though you can see the pressures shifting that as it happened in Aspen. Other resort towns vary in the level of "stuff" you can buy. It really depends on the type of people that frequent the area.

Roadside Vendors on the Navajo Reservation – Quality varies but you can find some interesting things at these stands. You do have to know what you are looking for. I once found an incredible fetish necklace at on in the Marble Canyon area. And you have a better story to tell about your 'find' too. *Try to buy true handmade items at these stands or in a trading post. The trading posts may sell overseas items - for a few dollars more you can often get something authentic.*

INTERESTING TOWNS

Aspen, CO - Although known as a top skiing resort and the high level of wealthy visitors, it has much more to offer than fancy boutiques and incredible skiing. During the summer world class scientists congregate at the Aspen Institute. There are a number of free lectures geared towards the lay person. Summer music programs for students bring highly talented youth to the town with free recitals and other events.

Bisbee, AZ - Another mining town in Southern Arizona that has become an artist community that has really interesting architecture as well as locals. Really worth exploring as it thrived longer than most mining towns and was one of the biggest cities in the west in its day. With steps leading everywhere up to houses on the sides of the canyon – it is the 'city of steps'.

Boulder, CO - Boulder is a fun city to explore, especially around the Pearl Street Mall. It has a funky, college feel like other mountain college towns like Flagstaff. Some of its character has been lost due to the onslaught of chain stores replaces the interesting icons that made it Boulder. But it still is

Boulder and wonderful things like the farmers market, bike trails, eateries and just the feel continue to keep it special.

Durango, CO - Though a heavy tourist area in the summer, I still love walking around the quaint downtown area. Or walking 3rd Avenue with all the old Victorian houses.

Flagstaff, AZ – It is a funky mountain city that has great people watching and a downtown area reminiscent of the turn-of-the-century. It is also on the historic Route 66. Art walk on the first Friday of the month is a wonderful time to visit.

Gallup, NM – Wonderful historic district with lots of shops selling Native American artwork and crafts.

Jerome, AZ - An old mining town (though mining left here only a few decades ago) that now has a couple of fun bars, wineries, and some neat artist shops.

Leadville, CO - Old mining town at 10,000 feet elevation that hasn't had the same level of high-cost tourist expansion that some of its ski town neighbors have had (I like ski towns too but they have lost some of their original character as tourism has totally taken them over). At the same time it is rougher on the edges since it doesn't have the polish of the higher end ski towns. Even visiting it years later, it is still wonderfully a bit rough on the edges!

Ouray, CO – I see it as the middle-class version of Telluride. Just as pretty and with its well-known hot springs. Shops are generally a bit less upscale but in many ways more fun. Plus 4th of July is a blast there.

Salida, CO – Has a really nice historic district – possibly the nicest in the state. Shops are more affordable than pricier ski towns.

Santa Fe, NM - One of the oldest cities in the country with lots of history and interesting shops and restaurants. **Taos** is also intriguing.

Springdale, UT – This serves Zion National Park and although touristy is cute & is a nice basecamp to explore Zion.

Telluride, CO – They have a fun array of summer weekend festivals from the famous bluegrass festival to jazz and wine. Take your pick. It is one of the prettiest towns in the state.

OUTDOORS/SCENERY

Remember if driving these routes in the winter to check on road conditions and weather. Plus be prepared in case you get stuck (see other notes under References).

The Grand Tour - North Rim Grand Canyon National Park, Zion National Park (via Kanab and Zion tunnel on State Route 9), Cedar Breaks (via Cedar City and State Route 14) and Bryce Canyon National Park. Allow several days for this trip. The drive from Jacob Lake to Flagstaff is beautiful as well. Dinner (get reservations) at the North Rim lodge is wonderful at sunset. Could also include a visit to Lake Powell. This loop could be started from Phoenix/Flagstaff or Las Vegas/St. George.

Chiricahua National Monument (Near Wilcox, AZ) - Take the time to hike this incredible spot, even if only for a mile.

Southeastern Utah - Drive from Cisco, Utah (exit on State Route 128 from I-70) to Moab along the Colorado River in the Little Professor Canyon and then Highway 191 down to Bluff, Utah. Several side trips to Hovenweep, Arches National Park or Arches National Monuments are possible. Breakfast/lunch at **EclectiCafe** in Moab.

Boulder to Escalante, Utah – I am listing this separately from the item directly below, since this little section of State Route 12 is not known to many and has to be one of the prettiest stretches of road in the world. Dinner at **Hell's Backbone**

Grille in Boulder, UT or coffee at the **Kiva Coffee House** (just west of the Calf Creek Trailhead) make it better.

Zion to Capitol Reef National Parks – Drive through the Zion tunnel on State Route 9 and then head towards Panguitch on Highway 89. Then drive on State Route 12, to Bryce Canyon and onto Tropic, Escalante, Boulder and finally Torrey (meal at **Café El Diablo** or **Rim Rock Patio**). If you want to go into Panguitch, you will have to retrace your steps a few miles south to get to SR 12. You will see some incredibly beautiful sections of road – some of the best in the world. In Springdale have a Mexican meal at the **Bit n' Spur** or **Oscar's**.

Southern Front Range Colorado Tour - Drive from Walsenburg (town on I-25) north on Highway 69 to Westcliff. Then head to Silvercliff and less than ¼ mile past Tony's Mountain Pizza you will see Oak Creek Grade (road 255) to the left – take this dirt road that normally should be easily passable with a passenger vehicle. Follow signs to Cañon City (generally when the road Y's, go left – you want to stay on Oak Creek Grade Road). When the road T's closer to town (now on pavement), you will go left and curve to the right which is 4th street and will take you to Highway 50. Since a dirt road, *I wouldn't drive this route in inclement weather and if early spring, check with locals if they've graded the road before driving it.*

Southwest Colorado Tour - Drive between Cortez, Dolores and Telluride on State Route 145. Then loop back then SR 162 to Ridgway then Ouray, Silverton and Durango on Highway 550, the Million Dollar Highway. Allow at least a full day for this trip. This includes **Mesa Verde National Park** – worth a day alone plus many like the **Durango-Silverton railroad**. When going through Mancos, stop at the wonderful **Absolute Bakery & Cafe** in the old part of town plus between Durango/Mancos is **Kennebec Restaurant**. You can easily spend a day in Durango and at least ½ day in Telluride and Ouray each.

Central Colorado Tour - Drive from Denver to Vail, then to Minturn, take Highway 24 from Minturn back to Leadville and into Colorado Springs. In the summer, the parking structure in Vail Village is free so park and walk into the village. Take Highway 83 back to Denver. You will see the heart of Colorado. Be aware of storms in the winter as some of the upper valleys (called parks) can be treacherous in a bad storm. Allow at least one very full day to accomplish this.

Gunnison Country Road 12 - Kebler Pass – Crested Butte, CO – Just East of Paonia is Kebler pass road (CR12) which is a summer seasonal road that goes all the way to Crested Butte. A beautiful drive on a well graded dirt road (can take a normal car). McClure Pass (Colorado 133) is also pretty which is the graded gravel road that goes between Paonia and Carbondale (you turn off of to go on Kebler pass). Breakfast in Paonia at the **Back Country Bistro** or at **Living Farm Café** is a good starting point.

I-70 - Glenwood Canyon – The section of I-70, just West of Glenwood Springs, Colorado. About half way through the canyon is the trail to **Hanging Lake** - a nice 1-2 hour hike up to an aqua colored pond bordered by felled trees (like a beaver pond). You can also bicycle the canyon. Then check out the **Yampa Spa & Vapor Caves** or the hot springs pools in Glenwood Springs.

State Route 89A - Sedona & Oak Creek Canyon - The canyon is located between Sedona and Flagstaff on Highway 89A. An easy day trip from Phoenix. If seeing Flagstaff and Sedona, drive the freeway to Flagstaff, shop there (get a cup of coffee at **Macy's**) and then drive down the canyon to Sedona (traffic typically flows better in that direction). Hiking **West Fork of Oak Creek** is always a treat (though the parking lot can fill up plus they charge for parking even with a normal Red Rocks Pass).

US 89 & State Route 89A - Phoenix to Sedona via Prescott - From Wickenburg (NW of Phoenix), take Highway 89 to Prescott going through Yarnell. The climb up the Yarnell Grade is spectacular. Then have lunch in Prescott and continue to Jerome via Mingus Mountain on 89A. Shop there and continue via Cottonwood to Sedona (Cottonwood has done a nice job of renovating part of its downtown area). They return to Phoenix from Sedona on State Route 179 (going through Village of Oak Creek) and then down I-17.

Train - Flagstaff to Las Vegas, NM - Take Amtrak either way, the Superliner cars are neato (they are two story cars with one car devoted to an observation lounge and snack bar). These trains are very unique - I have never seen them elsewhere in the world and the run from Albuquerque to Las Vegas, New Mexico is supposed to be pretty (only have been on the train from Albuquerque to Flagstaff). Sometimes they have a guide on the train discussing local lore - check which run that is.

Highway 60 - Salt River Canyon, AZ - It is located between Showlow and Globe, Arizona. It is well worth the drive (you go right through it) if traversing the state. You can also tube the section of the Salt River nearer to Phoenix in the summer — though be prepared to bake (sunscreen is mandatory!).

SPAS/HOT SPRINGS

I am by no means an expert on hot springs, but do enjoy a soak, especially after skiing or a long hike. I don't know if their therapeutic claims are real, but it sure helps my sore muscles. This list is by no means inclusive. There are good books out on the subject.

Durango, CO - Trimble Hot Springs - North on Highway 550 is a hot springs spot on the west side of the road (open year round).

Glenwood Springs, CO – The town has two spots. **Glenwood Hot Springs Pool** with 100 meter outdoor pool. And the separately owned **Yampa Spa & Vapor Caves,** natural steam baths in underground caves.

Ouray, CO - **Ouray Hot Springs Pool and Fitness Center** – Popular pools next to the Ouray Visitor Center. 1220 Main St - 970.325.7073. Also the privately run **Wiesbaden Hot Springs Spa & Lodgings** – you can just pay to use the hot springs. 625 5th St - 970.325.4347 Plus ones at **Box Canyon Inn** – Neat motel (you must stay there to use these pools).

Ridgway, CO – **Orvis Hot Springs** – Just south of Ridgway on Highway 550. Only clothing optional one on the list. Kitchen to cook meals in plus offer lodging and camping.

Ojo Caliente, NM – For many years my favorite, since it was clean and well run and at the same time not trendy. I sometimes made a special trip just to go there. *Though in recent years it has become much trendier and more expensive after renovations – still like it but prefer it before the changes.*

Near Salida, CO - **Mount Princeton Hot Springs Resort** - Nestled in a beautiful area at the base of the Collegiate Peaks. I wasn't impressed the last time I was there (other friends stayed there more recently and loved it). I plan to try **Cottonwood Hot Springs** that are west of Buena Vista. 1.888.395.7799

Scottsdale, AZ - **The Spa at Camelback Inn** - This is not a hot spring, rather a nice resort spa that allows you to pay a daily fee to use it.

Truth or Consequences, NM – The old part of town has numerous hot springs – see T or C section.

ARCHEOLOGY

Chaco Culture National Historic Park – Farmington, NM - This incredible ruin site is a must. Better to come in via Farmington (it is South of Farmington). No services at the site except water and a soda pop machine so prepare yourself.

El Morro NM – Gallup, NM – On State Route 53 is a small mesa with thousands of rock inscriptions from the Ancient Puebloans, Spaniards (1600-1700's) and Americans (1800's).

Hovenweep NM – Bluff, UT - In Southeastern Utah, very close to Arizona and Colorado. It has neat tower type ruins. Not a big site but one of my favorites.

Mesa Verde NP – Cortez, CO - The most famous of the ruin sites of the Southwest and <u>worth</u> it. It is a bit off of the highway and has enough to see to spend a day there. Plan a side trip to Durango, Hovenweep or Telluride while you're in the area.

Montezuma's Castle NM – I-17 - Right off of I-17 en route to Sedona or Flagstaff. It and Walnut Canyon are probably the most accessible cliff dwellings you can see in the SW. **Montezuma's Well** and **Tuzigoot NM** are other sites nearby that you might want to see depending on your driving itinerary.

Pueblo Grande Museum - Phoenix - Off of the 143 and Washington Avenue - just jorth and east of the Phoenix Skyharbor Airport. If in the area, it is a quick and interesting stop - though a bit hot in the summer.

Sego Pictographs & Petroglyphs – Thompson Springs, UT – See under I-70 Corridor.

Wupatki NM & Walnut Canyon NM - Flagstaff – See under Flagstaff.

SPIRITUAL SPOTS

I have found some interesting places in the region. **Sedona, AZ** is the best known as a New Age spiritual Mecca, though I find it a bit overdone.

Aztec NM – Azetec, NM – Sit in a reconstructed Anasazi Great Kiva – the type used for ceremonies.

Cerrillos, NM – St. Joseph Catholic Church in town has sweet garden area shrine to the Mother Mary.

Chapel of the Holy Dove – Flagstaff, AZ – On Highway 180 (heading north from Flagstaff), just before Kendrick Park. It burned once & was rebuilt. A testament to simplicity and faith.

Crestone, CO – This is kinda the Colorado version of Sedona, but it is more relaxed. A generous donor gave land to a variety of spiritual groups to build shrines or spiritual centers there so it has an eclectic mix of faiths.

Loretto Chapel - Santa Fe, NM – The wonderful spiral staircase built by a mysterious carpenter is just impressive.

Pecos Benedictine Monastery – Pecos, NM – It has been many years since I visited the site, but it just felt peaceful, great, & open. Also provide lodging. http://www.pecosmonastery.org/

Sacred Mountains - San Francisco Peaks (Flagstaff), Baldy Mountain, Navajo Mountain – To many Native Peoples, certain mountains are sacred. I try to resepect that if I visit those places. Some like Baldy in the Arizona White Mountains is officially not supposed to be hiked.

Santuario de Chimayo – Chimayo, NM – Beautiful adobe church in rural Northern New Mexico. These old churches just feel holy in a very human way since their decorations were hand-made by settlers who did not have the money to buy decorations. You may want to look into the "santero" traditions of that region.

RESOURCES

Traveling through this region takes a little more planning. There can be large gaps between towns so gas stations and other services can be less frequent. Additionally some facilities or spots may be seasonal in nature or close earlier in the day than expected.

GETTING ADDITIONAL INFORMATION

Federal and municipal visitor centers offer up great free information. I have noticed a few visitor centers that are run by businesses versus the community – their information may be biased by the local tourist companies they serve.

Plus if you have a specific activity you really like – I would recommend doing further web research and/or buying guides on those topics.

HIKING & TOUR BOOKS

I recommend getting other guides for the specific activities that suit you. This is especially true for hiking, bicycling, and river running. I personally have found the Falcon Guide books useful. Plus local writers can be very helpful – Cosmic Ray for instance writes about Arizona hiking and biking.

FEDERAL VISITOR CENTERS

There are a variety of federal lands you will encounter while traveling – National Parks, National Monuments, BLM, and Forest Service. Plus you may encounter state parks and lands as well. If hunting, the local state fish & game offices are also useful.

National Forest Service (USFS) Ranger Offices – Many of these have wonderful resources for hiking or exploring public lands.

National Park & National Monument Visitor Centers – These have information desks about park amenities, hiking and other information on exploring the parks. They also have wonderful book shops that have a plethora of information about the park and the region around it.

Escalante Interagency Visitor Center. Good spot for information on nearby federal lands. Also bathrooms – though locked after they close.

Kanab Visitor Center (BLM) - 745 US-89. Here you can pick up permits to hike the wave – check on their current process since you can't just show up and get a permit. Also the road to the wave can be tough going depending on weather.

Montrose Public Lands Center (USFS/BLM) - On 2505 S. Townsend Avenue has a wonderful bookshop that also sells topographic maps and has a help desk.

Red Canyon Visitor Center (USFS) – On State Highway 12 east a few miles of Highway 89. Closed in the winter 435-676-2676

MUNICIPAL & STATE VISITOR CENTERS

Many communities have very nice visitor centers. Some states have great Welcome Centers. Here are a few examples:

Blanding, UT – On Highway 191 on the north end of town.

Bluff, UT – In the Bluff Fort Historic site on the north side of US Highway 191.

Flagstaff – The center is located in the historic train station between Beaver and San Francisco streets, where the Amtrak trains also stop.

Florence, AZ – In the McFarland State Historic Park building.

Fruita, CO - Colorado Welcome Center – They have information for the entire state, organized by city/region. 340 CO-340 at Fruita exit for I-70 (also on in **Burlington** just west of Kansas state line). Nice spot with free coffee.

Grand Junction – Right off of I-70 and Horizon Drive is the city's visitor center (SW corner of that intersection). Plenty of information, some nice exhibits and clean restrooms.

Moab - Has the **Moab Information Center**, on 25 E Center Street - http://www.discovermoab.com/

Montrose – Built a new visitor center in the repurposed historic Elks Lodge on the SE corner of South 1st Street and Cascade downtown – even published a guidebook to the area that is very useful (http://visitmontrose.net/).

Ouray - Has a nice visitor center north of the hot springs pools on US Highway 550. Good place for a pit stop if you are traveling onward through town and not stopping.

Ridgway – Their visitor center is on the SW corner of the main intersection and only stoplight, includes a railroad museum that showcases the famous Galloping Goose train line. (http://ridgwaycolorado.com/)

Idaho Springs – Combined city & National Forest visitor center. 2060 Miner Street - http://visitidahospringscolorado.com/

Telluride – Recently moved their visitor center to wonderful new space in the center of town on Colorado Avenue across from the New Sheridan Hotel. It is short walk from the gondola up Oak Street (the last bit of Oak Street is a green space instead of a road).

Utah Welcome Center – I-70 Westbound Mile Marker 190 – Just before Thompson springs is a rest stop with a Utah specific visitor center.

Williams, AZ – Nice visitor center on 200 W Railroad Ave.

Yuma – In the **Yuma Quartermaster Depot State Historic Park.**
It is on 4th Ave next to the bridge crossing the Colorado River.

GROCERY STORES

Some travelers have more challenging food requirements.
Below is a list of grocery stores that have organic or gluten free
foods. I also included some places that source locally when
possible. Please realize smaller communities may not have the
selection large natural food stores typical to bigger cities. I
also recommend calling ahead so you can confirm their hours
if they carry what you will need.

Alamosa, CO – Valley Food Coop – 3211 Main St. Suite.
719.589.5727

Boulder, UT – Hills & Hollows – Gas station with a market that
has a lot of organic or healthy options. 435.335.7349.

Crested Butte, CO - Mountain Earth Whole Foods - 405 4th St
- 970.349.5132

El Morro National Monument, NM – El Morro Market – East of
the monument a few miles on State Route 53 is an organic
grocery store across from the Ancient Way Café.
505.783.4777

Escalante, UT - Escalante Mercantile - 210 W Main St -
435.826.4114

Flagstaff, AZ - Flagstaff CSA & Local Market – 116 W. Cottage
Ave – 928.213.6948

Gallup, NM - La Montañita Co-op Food Market - 105 E Coal
Ave - 505.863.5383

Kanab, UT – Kanab Natural Foods – Open Noon-7PM - 310
S 100 E, Kanab - 435.644.3636

Montrose, CO – The Vine Market & Bistro - 970.812.7977

Paonia, CO - Indigo Autumn – Currently open late morning 7 days a week. 230 Grand Ave, Paonia, CO - 970.527.3663

Ridgway, CO – Ridgway Mountain Market – 490 Sherman.

Springdale, UT - Sol Foods Supermarket - 995 Zion – Mount Carmel Hwy - 435.772.3100

Saguache, CO – Community grocery store - 404 N. Main St.

Telluride, CO – Clark's Market - 700 W Colorado. Also a location in Norwood. Also Market at Mountain Village – off Parking Lot Gondola.

Natural Grocers – A chain of health food stores that sells organic produce, gluten free products and supplements. Stores in Tucson, Phoenix, Flagstaff, Albuquerque, Santa Fe, Durango, Montrose, Grand Junction, Glenwood Springs, Frisco, and Denver.

Trader Joe's – A chain that sells an eclectic variety of foods. Some ready to go foods like salads and wraps. Shops in Tucson, Phoenix, Prescott, Albuquerque, Santa Fe, Denver, Boulder, Colorado Springs, and Salt Lake City. Great place to buy wine, beer and some stores sell spirits. Utah stores don't sell wine/beer and the only Colorado store selling wine/beer is the one at 790 N. Colorado Blvd in Denver. www.traderjoes.com

Sprouts – Another chain with locations throughout the SW.

Whole Foods – This large chain is well known to many. I find them a bit pricey. But I like the convenience of these two locations: Basalt, CO (off of State Route 92 and Willits Lane) and Frisco, CO (right off of I-70 and Summit Blvd).

Ski Areas

I have worked at several resorts in Colorado and Arizona. Ensuring the snow conditions are good for a planned trip can be challenging. Generally snow is better later in February or the month of March when the more common spring storms hit Arizona and Colorado.

The toughest mountains in the region are: Aspen Highlands (hike up the bowl), Crested Butte (though it lacks mid-range expert terrain), Taos, and Telluride (new hike to terrain to Palmyra Peak added a few years back!). Good beginner spots are Snowmass, Telluride, Vail (Lionshead), Keystone, and Buttermilk.

Ski Rush-Hour Traffic – Ski areas near metro areas can have heavy traffic on weekends or holidays.

Denver - If you are flying into Denver and traveling to ski resorts be aware of the horrendous traffic on I-70 Friday nights or mornings Saturday/Sunday to ski. And the afternoon traffic back to Denver on Saturday or Sunday evenings. Resorts closer to Denver (including Vail) will be super busy on weekends.

Phoenix - Arizona Snowbowl by Flagstaff also can get heavy traffic but more the last bit up to the ski area – I recommend getting up to the ski area around 8AM if you are renting gear and ready to ski by 9AM as the lift lines get longer in late morning on weekends. Similar situation for going to Sunrise in eastern Arizona.

Lift Tickets - Each ski area can have deals/specials on season passes or other packages. You often have too book these early – September/October. For instance, Telluride has in the past has had great deals for kids season passes purchased early, which work out much cheaper than buying even a couple of day tickets.

Epic Pass – It is is a good deal if you are going to ski areas owned by Vail Resorts or partner with the program (Vail, Beaver Creek, Keystone, Arapahoe Basin, Breckenridge, Park City plus resorts on Lake Tahoe, the Midwest, and some passes include International locations) - http://www.snow.com/epic-pass/.

GEMS Card – Provides discounts at nine of Colorado's Gems resorts. These are smaller resorts that don't have the destination draw that Aspen, Telluride, and Vail have. It includes Arapahoe Basin (great late season skiing), Loveland (known for its early season skiing), Powderhorn and Sunlight. http://coloradoski.com/gems-card/

GEAR

Weather can change quickly. If exploring the outdoors, having the right gear with you is important. I have run into more than one hiker with no rain gear on hand and over an hour from their car. On top of that, some were only wearing cotton clothing which once wet doesn't dry easily. Going to a shop that caters to outdoor clothing and gear can be helpful. Cabelas is a good source if you are more hunting oriented. REI Coop works better if you are hiking, bicycling, backpacking oriented. I also recommend visiting local shops as they know their region better and can help pick things you really need.

Binoculars – You might want to consider having a set of binoculars to look at ruins, points of interest, animals and birds. Plus kids love to play with them – giving them something to do besides a smart phone.

Rain Jacket – A light, single layer rain jacket that is easy to carry is recommended when hiking. Make sure it is something that repels water – many windbreaker jackets don't cut it.

Walking Shoes – If you plan on doing any longer walks, I recommend a pair of really solid walking or hiking shoes. They can still be a low cut pair. Tennis shoes in my opinion just don't work as well on rough terrain. Shops that specialized in fitting walking/hiking shoes may be helpful (Hiking Shack in Prescott, Summit Hut in Tucson, and Backcountry Experience in Durango).

Walking Sticks – Several companies including Black Diamond and Leki make ski pole like walking sticks. I love these tools and use them frequently. Some sets will pack in carryon luggage. An adjustable set may better so you can dial in what works for you.

Dogs – Make sure to take plenty of water for your dogs. Some areas require leashes for dogs or have other rules. At least in Colorado I learned that ranchers can shoot dogs chasing their livestock. So if you have a dog that might do that, bring a leash if in areas you might encounter livestock. I know this sounds silly but I met a woman hiking that lost one of her animals that way.

Equipment Rental – Many communities have equipment rental. Bicycles can be rented in Aspen, Moab, and Grand Junction. Water sports equipment can also be rented. For instance, **Montrose Kayak & Surf** on 302 W Main St is open seasonally to rent stuff for the park or other rivers/lakes in the area - 970.249.8730. If you don't have river experience, a river tour might be a better option – the Moab and Salida areas have tours on the Colorado and Arkansas rivers that include day trips that might be a better option for a first time experience.

TRAVELING BY CAR

Water - Make sure to take enough water for your planned outing. Carry some in your car too!

Gasoline – Many areas in the west have big gaps between services, even on the Interstate system. Distances can be greater between gas stations than where you are from.

Extra Cushion – I wouldn't recommend running your car to empty between gas stops. Plus if driving over mountain passes in the winter, make sure to have a full tank when heading into mountain country (e.g., fill up in Cortez when heading north to Telluride). *An old timer here in Montrose told me a story when he was driving in a storm and was stuck for hours due to weather - other stranded travelers jumped in his car to stay warm. One of his friends almost died in a similar situation where he didn't have enough gas. Of course if you do keep your car running make sure your exhaust pipe doesn't get buried in snow. And carrying extra clothes, food, and water are also important.*

Gas Prices - On I-70, between Denver and Grand Junction, gas prices can be higher. Grand Junction and Delta on the Western Slope of Colorado generally have better prices then other towns nearby. Ski and tourist towns in Colorado can really be pricey. Nebraska has some independent gas stations with a low price on their highway sign that may only be for one pump – the others are pricier. Flagstaff's gas stations on Highway 89 near the shopping mall tend to be much lower than other areas.

Communication – Sometimes it is a good idea to let people know exactly where you are going. This is especially true if hiking, biking or exploring a wilderness area. Many of these areas do not have cell phone coverage so getting help if you need it could be problematic.

Winter Roads – If driving where winter storms can hit, best to check on road conditions.

Mountain Passes - High mountain passes in Colorado can get storms as early as October and easily into April.

Exploring the Four Corners Region

Plowing - Once you leave the interstates, also be aware some highways are not plowed at night or just once a day.

Cruise Control on Slippery Roads - I learned from a neighbor who was a sergeant in the highway patrol that if wet or slippery roads that is best to turn off your cruise control.

Keep Gas Tank ½ Full – This is smart so you don't run out of gas. But if temperatures get really cold, you can avoid gas lines freezing by keeping your gas tank full.

Weather – Knowing current weather conditions is important. Especially if driving in the winter in the mountains, driving on dirt roads, or engaging in outdoor activities. Be aware that some roads may not be plowed at night – in Western Colorado this includes a couple of state highways (e.g., going over Grand Mesa). My favorite site for weather is the NOAA National Weather Service site: http://www.weather.gov/. And for road conditions I like the state highway sites. For instance in Colorado, CDOT has a wonderful site with a map showing road conditions. http://www.cotrip.org/map.htm

KIDS

Bringing kids along has its own challenges, even more so in the on-line world we live in. Many areas will not have cell phone coverage and even getting internet access can be spotty so you need a "plan B".

Binoculars – Mentioned earlier are fun to look at things.

Food – Make sure to have snacks and drinks with you if in rural areas so that you can even span a meal if you are spending longer than anticipated exploring (it is easy to take much longer than you planned to explore). It can be 50 miles between grocery stores and in small towns they could close early.

National Parks Passport – If visiting National Parks or Monuments, getting a passport for them to fill in at each stop could be a hit.

Non-Electronic Games – Having some board games or other activities (if space allows for you to bring along) can fill time in off-line spots.

Hands-On Experiences – Some places let kids interact exhibits such as science museums. Many outdoor sites are great for kids such as playing at **Goblin Valley State Park** or the pit house at **Fremont State Park**.

Museums & Indoor Events – Some spots are great for kids.

Arizona Science Center – Downtown Phoenix.

Arizona Sonora Desert Museum - Tucson

Denver Museum of Nature and Science – Denver – Dinosaur skeletons are cool.

Lowell Observatory – Flagstaff – Night viewing.

Meow Wolf – Santa Fe – Fun interactive art experience.

Museums of Western Colorado: Dinosaur Journey – Fruita

Hiking – Hiking can be a lot of fun. Though, choosing kid friendly trails is important. A shorter, less difficult route with interesting things to see is generally important for initial hikes. So old cabins, petroglyphs, cool views, or small streams to play in could all make the day a lot more fun. You want your kids safe. Around water, check if kid friendly – some rivers move faster than you might think and may not be kid friendly. Old buildings are fun to visit but most are not safe to explore. If the kids haven't walked a lot – maybe do some short walking outings back home so there are used to the idea.

Arches National Park - Moab – There are a lot of areas which short walks to see the different arch formations.

Dominguez Canyon (between Grand Junction and Delta) – Follows active railroad tracks (so make sure to discuss safety with them when around trains and not walking on the tracks) then crosses the river up to a beautiful canyon complex with wading ponds. The ponds are about 4 miles RT so this might not be a first trip out hiking.

El Morro NM – Gallup, NM – Take the full two mile trail past the inscriptions and then up to the pueblo ruins. There is about a 200 vertical foot elevation gain on the hike. I would follow the route in the direction on the map as it will keep you in the shade as you walk up hill. Make sure to take the laminated guide they give you as it has a lot of interesting information.

Mushroom Rocks – Kanab, UT – Between Page and Kanab, the Toadstool Trailhead is an easy hike (about 2 miles RT).

Nature Trail – Piestewa Peak Park - Phoenix – This trail is at the end of Squaw Peak Drive that access the park off of East Lincoln Drive.

Taylor Creek Trail (Kolob Section Zion National Park I-15) – Is another where you follow a stream to a dramatic rock alcove passing an abandoned cabin.

Veit Springs Trail - Flagstaff - Is a great example with an old cabin and Petroglyphs. Need a permit to park.

Maps – Get them a map (or several) of where you will be going and mark routes accomplished with a sharpie. This can be something they put on their walls when they get home. I do this with my younger clients in Telluride, marking up the ski are map as we tackle new runs.

Geocaching – This isn't everybody's cup of tea but could be a way to get kids out in the woods. Some current video games seem to mimic this activity and may have spots along your trip as well.

CPSIA information can be obtained
at www.ICGtesting.com
Printed in the USA
LVOW13s0002280617

539620LV00009B/170/P